DATE			

THE GREAT REHEARSAL

BOOKS BY CARL VAN DOREN

ANTHOLOGY

The Portable Carl Van Doren

HISTORY

Mutiny in January

Secret History of the American Revolution

American Scriptures

AUTOBIOGRAPHY

Three Worlds

BIOGRAPHY

Benjamin Franklin · *Swift* · *Thomas Love Peacock*

James Branch Cabell · *Sinclair Lewis*

FICTION

Other Provinces · *The Ninth Wave*

LITERARY HISTORY AND CRITICISM

The American Novel · *Contemporary American Novelists*

The Roving Critic · *Many Minds*

American and British Literature Since 1890

(with Mark Van Doren)

What Is American Literature?

BOOKS EDITED BY CARL VAN DOREN

The Cambridge History of American Literature

Modern American Prose · *An Anthology of World Prose*

Benjamin Franklin's Autobiographical Writings

Letters and Papers of Benjamin Franklin and Richard Jackson

The GREAT REHEARSAL

The story of the making and ratifying
of the Constitution of the United States

BY CARL VAN DOREN

GREENWOOD PRESS, PUBLISHERS
WESTPORT, CONNECTICUT

Library of Congress Cataloging in Publication Data

Van Doren, Carl, 1885-1950.
   The great rehearsal.

   Reprint. Originally published: New York : Viking
Press, 1948.
   "The Constitution of the United States": p.
   Bibliography: p.
   Includes index.
   1. United States. Constitutional Convention (1787)
2. United States--Politics and government--1783-1789.
I. United States. Constitution. 1982.   II. Title.
[JK146.V3 1982]   342.73'029   82-9160
ISBN 0-313-23492-2 (lib. bdg.)   347.30229   AACR2

This edition published by arrangement with The Viking Press

Reprinted in 1982 by Greenwood Press
A division of Congressional Information Service, Inc.
88 Post Road West, Westport, Connecticut 06881

Printed in the United States of America

10 9 8 7 6 5 4 3 2 1

FOR
BRADFORD AND ANNE BEVANS,
ANDREW ROSS, JOANNA KLAW

PREFACE

THE MOST momentous chapter in American history is the story of the making and ratifying of the Constitution of the United States. The Constitution has so long been rooted so deeply in American life—or American life rooted so deeply in it—that the drama of its origins is often overlooked. Even historical novelists, who hunt everywhere for memorable events to celebrate, have hardly touched the event without which there would have been a United States very different from the one that now exists; or might have been no United States at all.

The prevailing conceptions of those origins have varied with the times. In the early days of the Republic it was held, by devout friends of the Constitution, that its makers had received it somewhat as Moses received the Tables of the Law on Sinai. During the years of conflict which led to the Civil War the Constitution was regarded, by one party or the other, as the rule of order or the misrule of tyranny. In still later generations the Federal Convention of 1787 has been accused of evolving a scheme for the support of special economic interests, or even a conspiracy for depriving the majority of the people of their liberties. Opinion has swung back and forth, while the Constitution itself has grown into a strong yet flexible organism, generally, if now and then slowly, responsive to the national circumstances and necessities.

The Constitution was made and ratified during one of the two periods of American history in which the American people have been most occupied with fundamental principles of government. In 1787 the problem was how the people could learn to think nationally, not locally, about the United States. In 1948 the problem is how the people can learn to think internationally, not nationally, about the United Nations.

The present problem has turned many minds back to 1787 in

vii

search of a historic parallel to serve as an example. In that year the former colonies of Great Britain, now independent states, were recovering from a war. During the war they had been drawn together by a common danger, but afterward they had sagged apart. The Confederation under which they lived was not so much a government as a league of states, in which the individual states retained a large part of their sovereignty. Congress was not a general legislature, but a diplomatic assembly, in which the states had equal votes. There was no general executive, no general judiciary. Congress could raise money only by asking the states to contribute their quotas for Confederation expenses. The Confederation government did not operate directly on the people of the United States, but only through the states themselves, bristling with sovereignty or absorbed in their own concerns.

The situation was, in any number of respects which can be seen at a glance, much like that of the sovereign states of the United Nations in 1948.

In 1787 the Federal Convention, called to alter and amend the Articles of Confederation, boldly created a federal government which should have authority and power to regulate federal affairs, while leaving local affairs to the states. This was no longer a league. It was a government. And many citizens of many nations are now convinced that only by some similar alteration of the Charter of the United Nations can the United Nations develop from a league of states into a government capable of securing the peace and welfare of the world.

The parallel between 1787 and 1948 is naturally not exact. Even if it were, 1787 would have no authority over 1948. Each age must make or keep its own government and determine its own future. Nor do those citizens of the world who in 1948 desire to see a federal world government created assume that the process would have to follow the example of the United States of 1787 in the details of the new government. The Federal Convention did not follow any single example. Neither should a General Conference of the United Nations be expected to.

But it is impossible to read the story of the making and ratifying of the Constitution of the United States without finding there all the arguments in favor of a general government for the United Nations, as well as all the arguments now raised in opposition to it.

The opponents of the Constitution argued in 1787 that the United States, ten times larger in extent than any federation in previous history, was too large ever to be held together by a common government. The three natural sections of the country, Northern, Middle, and Southern, it was argued, might be formed into three federations which could maintain and promote the interests of those sections. But any government strong enough to dominate the whole country, it was insisted, would have to be a tyrannical super-state, supported by a standing army in a fortified capital which would have no respect for the liberty of individual citizens.

The supporters of the proposed Constitution argued that the larger a federation was, the less chance there must be that one part of it could dominate the others. To set up three regional federations was to set up political and economic rivalries which did not need to exist, because they did not represent essential conflicts in the interests of the people. The central government of a single great federation would have been designed by the people, through their representatives, would be administered by officers the people had chosen, and would be subject to control or change at the will of the people.

The opponents of the Constitution insisted that the smaller states would be swallowed up by the United States; the supporters pointed out that a small state is always likely to be swallowed up by a hostile state, but that it finds security and liberty in voluntary union with friendly states. The opponents of the Constitution declared that the larger states would disturb the United States by their powerful contentions; the supporters replied that those contentions were sure to disturb the continent if the larger states were not united, much less sure to do it if they were united and so could be expected to arrive at peaceable agreements.

The opponents of the Constitution were convinced that the people of the individual states could be protected only by their states armed with full, or at least substantial, sovereignty. The supporters of the Constitution knew that conflicting sovereignties had been the causes of most wars, in which the people have regularly suffered.

The opponents of the Constitution in 1787 could talk only of the difficulties of forming a new government. The supporters of the Constitution, aware of the dangers facing the Confederation, de-

manded that a new government be attempted, no matter what
the difficulties.

In this respect those antagonists were precisely like the enemies
and the friends of world federation in 1948, now when it is obvi-
ous that no difficulty in the way of a world government can match
the danger of a world without it.

The story as here told brings those older arguments and coun-
ter-arguments once more to the light. The supporters of the Constitution in 1787 knew that they were planning a government
only for the United States, but they believed their experiment
would instruct and benefit all mankind. Their undertaking might
be, though of course no one of them ever used the term, a rehearsal for the federal governments of the future.

This story shows the arguments in action, not in a philosophic
vacuum. The arguments are the story. Arguments must always be
seen as actions if they are to reach through the minds of men to
their hearts and habits.

CONTENTS

THE ILLUSTRATIONS

(Above.) INDEPENDENCE HALL IN 1778. From a drawing by Charles Willson Peale. *(Below.)* INDEPENDENCE HALL IN 1799. From an engraving by W. Birch.

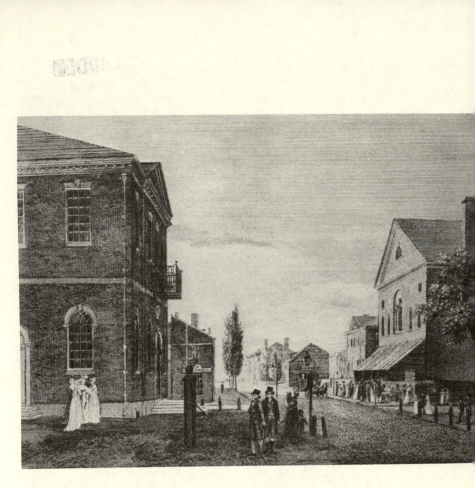

CONGRESS HALL

Which was being built at the time of the Federal Convention. From an engraving by W. Birch.

THE WALNUT STREET PRISON
Facing the State House Yard, now Independence Square. From an engraving by W. Birch.

The City Tavern

Where the delegates to the Federal Convention dined on the last day of the session. From a print made a few years later.

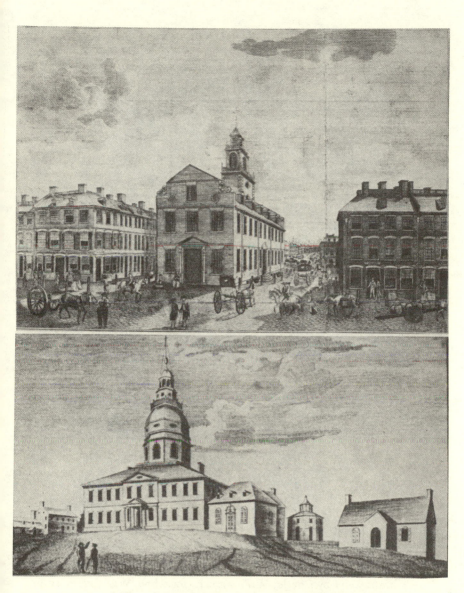

(*Above.*) The Massachusetts State House

Where the Massachusetts convention for the ratification of the Constitution first met.

(*Below.*) The Maryland State House

Where the Constitution was ratified in April 1788. From a contemporary print in the *Columbian Magazine* for 1789.

GEORGE WASHINGTON IN 1787

"Let us raise a standard to which the wise and honest can repair." (Page 9.) A mezzotint by Charles Willson Peale, for whom Washington sat in the early days of July.

BENJAMIN FRANKLIN IN 1787

"We are sons of the earth, and, like Antæus in the fable, if, in wrestling with a Hercules, we now and then receive a fall, the touch of our parent will communicate to us fresh strength and vigour to renew the contest." (Page 1.) From a mezzotint executed by Charles Willson Peale early in the year, from a painting made probably at about that time.

James Madison

He is the indispensable chronicler of the Convention, and sometimes the skeleton of his narrative, to the eye of any imaginative reader, puts on flesh and blood and walks through days that without him would be lost to memory. (Page 30.)

This etching and the seven following, with the exception of that of James Wilson, were made in 1888 by Albert Rosenthal. The Wilson was made in 1890 by Max Rosenthal.

ALEXANDER HAMILTON

"He enquires into every part of his subject with the searchings of phylosophy, and when he comes forward he comes highly charged with interesting matter, there is no skimming over the surface of a subject with him, he must sink to the bottom to see what foundation it rests on." (Page 91.)

GEORGE MASON

Mason ranked with Washington or Jefferson as one of the three most
eminent Virginians of their day. (Page 17.)

ROGER SHERMAN

He now came to the Federal Convention with all the simplicity, cunning, and courage of a rural Yankee. (Page 32.)

JAMES WILSON

"Government seems to have been his peculiar Study, all the political institutions of the World he knows in detail, and can trace the causes and effects of every revolution from the earliest stages of the Grecian commonwealth down to the present time." (Page 38.)

Gouverneur Morris

Morris, who spoke more often than any other delegate to the Convention, seemed exotic there, with his wit and arrogance, his reputation for gallantry, and his wooden leg. (Page 39.)

WILLIAM PATERSON

He was a very short, acute man, an experienced lawyer, and a speaker who, according to Pierce, was "very happy in the choice of time and manner of engaging in a debate." (Page 72.)

EDMUND RANDOLPH

Randolph brought youth, energy, the prestige of his governorship, and the advantage of his relations with the most powerful families in Virginia. (Pages 16-17.)

COMMANDER
AND PHILOSOPHER

"No morn ever dawned more favourably than ours did;
and no day was ever more clouded than the present."
*George Washington to James Madison, November 5,
1786.*
"We are sons of the earth: and, like Antæus in the fable,
if, in wrestling with a Hercules, we now and then receive
a fall, the touch of our parent will communicate to us
fresh strength and vigour to renew the contest." *Benjamin
Franklin, Comfort for America, January 1787.*

O N THE bright, noisy afternoon of Sunday, May 13, 1787,
George Washington, late commander in chief of the Continental Army, arrived in Philadelphia as a Virginia delegate to
the Federal Convention which was due to open the following
day. He had been met at Chester by three generals, two colonels,
and two majors of his former command, and at Gray's Ferry
across the Schuylkill by Philadelphia's smart troop of light horse,
the City Cavalry. Under ceremonious escort, to the sound of
chiming bells and cheering citizens, Washington proceeded in
his carriage to the lodgings he had reserved at Mrs. House's, at
Fifth and Market Streets. But "being again warmly and kindly
pressed by Mr. and Mrs. Robt. Morris to lodge with them," he
did so, and had his baggage removed to their house, the finest
in the city, in Market Street nearer to Sixth. The house had
belonged to Richard Penn, once proprietary governor of Pennsylvania, and had been headquarters in turn for Sir William
Howe and Benedict Arnold during the military occupations of
Philadelphia in the Revolution. Robert Morris, as superintendent
of finance for the Continental Congress, had won the confidence
of Washington and they had remained firm friends. They were
of the same opinion on the necessity of supporting the public

credit of the United States, and Morris was one of the Pennsylvania delegates to the Convention.

As soon as Washington got to town, he noted in his diary, he "waited on the President, Doctor Franklin." Benjamin Franklin, late minister to France, was now president of the Supreme Executive Council of Pennsylvania, which made him in effect governor of the state. By virtue of his office he was host to all the Convention delegates. But Washington, so prompt and punctilious in going to call on the president, was at the same time showing the regard in which he held the philosopher for his age and eminence. Washington was fifty-five, Franklin eighty-one. The two had first met at the time of the Braddock expedition in 1755. A few days then and the year after, six weeks as members of the Continental Congress and a brief conference in camp at Cambridge in 1775: these were all the meetings they had ever had. But their mutual esteem and affection had grown steadily through the long years, without a doubt or a cloud. They had borne the two heaviest burdens of the Revolution, Washington at home and Franklin abroad, each of them too honest to feel suspicion, too great to feel envy.

Franklin, already world-famous as a scientist when Washington was still an obscure young soldier in Virginia, had rejoiced in the rise of Washington's reputation, and in March 1780 had invited him to come to Europe, where, Franklin said, "you would know, and enjoy, what Posterity will say of Washington. For 1000 Leagues have nearly the same Effect with 1000 Years." When Franklin returned to America in September 1785, Washington had at once written from Mount Vernon to assure him that "as no one entertains more respect for your character, so none can salute you with more sincerity, or with greater pleasure, than I do on the occasion. . . . It would give me infinite pleasure to see you."

The miles between them had so far made this impossible. But today Washington had only to go along Market Street, beyond Fourth Street, turn in through an arched passage to Franklin Court, and there, probably, find Franklin in his garden "with grass plots and gravel walks, with trees and flowering shrubs," and particularly a large mulberry tree under which he often sat in pleasant weather. Here they might have tea, served by Franklin's daughter, and exchange compliments and reflections on

American affairs and the prospects of the Convention. For Franklin also was a delegate.

Whether the Convention's two most famous delegates that afternoon actually spoke of public business, or what they said, is not known, but there is no question as to what they thought. Franklin had spent twenty-five of the past thirty years in Europe, aware of the poverty of peasants, laborers, artisans, and tradesmen there, and cheerful over the general prosperity he had observed among the people in Pennsylvania since his return. "All among us may be happy," he had recently written to an English friend, "who have happy dispositions; such being necessary to happiness even in Paradise."

To a French friend he had written, less than a month ago, that "the grand Federal Constitution," by which he meant the Articles of Confederation, "is generally blamed as not having given sufficient powers to Congress, the federal head. A convention is therefore appointed to revise that constitution, and propose a better." In these and in other letters to Europe, Franklin insisted that the Americans were happy in their independence and that the British newspapers, full of accounts of distress, confusion, and disorder in the United States, were either ignorantly or deliberately misleading. The Americans had made mistakes, but these were being corrected; they had need "of more skill in financiering," but they would learn by experience. To Thomas Jefferson, who had succeeded Franklin as minister to France and was now in Paris, Franklin on April 19 had been reflective and foresighted. The delegates to the Convention, he said, were men of character and ability, "so that I hope Good from their Meeting. Indeed if it does not do good it must do Harm, as it will show that we have not Wisdom enough among us to govern ourselves; and will strengthen the opinion of some Political writers, that popular Governments cannot long support themselves."

There was nothing which Franklin more earnestly desired for his country than that its people should continue to govern themselves, with increasing wisdom and justice. Many of his political antagonists during the Revolution, both in Europe and in America, had contended that the English colonies must be governed by the Crown and Parliament in London or else fall into public chaos. Franklin, arguing with all his passion, skill, and wit that Americans were capable of the self-government which they claimed as their natural right, had extended his argument to include mankind. The rights of Americans were the rights of men. If the Americans, once independent of Great Britain, should fail to justify his faith in them, he would be discredited not only as an American statesman but also as a cosmopolitan philosopher. What was more important, America and mankind would suffer from any such failure. Franklin did not expect this, but he knew from a lifetime of observation that successful self-government depends on the constant work and vigilance of public-spirited citizens. Old as he was, suffering from gout and stone so severely that he could not ride in a carriage but had to be carried through the streets in a sedan chair, he was willing to take up this final labor in behalf of his country and the world.

For nearly sixty years he had devoted much of his time to drawing men together and negotiating difficult agreements: his little Junto of tradesmen in Philadelphia, the American Philosophical Society, the Albany Congress which had adopted his Plan of Union in 1754; the Continental Congress, to which he had offered a first draft of Articles of Confederation and perpetual Union; the Declaration of Independence, which he had helped to draft and had signed; the treaties of alliance and friendship with France and the treaty of peace and independence with Great Britain, in which he had been a principal negotiator. The Federal Convention would be another chapter in his great career, the same methods, the same aims. He had at first doubted that his health would permit him to serve, when the Pennsylvania legislature, on Robert Morris's nomination, had late in March unanimously chosen their venerable "statesman and philosopher" to be a delegate. But now his perennial energy was stirring freshly in him as it had always done when the times called him into action. He had not, however, thought in detail about the defects of the Confederation or drawn up any plan for amending or changing it. He would wait to see what the younger men had in mind, then give them the benefit of his older knowledge and judgment.

Washington was more disturbed than Franklin about the state of the Confederation, more convinced of the need of major changes in its structure. Franklin as a scientist might wait patiently for nature to reveal its secrets, or as a diplomatist be willing to rely on the gradual arts of persuasion; but Washington was by temper and experience a soldier, disciplined himself and expecting discipline in others. For the eight years when he had been, in title, commander in chief of the Continental Army, he had in fact commanded thirteen allied armies, enlisted by the individual states, supplied and paid by them, and never furnished in the numbers asked for by the Continental Congress. Even under the pressure of war and invasion, the states had been slow in forming any kind of political union, and then had formed a weak one, adopted in 1777 but not finally ratified until 1781.[1]

The Confederation, a league of more or less sovereign states, had delegated to Congress only a minimum of power. Without a federal executive or a federal judiciary to support it, Congress was no better than an advisory body, in which each state, no matter what its population, had one vote; nine votes were required for any major decision by Congress, and a unanimous ratification by the states for any amendment. The Continental Congress could give so little support to the Continental Army that as the war went on, Washington, as commander in chief, had himself become the most effective bond, as well as the most conspicuous symbol, of union. Nothing had contributed so much to his fame as his voluntary surrender of power and his retirement to private life. Ancient Rome had had its Cincinnatus, modern America had its Washington, all his contemporaries agreed.

When Washington resigned his commission in December 1783 he told Congress that he was withdrawing "from the great theatre of Action" and taking his "leave of all the employments of public life." But his renown denied him the privacy he looked forward to, and his character obliged him to feel a continuing responsibility for the welfare of the whole country. Hoping for the best, he had feared the worst even before his retirement. Afterward, his letters more and more frequently reflected his deep concern over the incompetence of Congress, the prejudices and jealousies of the states, the weakening of the union once the war was over, the want of money and of public credit, the military insecurity of the Confederation facing possible enemies in the British on the north and the Spanish on the south and west. By August 1785 he had come to a definite conclusion: "We are either a united people under one head, and for federal purposes;

[1] See Appendix 1.

or we are thirteen independant sovereignties, eternally counter-acting each other." How could the United States enter into commercial or other treaties with foreign nations "who must see and feel that the Union, or the States individually are sovereigns as best suits their purpose; in a word, that we are one nation today, and thirteen to-morrow"?

"The discerning part of the community," he wrote in May 1786, "have long since seen the necessity of giving adequate powers to Congress for national purposes; and the ignorant and designing must yield to it ere long." Washington that month had not made up his mind as to the wisdom of immediately calling a general convention to revise and amend the Articles of Confederation. The ignorant people had been misled by the designing, but perhaps "not yet sufficiently misled to retract from error." In republican governments, evils "must be sorely felt before they can be removed." By August he could "not conceive" that the United States had a chance to survive without some federal power which would "pervade the whole Union" with an authority like that of the individual state governments over their citizens. In the present circumstances, "I am told that even respectable characters speak of a monarchical form of Government without horror. From thinking proceeds speaking, thence to acting is often but a single step. But how irrevocable and tremendous! what a triumph for our enemies to verify their predictions! what a triumph for the advocates of despotism to find that we are incapable of governing ourselves, and that systems founded on the basis of equal liberty are merely ideal and fallacious!" Here he was speaking the same thoughts as Franklin's, in close to the same words.

"Yet," Washington wrote to John Jay on August 1, "having happily assisted in bringing the Ship into Port, and having been fairly discharged; it is not my business to embark again on a sea of troubles"; nor did he suppose he would have much influence with his countrymen, who knew his sentiments and had neglected them. For some months he held to this resolution, in spite of what was happening.

Virginia proposed a convention, to meet in Annapolis in September, to discuss the regulation of trade among the states. Only five states sent delegates. The Annapolis Convention accomplished nothing except the recommendation, drafted by Alexander Hamilton of New York, that the states should appoint commissioners to meet at Philadelphia the second Monday of the following May "to devise such further provisions as shall appear to them necessary to render the Constitution of the Fœderal Government adequate to the exigencies of the Union." Seven of the states, Virginia first, had selected delegates before Congress, on February 21, 1787, passed a cautious Resolve which limited the proposed Convention to "the sole purpose of revising the Articles of Confederation, and reporting to Congress and the several Legislatures, such alterations and provisions therein, as shall, when agreed to in Congress, and confirmed by the States, render the Federal Constitution adequate to the exigencies of Government, and the preservation of the Union."[1]

Even after the Convention had official support, Washington still hesitated to accept Virginia's nomination as a delegate. He had publicly announced that he would have no more to do with public affairs. How could he go back on his explicit words? He had declined to be present at the meeting of the Society of the Cincinnati, his former comrades in arms, in Philadelphia in May. How could he decline one invitation and accept another at the same time and place? He was in acute and handicapping pain from a rheumatic shoulder which obliged him to carry one arm in a sling for days on end. His brother died in January. His mother and sister were ill at Fredericksburg and either of them might die in his absence. But late in March, almost the same day on which Franklin was chosen a delegate in Philadelphia, Washington consented to serve. One thing which finally influenced his decision was a thought that kept running through his mind and conscience: if he did not attend the Convention, and make it plain that he was in agreement with its aims, his countrymen might suspect he had lost faith in a republican form of government. At whatever cost to himself, he must prevent any such suspicion. So at sunrise on May 9 he left Mount Vernon, and arrived in Philadelphia a day before the stated opening of the Convention.

The meeting of Franklin and Washington that Sunday afternoon was, symbolically, the beginning of the Convention. They could not help knowing that they were the most influential Americans of their time, and that without their presence and

[1] See Appendix 2.

support the Convention would never command the full respect of the people. Neither could they well help fearing that if the Convention were to fail, even with the sanction of Washington and Franklin, the cause of popular government in the United States would certainly suffer for the present, and possibly be lost for a long and ominous future. It might already be too late to try to strengthen the union, but then also it might be too early.

The people at large took the Confederation for granted. The league established by the Articles, such as it was, was becoming a habit. Certain of the states, once independent of the general rule of Great Britain, were suspicious of the Confederation government, and chose to pursue their own selfish advantage with little concern for the interests of the other states. The selfish states might resist any move to bring them into a union more just and orderly than the one they had. The people, if their political habits were disturbed, might lose faith in any general government. Franklin and Washington were both aware of the unstable situation. The wisest statesmen, in timing their actions, have to realize that they are guessing in the dark. Though they may gamble gloriously, they still are gamblers, with none of the easy knowledge of the outcome which may make posterity, having that knowledge, wonder how they could have been so apprehensive.

Fortunately, Franklin and Washington had lived through many years of uncertainty, had taken many bold risks and often triumphed, and were now willing to venture again. They had come by different routes to their position of influence. Franklin, born a tradesman, was the most celebrated scientist and wit alive; Washington, born a gentleman, was the most illustrious soldier. But they were perfectly alike in their sense of political responsibility, their devotion to the general welfare, and their generous freedom from prejudice and self-interest. Neither of them had shaped in advance any obstinate plan for a new constitution. Both were prepared to work with other men for the best frame of government that could come out of these days and these men.

2

PRELIMINARY PLANNING

"Let us raise a standard to which the wise and honest can repair." *George Washington, as quoted after his death by Gouverneur Morris, December 31, 1799.*

"But we must not expect, that a new government may be formed, as a game of chess may be played, by a skilful hand, without a fault. The players of our game are so many, their ideas so different, their prejudices so strong and so various, and their particular interests, independent of the general, seeming so opposite, that not a move can be made that is not contested; the numerous objections confound the understanding; the wisest must agree to some unreasonable things, that reasonable ones of more consequence may be obtained; and thus chance has its share in many of the determinations, so that the play is more like *tric-trac* [backgammon] with a box of dice." *Benjamin Franklin to Pierre-Samuel Dupont de Nemours, June 9, 1788.*

IN 1787 the State House in Philadelphia had not yet come to be called Independence Hall, though the name was sometimes given to the white-paneled council chamber in which the Declaration of Independence had been voted and signed eleven years before. The central building turned its plain dignified face to Chestnut Street, its wings extending almost to Fifth and Sixth Streets on either side, and the bell tower at the rear overlooking the State House Yard (now Independence Square) which reached to Walnut Street. The Yard, long rough and bare but recently planted with a few elm trees, was surrounded by a wall seven feet high. The high wall gave an air of privacy, if not of secrecy, to the State House and the affairs transacted there. The Federal Convention, first meeting on the morning of May 14, was so uncertain, as to its intentions and its prospects, that it was still a kind of mystery.

Washington came punctually to the opening session; and so probably did Franklin, who was that day absent from the regular meeting of the Pennsylvania Council. His sedan chair, the earliest in America, made for him after his return from France and usually borne by trusty convicts from the prison, was a familiar sight in Philadelphia, and no doubt attracted less attention than Washington in his carriage coming the short distance from Robert Morris's house only one square away. With them, it is certain, were George Wythe, John Blair, and James Madison of the Virginia delegation, who with Washington gave their state one more member than was required for its quorum. Madison, then a member of Congress sitting in New York, had been in Philadelphia since the 3rd, the earliest of all the delegates to arrive from out of town. Wythe and Blair, because of the "badness of their cavalry," had been furnished by order of their governor with a sailing vessel which carried them from Yorktown to the head of Chesapeake Bay, to complete the journey overland. There were three more Virginia delegates to come, and they were on their way.

Except for Virginia, only Pennsylvania was represented by a quorum, in this case four, of its delegates. All of them lived in Philadelphia and might easily be present; but for the same reason all of them could easily know how little would be done that day, and so have an excuse for not attending. While there are no records of the meeting, Robert Morris as Washington's host was sure to be there; and the others beside Franklin most likely to attend were James Wilson, Gouverneur Morris, and Thomas FitzSimons.

Of the eight or ten men probably present, Franklin, Robert Morris, Wilson, and Wythe had signed the Declaration of Independence; and Robert and Gouverneur Morris had signed the Articles of Confederation. All of them but Blair had at one time or other been members of the Continental Congress, and Madison now was. Washington was a soldier and planter; Franklin, printer, diplomat, was chief executive of Pennsylvania; Robert Morris and FitzSimons were merchants and financiers; Blair and Wythe were judges, and Wythe was also professor of law at William and Mary; Madison, Gouverneur Morris, and Wilson were lawyers, who had held official posts in New York, Pennsylvania, and Virginia, and concerned themselves with public affairs more than with their practices. Wilson had been born in Scotland, FitzSimons in Ireland, Robert Morris in England. The Virginians were natives of their state; Franklin had left Boston, a runaway apprentice, and Gouverneur Morris had left the manor of Morrisania, New York, to live in Philadelphia. Franklin, Washington, Robert Morris, and FitzSimons were largely self-educated. Wythe and Blair had attended William and Mary, and Blair had studied law at the Middle Temple in London. Madison was a graduate of Princeton, Gouverneur Morris of Columbia; Wilson had been at two and possibly three Scottish universities. Franklin was older by twenty years than Wythe, the oldest of the rest; Gouverneur Morris was the youngest, thirty-five, a year younger than Madison.

With only two states represented, the delegates could do no more than stand or sit in the famous room with its high sunny windows which was so familiar to most of them, greeting or meeting one another, wondering when further delegates would put in an appearance, sharing preliminary views on the political circumstances which brought them together. If they were not too impatient over the delay of the delegates from the North and South it was because they were not accustomed to rapid travel. The journey from New Hampshire to Philadelphia took usually a good part of two weeks, from Georgia a good part of three. Moreover, there was said to be bad weather elsewhere along the coast. This first day was disappointing but not alarming. The Virginians and Pennsylvanians agreed to meet again tomorrow at eleven.

On Tuesday the 15th again only the two states had quorums, but there were individual delegates from Delaware, North Carolina, and New Jersey. Again the delegates present adjourned to the next day. Washington went to dine with the members of the Society of the Cincinnati who had come to Philadelphia for the general meeting called for May 7 and were in session in Carpenter's Hall, up a court opening out of Chestnut Street. At some time during the day, apparently in the afternoon, Edmund Randolph, a fifth Virginia delegate to the Convention, reached Philadelphia. Still younger than Gouverneur Morris, he had been a member of Congress and was now governor of his state.

On the 16th a sixth Virginia delegate appeared. He was James McClurg, a Virginia-born physician with a medical degree from the University of Edinburgh who had been a surgeon in the Virginia militia during the Revolution. He had had little political experience, and had been belatedly appointed to this post by

Governor Randolph only after Patrick Henry, elected by the legislature, had declined to serve. Henry was one of the few great Virginians opposed to the Convention. He remained at home, Madison was afraid, in order to be free to approve or disapprove "the results of the Convention" which might then "receive its destiny from his omnipotence." The Convention delegates in Philadelphia on the 16th agreed that till there should be a majority of seven states represented they would meet at one each afternoon. Then those present went to dine with Franklin.

At an age when most men are content to sit quiet in their houses, Franklin had lately built an addition to his, which since his return from Paris had come to seem too small for him, his daughter Sarah Bache and her husband, and six grandchildren. He needed a library to accommodate the many books he had brought home from Europe, and a room large enough for guests at dinner or conference. In this room, he carefully explained to his sister Jane Mecom in Boston, he could "dine a Company of 24 Persons, it being 16 feet wide and 30½ long; and it has 2 Windows at each End, the North and South, which will make it an airy Summer Room; and for Winter there is a good Chimney [fireplace] in the Middle, made handsome with marble Slabs." According to an unpublished inventory of his household goods, he had eighteen new mahogany and twenty-four white Windsor chairs. Here the Supreme Executive Council occasionally met instead of at the State House; and the American Philosophical Society, of which Franklin was president. Here the newly organized Society for Political Enquiries had met on May 11, to hear and discuss a paper by Tench Coxe on a commercial system for the United States. And now the delegates to the Federal Convention for the first time sat down to dine together at Franklin's long mahogany table with the silver and fine porcelain he had accumulated in England and France as well as in America. Busts of great men (including Houdon's and Caffieri's of Franklin himself) looked down from their places on the walls, and a tall clock, which had Franklin's portrait painted on the dial, ticked at the foot of the stairs outside the door.

Whatever the diners may have had to say about their federal undertaking, no record of it has survived. Franklin, two days later, wrote to an old English friend, Thomas Jordan, to acknowledge the gift of a cask of beer from Jordan's brewery in London.

"We have here at present," Franklin reported, "what the French call *une assemblée des notables,* a convention composed of some of the principal people from the several States of our Confederation. They did me the honor of dining with me last Wednesday, when the cask was broached, and its contents met with the most cordial and universal approbation. In short, the company agreed unanimously, that it was the best porter they had ever tasted."

On the 17th the last Virginia delegate was at the meeting at the State House. George Mason, though he had avoided public office so far as possible, had been immensely influential in Virginia affairs and through them on the Revolution in general. He had drafted the Virginia Declaration of Rights in May 1776 which Jefferson had drawn upon for the Declaration of Independence in July; and had framed the major part of the Virginia Constitution of 1776 by which the state was now governed. Coming to the Federal Convention, he brought the very essence of reasonable, republican Virginia, and a particular opposition to the institution of slavery.

On this same day, with the last of the Virginians, the first members of the powerful South Carolina delegation arrived. They were John Rutledge, war governor of the state and member of the First and Second Continental Congresses, who came from Charleston, and Charles Pinckney, not yet thirty, who had been serving in Congress and came from New York.

Friday the 18th saw New York represented in the Convention, by Robert Yates, a justice of the State Supreme Court, and by the immensely gifted Alexander Hamilton: thirty, born in the West Indies, an effective Revolutionary pamphleteer while he was still a student at King's (later Columbia) College, aide and secretary to Washington for three years during the war, lawyer, former member of Congress, and among the earliest Americans to perceive the weakness of the Confederation and to urge the need of a strongly centralized authority supported by a new constitution.

For another week the Convention marked time while the opening was daily put off for want of a majority of state delegations. Some of the delegates who drifted in are hardly more than names on a famous record, but they had their day and deserve to be announced as they appear, though not to be laboriously memorized, like the names of the ships in Homer.

Delaware had its quota present on the 21st, with George Read, who had signed the Declaration, Richard Bassett, soldier and ardent Methodist, and the inconspicuous Jacob Broom. On the 22nd the North Carolina quorum was made up. Alexander Martin had been governor of the state; Richard Hobbs Spaight was speaker of the Commons house in its legislature; William Richardson Davie had been a distinguished Revolutionary soldier; Hugh Williamson was a physician and a promising experimental scientist. On the 24th two more South Carolina delegates came in, by packet from Charleston. Charles Cotesworth Pinckney had been educated in England, at Westminster, Oxford, and the Middle Temple, and was a brigadier general by brevet in the Continental Army. Pierce Butler, born in Ireland and formerly a major in the British Army, had since 1771 been a planter and politician in South Carolina. Finally, on the 25th, New Jersey, only across the Delaware from Philadelphia, achieved its quorum: David Brearley, former soldier and now chief justice of the state; William Churchill Houston, who had been professor of mathematics at Princeton; and William Paterson, formerly the state's attorney general. Of these men, Read, Spaight, Williamson, and Houston had all been members of Congress. Two other delegates, from states not yet represented by quorums, were now members and had come from New York: William Few of Georgia, Quaker and soldier, and Rufus King of Massachusetts, a rising statesman and orator.

New Jersey brought to the Convention the seventh quorum of delegates. Virginia, Pennsylvania, South Carolina, New York, Delaware, North Carolina, and New Jersey made up a majority of the thirteen states. The Federal Convention on May 25 closed the doors of its chamber and opened its first official session.

On some day or other between May 14 and May 25 Washington presumably spoke the classic words of those days. It could not have been later, for on the 25th he became president of the Convention and thereafter did not join in its debates till the last day. His actual words cannot have been exactly those which tradition has made well known, for they were never reported till after his death, when Gouverneur Morris quoted them, in his funeral oration, from memory. But it is possible enough that Washington did say something very like these words, at some gathering of the delegates where he had heard his less resolute colleagues talk of the need of caution, of being careful to propose nothing bold and fundamental for fear of rousing opposition which might defeat their plan. Better, they said, offer half-measures that were sure to succeed than risk whole-measures that might fail and discredit the delegates to the Convention. Of such counsels Washington would have thought what Gouverneur Morris quotes him as saying:

"It is too probable that no plan we propose will be adopted. Perhaps another dreadful conflict is to be sustained. If to please the people, we offer what we ourselves disapprove, how can we afterwards defend our work? Let us raise a standard to which the wise and honest can repair. The event is in the hand of God."

II

Behind the scenes, in the eleven days of waiting, the delegates were active in private discussions, exchanging information and opinions. Few of them were widely aware of what had been going on outside their own states. Madison, perhaps better informed than any other, had said on April 12: "Of the affairs of Georgia I know as little as of those of Kamskatska." Pierce Butler of South Carolina soon came to the conclusion that the "manners and modes of thinking" of the several states differed "nearly as much as in different Nations of Europe." Rufus King of Massachusetts was at first distrustful of the Convention and opposed to any radical alteration of the Articles, but he listened to Hamilton of New York, who "revolutionized his mind," Hamilton afterward declared. Mason of Virginia got the impression that the Southern and Middle states were more republican in sentiment than the Eastern—that is, New England—where "the people, setting out with more republican principles, have consequently been more disappointed than we have been." George Read of Delaware as early as the 21st had begun to suspect that delegates from the small states must "keep a strict watch upon the movements and propositions from the larger States, who will probably combine to swallow up the smaller ones by addition, division, or impoverishment." He urged John Dickinson of Delaware to come to Philadelphia without delay.

Whether or not Read had yet heard of it, the Pennsylvania and Virginia delegations were already asking whether it could be just for a small state to have the same vote as a large state in the

Convention. Delaware, with its population of under 60,000, would have as much to say as Virginia, with nearly 750,000 (not counting Kentucky, which had more inhabitants than Delaware but was still a part of Virginia). Pennsylvania, with about 430,000, was the third largest of the states as to population, roughly equal to the combined numbers of New Hampshire, Rhode Island, New Jersey, Delaware, and Georgia. Gouverneur Morris and other delegates from Pennsylvania proposed that the large states should unite "in firmly refusing to the small States an equal vote," as unreasonable in itself and sure to "negative every good system of Government," which in the nature of things could not permit a few people here to have the same voice as many people there. The delegates from Virginia thought that to raise the issue at the beginning might "beget fatal altercations" between the small and large states before anything had been accomplished. Let the small states have equal votes at the outset, on the chance that they might in time see the wisdom of voluntarily giving up their artificial equality "for the sake of an effective Government." Consequently Virginia "discountenanced & stifled" the Pennsylvania project.[1]

The Virginia delegates, all being in Philadelphia and all having no private affairs to occupy their time, were free to begin systematic preparations for the Convention. As George Mason wrote on the 20th, they met and conferred two or three hours every day "in order to form a proper correspondence of sentiments"—that is, to agree on a common program. Washington, who never mentions these conferences in his diary, may not have attended all of them; but even without him his colleagues had a weight and range of political knowledge, experience, and ability which could not have been surpassed in any other state. Randolph

[1] The actual population figures for 1787 are not known, but they were not far from the figures, themselves approximate, given by the first census of 1790: Virginia (including what is now West Virginia), 747,610 (292,627 of them slaves), not counting Kentucky, 72,677 (12,430 slaves); Massachusetts, 378,787 (no slaves) within its present limits, and 95,590 in Maine; Pennsylvania, 434,373 (3,757 slaves); North Carolina, 393,751 (100,571 slaves), not counting Tennessee, which without recognition from North Carolina called itself the independent State of Franklin, 35,691 (slaves estimated at one to every twenty whites); New York, 340,120 (21,324 slaves); Maryland, 319,728 (103,036 slaves); South Carolina 249,073 (107,094 slaves); Connecticut 237,946 (2,764 slaves); New Jersey, 184,139 (11,423 slaves); New Hampshire, 141,885 (158 slaves); Georgia, 82,548 (29,264 slaves); Rhode Island, 68,725 (948 slaves); Delaware, 59,094 (887 slaves).

brought youth, energy, the prestige of his governorship, and the advantage of his relations with the most powerful families in Virginia. Wythe was the foremost classical scholar of the Commonwealth and learned in Roman and English law. Mason ranked with Washington or Jefferson as one of the three most eminent Virginians of their day. Jefferson was in Paris, but he was in close correspondence with Madison, who had done as much as any single man to bring the Federal Convention into being and more than any other to prepare the ground for the course that was to be taken. Madison, sending to Jefferson for books on the laws and history of confederated republics in all ages, had found all their most damaging defects repeated in the Articles of Confederation.

The General Assembly of Virginia, choosing delegates to the Federal Convention the past October, had held that the people of America must now decide whether to consolidate the Revolution or to fall into jealousies, prejudices, and transitory interests and so lose the "just fruits" of independence. Agreeing to the Assembly's statement of the crisis and the dilemma to which the United States had come, the Virginia delegates in Philadelphia proceeded to draft a plan for a new government which could be ready for the Convention when it sat down to its complex undertaking.

Instead of merely revising or altering, the Virginia plan boldly aimed at correcting and enlarging, the Articles of Confederation. It proposed that a national legislature, a national executive, and a national judiciary be established, to take over the work hitherto done, or left undone, by the Continental Congress. The new legislature would consist of two houses, in which the states would vote, not all equally, but in proportion to the amount of their several contributions to the national government or the number of their free inhabitants. The new national executive would be chosen by the legislature. The executive, with certain "members" of the national judiciary, would have the right to examine, approve, or in some cases negative the laws passed by the national legislature or by the state legislatures. The national judiciary would consist of supreme and inferior tribunals which should have jurisdiction in various specified cases and in unspecified controversies that might involve "the national peace and harmony." Provision should be made for the admission of new states to the union. The national government should guarantee to each state a republican form of government. The proposed new "Articles of Union" should be subject to amendment by the people, with or without the consent of the national legislature. When the "amendments" agreed on by the present Convention had been approved by the Continental Congress, they should then be submitted to assemblies chosen by the people, for ratification

Since Virginia had taken the lead in urging the Federal Convention, its delegates supposed that they would be expected to offer some such outline as this of a government under which, in Virginia's opinion, the United States might be "as happy in peace as they have been glorious in War." Their plan was only an outline, which "committed no one to their precise tenor or form"; and the Virginia delegates would be as free as any others to discuss and shape them. In ordinary circumstances Washington would have been chosen to present them to the Convention. But the delegates foresaw that he would be the presiding officer, and so instead chose Randolph. He was governor of the state, "of distinguished talents, and in the habit of public speaking," as Madison long afterward explained.

Statesmen as the Virginia delegates were, they were politicians enough to know that the first plan presented to the Convention might have an advantage over any that came later. The smaller states would naturally object to the Virginia plan for representation in the national legislature, which would give Virginia the largest number of votes—even though it would also oblige Virginia to make the largest contribution to the national revenues. Virginia, through its delegates, was properly attentive to its own interests, which had suffered from the one-state one-vote rule of the Articles of Confederation. But on the whole the Virginia delegates had taken their stand above Virginia's local interests, and did not consider them in the long run to be in conflict with the general interests of the United States. One state could not be rich or poor, orderly or disorderly, without affecting the other states. And as to population, Virginia had already consented to the independence of Kentucky, and had ceded to Congress all her claim to the Northwest Territory (the present Middle Western states between the Ohio and the Mississippi).

The punctuality of the Virginia delegates and their concerted planning before May 25 had put them by that time in a position of leadership. But delegates from other states too had been active. Charles Pinckney of South Carolina had come from Congress in New York with a plan of his own. In Congress he had served on a committee charged with recommending amendments to the Articles of Confederation, and his plan, though now lost as a whole, appears from surviving parts of it to have aimed at amending the Articles rather than supplanting them, as the Virginia plan did. George Read of Delaware, who had seen a copy of the Pinckney draft by May 21, saw that its plan for proportional representation might give Delaware only "one member in eighty" in the national legislature. Even if he liked such a scheme he could not vote for it, because the Delaware delegates had been explicitly forbidden by their instructions to join in any alteration of the Articles which should affect the one-state one-vote rule.

Much discussion, unrecorded and so only to be guessed at, went on at the Indian Queen, a tavern in Fourth Street near Chestnut which had already begun to be the informal headquarters of Convention delegates. Before May 25 Mason and Madison of Virginia had taken lodgings there. So had Rutledge and Charles Pinckney of South Carolina; Governor Alexander Martin and Hugh Williamson of North Carolina; Richard Bassett of Delaware, Hamilton of New York, and perhaps others; and they were to be joined before the 28th by Nathaniel Gorham and Caleb Strong of Massachusetts. In time the delegates had a "Hall" or common room to themselves, where they could talk at ease about Convention matters that must be kept secret from the public.

A guest who stopped at the Indian Queen in July said that it was "a large pile of buildings, with many spacious halls, and numerous small apartments, appropriated for lodging rooms." He was impressed by the liveried Negro servant who expertly took charge of him when he inquired of the "barkeeper" (clerk) about lodgings. This servant was "a young, sprightly, well-built black fellow, neatly dressed—blue coat, sleeves and cape red, and buff waistcoat and breeches, the bosom of his shirt ruffled, and hair powdered." He conducted the visitor to a "rather small but very handsome chamber (No. 9), furnished with a rich field bed, bureau, table with drawers, a large looking glass, neat chairs, and other furniture." It was on the third floor, faced the east, and commanded a "fine prospect" of the Delaware and the Jersey shore. After the servant had carried up the baggage, "he brought two of the latest London magazines and laid on the table. I ordered him to call a barber, furnish me with a bowl of water for washing, and to have tea on the table by the time I was dressed."

George Mason, who was used to more comfortable quarters on his Virginia plantation, thought well of the Indian Queen. He and his son John, he wrote on May 20, were "very well accommodated, have a good room to ourselves, and are charged only twenty-five shillings Pennsylvania currency per day, including our servants and horses," not liquor and extra charges. By the 27th, however, Mason had begun "to grow heartily tired of the etiquette and nonsense so fashionable in this city. It would take me some months to make myself master of them, and that it should require months to learn what is not worth remembering as many minutes, is to me so discouraging a circumstance as determines me to give myself no manner of trouble about them." Other delegates from the country or smaller towns felt the same way. Philadelphia had less than 30,000 inhabitants, excluding the suburbs, but it was the largest city in the United States, and the capital so far as there was one. A kind of official society had grown up, more fashionable and formal than the Quakerly society of the days before the Revolution. Even Washington, who lived handsomely at Mount Vernon, commented on the "great splendor" in which he dined at William Bingham's on May 21.

Philadelphia was proudly aware that month of its position in American affairs. The "collective wisdom of the Continent," according to the *Pennsylvania Herald,* had met there to deliberate "upon the extensive politics of the confederated empire." The Society of the Cincinnati, "those veterans whose valour established a mighty revolution," were "once more assembled to recognize their fellowship in arms and to communicate to their distressed brethren the blessings of peace." The Presbyterian Synods of New York and Pennsylvania also were meeting in the city, to "clear and distribute the streams of religion through the American world," as the *Pennsylvania Journal* put it.

Outside of Virginia, probably no other state had given more thought than Pennsylvania to the ineffectiveness of the central government under the Articles of Confederation. There were former loyalists in Philadelphia who remembered peaceful days under the British Crown and wished, privately, for the establish-

ment of a monarchy in America. Only the past April the Philadelphia newspapers had published a letter from an unidentified
correspondent, asking if it might not be wise to give up the
attempt to form "one General Government for the whole community" and instead "to distribute the United States into three
Republics, who would enter into a perpetual league and alliance
for mutual defence." This suggestion, reprinted and discussed in
newspapers both north and south of Philadelphia, seems to have
made considerable headway. Philadelphia, with its experience as
a capital, preferred a federal government for the whole country,
and no doubt hoped its seat would be Philadelphia.

Dr. Benjamin Rush of Philadelphia had the past January given
voice to the most ardent federal principles in his *Address to the
People of the United States,* which opened with words that have
long been famous: "There is nothing more common," he said,
"than to confound the terms of the American revolution with
those of the late American war. The American war is over: but
this is far from being the case with the American revolution. On
the contrary, nothing but the first act of the great drama is closed.
It remains yet to establish and perfect our new forms of government; and to prepare the principles, morals, and manners of our
citizens, for these forms of government, after they are established and brought to perfection."

Rush's words here summed up the opinion of many Americans,
whether in Philadelphia or elsewhere, who were thinking about
the future of the republic. Both in Philadelphia and elsewhere
there were many more who were uninformed or indifferent as to
any need of change; a good many who were jealous for the
sovereignty of their separate states; some who feared that a
stronger federal constitution might create a super-state in which
local self-government would be lost; a few who had come to the
conclusion that the people of so widespread a confederation
could never govern themselves. In the circumstances perhaps
nothing did so much to encourage public faith in the Federal
Convention as the presence of Washington among the delegates.
He had been the symbol of American union as commander in
chief. He would be a symbol of union as president of the Convention.

Testimony to the general confidence in him comes from a gos-
siping observer, Susannah Dillwyn, who in May wrote her

father a hitherto unpublished letter from Philadelphia.[1] "There is now sitting in this city a grand convention—who are to form some new system of government or mend the old one—I suppose it is a body of great consequence—as they say it depends entirely upon their pleasure—whether we shall in future have a congress.

"They are collected from all the States and their equipages &c make some addition to the usual bustle—General Washington is among them—he is certainly a very good character—but the common people dont know how to admire without adoring him.

"I heard there were a few days ago half a dozen Gentlemen— who hearing he was going a little way out of town—follow'd him, intending to take his horses out of his carriage and draw it to the city themselves—but a friend of his who knew it would be disagreeable gave him private notice of their design—upon which he went another road & disappointed them—I have not seen him and shall be sorry to return without having had that pleasure."

---

[1] Dillwyn Papers, Library Company of Philadelphia.

3

REVISION OR CREATION

"The Crisis is arrived at which the good People of America are to decide the solemn question whether they will by wise and magnanimous Efforts reap the just fruits of Independence which they have so gloriously acquired and of that Union which they have cemented with so much of their common Blood, or whether by giving way to unmanly Jealousies and Prejudices or to partial and transitory Interests they will renounce the auspicious blessings prepared for them by the Revolution." *General Assembly of Virginia, October 16, 1786.*

"An Union of Sovereign States, preserving their Civil Liberties and connected together by such Tyes as to Preserve permanent & effective Governments is a system not described, it is a Circumstance that has not Occurred in the History of men." *North Carolina delegates to Governor Richard Caswell, June 14, 1787.*

THE CARRIAGES of the delegates, and some of the delegates on foot or on horseback, made their way to the State House through a heavy rain on the morning of Friday, May 25. With a majority of the thirteen states at last represented, it was at last necessary to set down the names of the delegates in attendance. The whole of New England had only one delegate: King of Massachusetts. Hamilton and Yates of New York, Brearley, Houston, and Paterson of New Jersey, Robert and Gouverneur Morris, FitzSimons, and Wilson of Pennsylvania, were present. Franklin was absent because of the weather and his infirmities. Delaware had Read, Bassett, and Broom. Maryland was not yet represented, but all seven Virginia delegates were solidly on hand: Washington, Randolph, Wythe, Mason, Madison, Blair, McClurg. For North Carolina there were four out of the total of five elected: Spaight, Davie, Martin, Williamson. All four of the South Carolina delegates had come: Rutledge, the two Pinckneys (who were second cousins), and Butler. Few of Georgia was still his state's only representative.

As soon as they were settled in their chairs, ranged probably in arcs not rows facing the speaker's chair at the east side of the square room, they proceeded to the election of a president. Franklin, the only delegate besides Washington who could have been thought of for the post, had intended to put Washington's name in nomination. In Franklin's absence, Robert Morris moved, as for Franklin and Pennsylvania, that a president be elected by ballot. When this was agreed to, Morris nominated Washington, as everybody expected and desired. Rutledge, seconding the motion, observed that in view of Washington's presence there could be no discussion. The ballots were taken, each state casting one vote, and Washington was found to have been unanimously chosen. Morris and Rutledge conducted him to the president's chair, standing on its low dais behind the desk on which the Declaration of Independence had been signed. That memorable chair, which belonged to the Pennsylvania Assembly, had been used by all the presidents of the Continental Congress when it met in Philadelphia. On the crown which surmounted the chair's high back was carved and gilded a rising (or was it a setting?) sun.

Sitting here in the room in which he had been chosen commander in chief, Washington now accepted the new honor with words as modest as those he had spoken then. He thanked the delegates, reminded them that he was undertaking this task without experience, and hoped that his errors, which would be unintentional, might be excused. Some of the delegates present had never seen him before this Convention, but already they saw him as heroic and prophetic, hardly noticing in detail his tall, heavy body, ruddy face, grave blue eyes, sloping shoulders, large hands and feet, and long horseman's legs; hardly aware that his badly fitted false teeth made his words indistinct, as an admiring French lady had noted the past October at Mount Vernon. All these things were unimportant in comparison with his general look of command. It was as natural for Washington to command as for Franklin to think.

Wilson of Pennsylvania moved that a secretary be appointed, and nominated Franklin's grandson, William Temple Franklin, who had been secretary to his grandfather in Paris and to the commissioners who negotiated the treaty of peace with England. Colonel Hamilton of New York nominated Major William Jackson of South Carolina, who had been a lieutenant in the Continental Army before he was eighteen, had served for two years as assistant secretary of war, and now wished to re-enter the public service in a capacity that might lead to something more substantial under the new government. Jackson was elected over Temple Franklin, and was called in to take his seat.

His first duty was to read the credentials which the various delegates had brought from the Commonwealths of Massachusetts, Pennsylvania, and Virginia; the States of New York, New Jersey, Delaware, North Carolina, South Carolina, and Georgia (of which the official style was "The State of Georgia by the grace of God, free, Sovereign and Independent"). The credentials were greatly different in language but they generally agreed in instructing the delegates to consider and report revisions of the Articles of Confederation. Not even Virginia clearly authorized any attempt to draft a new constitution. Delaware enjoined its delegates against consenting to any change in the rule of equal representation of the states in Congress.

Here was a serious obstacle at the very outset. Suppose the Convention should decide in favor of amending the rule of representation, against the vote of Delaware. The amendment would have to be submitted to Congress. Suppose Congress should approve. The amendment would then have to be sent to the states for ratification, and could not become a part of the Articles unless it was "confirmed by the legislatures of every state." Delaware could refuse to confirm it. The 60,000 people of Delaware would have the right, under the Articles, to defeat the will of an overwhelming majority of all Americans.

For the present there was nothing to be said about this difficulty. The Convention appointed a messenger and a doorkeeper. Charles Pinckney moved that a committee be appointed to draw up rules of order for the conduct of Convention business. The choice, by ballot, fell on Wythe of Virginia, Hamilton of New York, and Charles Pinckney of South Carolina. Then the Convention adjourned to ten o'clock on the morning of Monday the 28th.

On Monday nine more delegates were present. Massachusetts was now officially represented by the punctual King and the tardier Nathaniel Gorham and Caleb Strong. Connecticut had sent its first delegate in Oliver Ellsworth. Gunning Bedford joined the other delegates from Delaware. James McHenry, Irish-born aide to Washington and to Lafayette during the Revolution, was Maryland's first representative to attend. Franklin, after Friday's illness, was again present, and with him three more delegates who made up for Pennsylvania the largest delegation in the Convention: George Clymer, who had signed the Declaration, the Quaker Major General Thomas Mifflin, and the Connecticut-born Jared Ingersoll, who for the past two years had been insistent in speech and in print on the need of revising or supplementing the Articles of Confederation. Every one of the nine except Strong had been, or now was, a member, and Gorham and Mifflin had each been a president, of Congress. Gorham and Clymer were merchants, McHenry was a physician, and Strong, Ellsworth, Ingersoll, and Bedford were all lawyers who had been active in state or Confederation affairs.

Wythe, as chairman of the committee appointed on Friday, reported the rules that had been drafted. He read them through "in his place" and then gave them to the secretary. The Secretary read them through again, and once more one by one for the consideration of the house. Two of them were rejected. One of these would have authorized any delegate to call for the "yeas and nays" on any vote and have them entered on the minutes. King, objecting to the rule, "urged that as the acts of the Convention were not to bind the constituents it was unnecessary to exhibit this evidence of the votes; and improper as changes of opinion would be frequent in the course of business & would fill the minutes with contradictions." Mason seconded the objection, "adding that such a record of the opinions of members would be an obstacle to the change of them on conviction; and in case of its being hereafter promulged must furnish handles to the adversaries of the Result of the Meeting."

The proposed rule was unanimously rejected. All the delegates were aware that the work ahead of them was unprecedented as well as intricate. Not one of them had more than a tentative conception of the government he desired for the United States. Different delegates had different conceptions, saw them in different lights, and expressed them in different terms. They differed in their degrees of attachment to the government now in being, and in the amounts of confidence with which they faced the prospect and risk of change. Some had local patriotisms, some had personal ambitions. Uncertain of themselves, they were uncertain of one another. Even if it should be possible to come to a general understanding of the situation, it might not be possible to agree on the best steps to be taken. Their problem could not be merely reasoned out; it had to be felt through, by some process of growth in the corporate body of this assemblage. Nor was their own growth the whole matter. If they went beyond the wishes of their constituents, they might find their proposals unacceptable and their work wasted. They knew there was certain to be opposition to every specific alteration that might be proposed, and a stubborn inertia resisting any new creation. When they rejected the rule about recording the votes in the minutes, they were keeping their own hands free inside the Convention, and withholding weapons from their adversaries outside it.

For the most part, the other rules were routine provisions for convenience and courtesy in the meetings. The first rule was likely to call for protest, and later did so, from the states. Seven state delegations were to make up a quorum in the Convention, and a majority of the states represented on any day could decide all questions before the house. This meant that the delegates from only four states might recommend amendments to the Articles of Confederation. But of course such amendments were subject to approval by Congress and ratification by the states.

The Convention delegates knew, many of them from experience, that Congress was often delayed by the non-attendance of its members. Butler of South Carolina moved that the Convention provide against the interruption of business by the absence of delegates, and against "licentious publication of their proceedings." To this, Spaight of North Carolina added a motion to provide that the house might be free to change its mind on any question even after a vote, but also that decisions might not be too hastily rescinded. These motions were referred to the committee on rules, and the Convention adjourned to the next day.

On Tuesday the 29th Wythe for the committee reported further rules which were approved and adopted. As to attendance: no member was to be absent without leave unless his state would be fully represented without him. Committees were not to sit while the Convention was, "or ought to be, sitting." As to reconsidering or rescinding: after a majority had decided a question, any delegate on that same day might move to reconsider it, and this might be done if the house unanimously consented. After that day, a motion for reconsidering must be announced a day before it was made, and the Convention, if it agreed, might assign some future day for the motion.

As to the "licentious publication of their proceedings," the committee reported and the house approved and adopted the Convention's much controverted rule of secrecy. "That no copy be taken of any entry on the journal during the sitting of the House without the leave of the House. That members only be permitted to inspect the journal. That nothing spoken in the House be printed, or otherwise published, or communicated without leave."

Jefferson in Paris, when he heard of this decision by the delegates, was "sorry they began their deliberations by so abominable a precedent as that of tying up the tongues of their members. Nothing can justify this example but the innocence of their intentions, & ignorance of the value of public discussions." No man present in the Convention on May 29 objected or protested. Mason, reasonable and enlightened, wrote on June 1 that he thought the rule "a necessary precaution to prevent misrepresentations or mistakes; there being a material difference between the appearance of a subject in its first crude and undigested shape, and after it shall have been properly matured and arranged." Madison, forty-three years later, still believed the Convention had been right in sitting "with closed doors, because opinions were so various and at first so crude that it was necessary they should be long debated before any uniform system of opinion could be formed. Meantime the minds of the members were changing, and much was to be gained by a yielding and accommodating spirit. Had the members committed themselves publicly at first, they would have afterwards supposed consistency required them to maintain their ground, whereas by secret discussion no man felt himself obliged to retain his opinions any longer than he was satisfied of their propriety and truth, and was open to the force of argument." In 1830 Madison believed that no constitution would ever have been adopted if the Convention debates had been public.

Some such belief was held in advance by most of the delegates. This was, in a sense, less a convention than a committee, and in fact it sat at first as a committee of the whole house. In the debates the delegates were much of the time thinking out loud. If they desired not to be bound by their own first unformed opinions, still less did they desire to be bound by the expectations and disappointments which publicity might rouse in their constituents. Before news of temporary decisions could reach Georgia or New Hampshire, they could have been changed in Philadelphia. Antagonisms created here or there by wrong decisions, later rescinded, might sullenly persist, no matter what the eventual result. Particular states might feel bound to support the proposals of their delegates, and to oppose those made by delegates from rival states.

Above all, the delegates in the Convention wished to be judged by their final, total achievement, presented whole when it should be ready. Perhaps some of them hoped to hide within the Convention and so to avoid individual blame. Others were perfectly willing to forego individual credit if the public might be benefited. Many cross-purposes as were to arise during the summer, and had in May begun to be apparent, the Convention then and afterward thought of itself as a responsible political body engaged in an enterprise of great significance. They were not making laws for their country; they were trying to find the best form of government they could agree on, and then intending to offer it to their fellow citizens for their own decision. Certainly some of the delegates thought of themselves as engaged in a process like that of a creative artist, who insists on finishing his work before he exhibits it at all.

By the rule of secrecy the Convention may have done itself a service, but it did a disservice to history. The official Journal kept by the secretary—and never printed till 1819—is formal and unrevealing. Very few details leaked out through careless or disaffected delegates. When in time there seemed no further need of such discretion, and aging delegates talked to posterity, their memories were often inexact and conflicting. The most momentous single chapter in American history has to be detected and deduced from miscellaneous records in which the great drama is frequently obscure and almost always overlooked.

Fortunately, some of the delegates kept private records that slowly found their way into print from 1821 to 1904. Those by Yates, King, McHenry, Pierce, Paterson, Hamilton, Charles

Pinckney, and Mason are of varying degrees of usefulness, but none can compare with the notes kept by Madison.

From the first, Madison seems to have been regarded by his fellow delegates as a licensed private recorder of their proceedings. "I chose a seat," he later explained, "in front of the presiding member, with the other members on my right hand and left hand. In this favorable position for hearing all that passed I noted in terms legible and abbreviations and marks intelligible to myself what was read from the Chair or spoken by the members; and losing not a moment unnecessarily between the adjournment and reassembling of the Convention I was enabled to write out my daily notes during the session or within a few finishing days after its close. . . . It happened also that I was not absent a single day, nor more than a casual fraction of an hour in any day, so that I could not have lost a single speech, unless a very short one." Madison's colleagues in several cases gave him copies of their written speeches or motions, which now survive in his notes (published in 1840) if nowhere else. He is the indispensable chronicler of the Convention, and sometimes the skeleton of his narrative, to the eye of any imaginative reader, puts on flesh and blood and walks through days that without him would be lost to memory.

II

On this Tuesday when the rule of secrecy was adopted, the Convention seated two important new delegates: John Dickinson of Delaware, who had voted against the Declaration of Independence but had fought for it in the Continental Army; signer of the Articles of Confederation, president in turn of Delaware and of Pennsylvania; and Elbridge Gerry of Massachusetts, merchant and shipowner, signer of the Declaration and the Articles. Massachusetts and Delaware were now represented by all their delegates, as were also Pennsylvania, Virginia, and South Carolina. Connecticut (which permitted any one of its delegates to represent it), New York, New Jersey, and North Carolina were officially represented. Nine states in all, as many as were required for any major decision in Congress.

When the Convention was ready to begin its real business, Governor Randolph of Virginia laid before it—in the dry words of the Journal—"sundry propositions, in writing, concerning the american confederation, and the establishment of a national government."[1] But before presenting the Virginia plan, which he and his colleagues had drawn up in advance, Randolph spoke at length about the crisis in the United States, the need of an adequate government, and the defects of the Articles of Confederation. His arguments were arranged under five heads.

(1) An adequate government must be able to secure the country against foreign invasion. Congress under the Articles could not do that, because it could not control the individual states in their dealings with foreign states, and could not raise an army or levy taxes to carry on a war if it should come. (2) An adequate government must be able to prevent dissensions among the states or seditions in them. Congress under the Articles had neither constitutional right nor sufficient force to do these things. (3) An adequate government must be able to provide for general benefits, such as regulation of interstate trade, development of national works, inland navigation, agriculture, manufactures, which individual states could not accomplish alone. The Articles of Confederation had no means and no authority to provide the people with such "blessings." (4) An adequate government must be able to defend itself against the encroachments of the several states. The history of the Confederation had been full of steady resistance by the states to federal measures. (5) An adequate central government must be superior to local governments. Under the Articles there was no federal constitution which was paramount to the state constitutions, either in law or in effect.

Aware that four of the delegates listening to him—Gerry, Gouverneur Morris, Robert Morris, John Dickinson—had signed the Articles of Confederation, Randolph did not blame the defects of the Confederation on its authors. They had been wise and great men, he said, and had done all that patriots could do "in the then infancy of the science of constitutions, & of confederacies." They could not in 1777 have foreseen how difficult it would be to requisition men or money for federal purposes. Commercial discords had not then arisen among the states. No state had yet experienced a rebellion, such as the armed rebellion led by Daniel Shays in Massachusetts in 1786. Foreign debts had not become urgent, paper money had not become a threat to

[1] See Appendix 3.

commerce and finance, treaties had not been violated—"and perhaps nothing better could be obtained from the jealousy of the states with regard to their sovereignty."

Though Randolph read the fifteen resolutions of the Virginia plan, and explained them one by one, there was that day no discussion. The Convention merely voted to resolve itself, the day following, into a committee of the whole and to refer the Randolph proposals to the committee. Charles Pinckney of South Carolina introduced his "draught of a foederal government to be agreed upon between the free and independent States of America." The Pinckney plan also was referred to the committee of the whole "appointed to consider of the state of the american Union." Then the Convention adjourned to ten o'clock the next morning.

But before it adjourned, Hamilton of New York made what appears to be his first remark in Convention on the problem before them. It struck him, he said, "as a necessary and preliminary inquiry to the propositions from Virginia whether the united States were susceptible of one government, or required a separate existence connected only by leagues offensive and defensive and treaties of commerce." Here he put his finger on the essential point at issue. Were the United States to continue to be a mere league of states held together by a set of treaties, or were they to become a nation with a national government?

On Wednesday the 30th Roger Sherman of Connecticut attended and took his seat. He had begun life as a shoemaker, with little schooling, had prospered as shopkeeper, devoted most of his life to public service, signed the Articles of Association of 1774, the Declaration, and the Articles of Confederation; and he now came to the Federal Convention with all the simplicity, cunning, and courage of a rural Yankee.

Resolving itself into a committee of the whole, with Gorham of Massachusetts in the chair, the Convention at once took up the Randolph resolutions. Randolph, on the suggestion of Gouverneur Morris, moved that the first resolution, which was somewhat general in terms, be postponed till three more precise substitute resolutions could be discussed.

The first of these read: "that an Union of the States, merely foederal, will not accomplish the objects proposed by the articles of confederation, namely 'common defence, security of liberty, and general welfare.'" The second: "that no treaty or treaties among the whole or part of the States, as individual sovereignties, would be sufficient." Charles Cotesworth Pinckney pointed out that if the delegates agreed on the first, then their business was at an end. They had come together to revise the present Confederation. To say that no revision would make it adequate was to say there was no use in their going further. The other delegates felt the weight of his argument and decided to postpone both the first and second substitute resolutions. This brought them to the third, which was positive, not negative, and which included both the others and more besides: "That a national government ought to be established consisting of a supreme legislative, judiciary and executive."

For a few moments nobody spoke, till Wythe of Virginia said he presumed, "from the silence of the house," that they were prepared to pass on the resolution, and he suggested that it be put to a vote. It then appeared that the delegates were silent, not from consent to this revolutionary proposal, but from the conflict of their thoughts about it. Charles Pinckney asked if Randolph meant to abolish the state governments altogether. Randolph explained that the states would give up only the powers which they granted, under the proposed government, to the central authority. Dickinson of Delaware and Gerry of Massachusetts admitted that the Confederation was defective, but thought the delegates should limit themselves to trying to amend it, as they had been authorized to do. Gouverneur Morris of Pennsylvania objected that the delegates were not yet agreed upon the terms they used. They could not say that the present United States had a federal government, for it had not. A federal government would have "a right to compel every part to do its duty." The states and the federal government could not both be supreme. Two supremes were inconceivable. There must be one government or none. "We had better take a supreme government now, than a despot twenty years hence—for come he must" in the anarchy which would result from the present confusion.

Mason of Virginia made another essential point. The Articles were blamed for not providing for the coercion or punishment of delinquent states. But in the very nature of things, states could not be coerced or punished collectively. That was war. What was needed was a federal government which could "directly operate on individuals, and would punish those only whose guilt required it." That was law, though Mason may not have said this in so many words. He was saying that to undertake to coerce or punish a state is to bring all its citizens to the defense of their territory or liberty. To undertake to punish individual offenders is to distinguish between them and those who have not offended and so need not feel obliged to take up the offenders' cause in patriotic loyalty.

Without too much delay the committee of the whole resolved "that it is the opinion of this Committee that a national government ought to be established consisting of a supreme Legislative, Judiciary, and Executive." Sherman, representing Connecticut, cautiously voted no. New York was divided. New Jersey, for want of a quorum in attendance that day, did not vote. Massachusetts, Pennsylvania, Delaware, Virginia, and the Carolinas voted aye. The resolution was carried. The Convention, in committee, had cast its first vote in favor of creation, not revision.

But after this general statement, there had to be details. Randolph brought up the second of his original resolutions, which experimentally said: "that the rights of suffrage in the national legislature ought to be proportioned to the quotas of contributions, or to the number of free inhabitants, as the one or the other rule may seem best in different cases." As the resolution stood, it seemed to satisfy no one. Hamilton moved, with Spaight of North Carolina seconding, that representation be based solely on the number of free inhabitants. This was postponed. After some further skirmishing, which was really thinking, Madison moved, and Gouverneur Morris seconded, "that the equality of suffrage established by the articles of Confederation ought not to prevail in the national Legislature, and that an equitable ratio of representation ought to be substituted." This, "being generally relished," would have been agreed to. But Read for Delaware reminded the committee of the whole that he and his colleagues were restrained by their commission from assenting to any change of the rule of suffrage; and that if this were insisted on, they might feel it their duty to leave the Convention.

Here for the time being the discussion had to break up. Gouverneur Morris said that the Convention would be worse off without the help of the Delaware delegates; that the "secession of a State" so early as this would be a lamentable proof of discord; but that the change proposed was so fundamental it could not be dispensed with. Madison said that, whatever reason there may have been for equality of suffrage so long as the union was a confederation of sovereign states, it must cease to operate under a national government. This would make different numbers of representatives as reasonable for large states and small states within the union as for large counties and small counties within a particular state. Several delegates argued that, while the Delaware instructions forbade the delegates to join in any alteration of the one-state one-vote rule, they were not required to secede from the Convention if the matter came up. The delegates from Delaware would—and thought they could—not yield. Consideration of the resolution on the rule of suffrage was postponed, and the Convention adjourned to the next day.

Delaware, able to agree in principle that a national government ought to be established, could not agree to the first step toward creating such a government if this appeared at first thought to be disadvantageous to Delaware; and could not be persuaded that there need be no such conflict between general and local interests as Delaware now feared. Delaware believed it was fighting for its very existence, with no weapon but its sovereignty, which it would be suicide to give up. The Delaware instructions had forced Delaware to take, in the Convention, before any other of the small states, the position which was to make all of them the chief problem for weeks to come.

The Convention may have decided to create a new government, not revise an old one. But it had still to learn how hard it is for men to revise their own ways of thinking and feeling about an old government, and to change the habits it has formed in them, even while they are working for the change which their reasons and their wills desire.

4

THE LEGISLATURE
AND THE PEOPLE

"They [the members of Congress] are of the People, and return again to mix with the People, having no more durable pre-eminence than the different Grains of Sand in an Hourglass. Such an Assembly cannot easily become dangerous to Liberty. They are the Servants of the People, sent together to do the People's Business, and promote the public Welfare; their Powers must be sufficient, or their Duties cannot be performed." *Benjamin Franklin to George Whatley, May 23, 1785.*

"The election of the different branches of Congress by the Freemen, either directly or indirectly is the pivot on which turns the first Wheel of the government; a Wheel which communicates motion to all the rest." *George Washington, fragment of address never delivered, April (?) 1789.*

ON THURSDAY May 31, Major William Pierce of Georgia arrived from New York, where for four months he had been serving his state in Congress, to take a seat in the Convention along with his colleague William Few. Pierce had been an artillery officer in the Revolution, and was now a merchant in Savannah. Almost nothing is known of him outside of the bare facts of his military career and his few weeks in the Federal Convention. But while he was in the Convention, or shortly afterward, he made notes on the characters of the delegates which help posterity to look behind those closed doors and see the men of 1787 as they seemed and sounded at their work.

All of them, in their minds if not in ink on paper, must have been doing the same thing. Many of them were strangers to one another, or were known only by their names and public records. They came then to Independence Hall as they come now into the history of the Convention, mere outlines at first, to be filled in with living qualities and become familiar persons in the long debate. Readers of the Convention's history can do no more than follow that process, learning in time to fix their attention on the original and articulate members of the assembly, to disregard the negligible ones, and yet to be always aware that the whole was greater than the parts as the parts were slowly fused into a general agreement with only a few dissenting voices.

Washington was too renowned for Pierce to feel the need of saying much about him, and he said only what everybody was then saying: that the soldier had become a statesman, and that he was to be compared with Gustavus Vasa, Peter the Great, and Cincinnatus. About Franklin, who had been in Europe during most of Pierce's life and was almost legendary, Pierce was more specific. Of course Franklin was "the greatest phylosopher of the present age," but "he does not shine much in public Council,—he is no Speaker, nor does he seem to let politics engage his attention." Observers more experienced than Pierce had before this misjudged Franklin's skill as a politician, because he spoke so seldom and so briefly and with so little rhetoric, and because his wit might play over a whole field of speculation while other men were digging in one spot. Still, Pierce perceived that Franklin was "a most extraordinary man, and tells a story in a style more engaging than anything I ever heard. . . . He is 82 years old, and possesses an activity of mind equal to a youth of 25 years of age."

Pierce, who had known Madison in Congress, found him already a major figure in the Convention. There he sat, close in front of the President's chair, a small man plainly dressed, his blue eyes bright as a bird's, taking note of whatever went on and incessantly writing it down. "Mr. Maddison," Pierce thought and said, "is a character who has long been in public life; and what is very remarkable every Person seems to acknowledge his greatness. He blends together the profound politician, with the Scholar. In the management of every great question he evidently took the lead in the Convention, and tho' he cannot be called an Orator, he is a most agreeable, eloquent, and convincing Speaker." Here Pierce exposed his conception of oratory. "From a spirit of industry and application which he possesses in a most eminent degree, he always comes forward the best informed Man of any point in debate. The affairs of the United States, he perhaps has the most correct knowledge of, of any man in the Union. . . . Mr. Maddison is about 37 years of age, a Gentleman of great modesty,—with a remarkable sweet temper. He is easy and unreserved among his acquaintance, and has a most agreeable style of conversation."

To Pierce, consciously Southern and a gentleman, Roger Sherman of Connecticut was "the oddest shaped character I ever remember to have met with. He is awkward, un-meaning, and unaccountably strange in his manner. But in his train of thinking there is something regular, deep and comprehensive; yet the oddity of his address, the vulgarisms that accompany his public speaking, and that strange New England cant which runs through his public as well as his private speaking make everything that is connected with him gross and laughable;—and yet he deserves infinite praise,—no Man has a better Heart nor a clearer Head. If he cannot embellish he can furnish thoughts that are wise and useful. He is an able politician, and extremely artful in accomplishing any particular object;—it is remarked that he seldom fails."

Pierce's Sherman sounds like a country Puritan in a contemporary comedy; a shoemaker who has risen from his last but whose useful muscles have never learned to be graceful; a shrewd politician whose tongue may at any minute use pious words in his discourse, in a Yankee accent; yet a man, if you can see past his rough surfaces, of virtue and judgment. There was in him none of the easy charm which made Pierce forget that Franklin too had sprung from a Puritan stock much like Sherman's. The provincial politician and the cosmopolitan philosopher, the two oldest men in the Convention, were both Yankees of an earlier day, still wise and bold among the strong young men of this.

Pierce admired the "clear and copious understanding" of Mason of Virginia, and the "legal and political knowledge" of Wilson of Pennsylvania. "Government seems to have been his peculiar Study, all the political institutions of the World he knows in detail, and can trace the causes and effects of every revolution from the earliest stages of the Grecian commonwealth down to the present time." But for Pierce the dramatic hero (or, rather, the leading man) in the action on the stage of Independence Hall was Gouverneur Morris.

"Mr. Gouverneur Morris," Pierce noted, "is one of those

Genius's in whom every species of talents combine to render him conspicuous and flourishing in public debate:—He winds through all the mazes of rhetoric, and throws around him such a glare that he charms, captivates, and leads away the senses of all who hear him. With an infinite stretch of fancy he brings to view things when he is engaged in deep argumentation, that render all the labor of reasoning easy and pleasing." Still, Pierce could not help noting that Morris was "fickle and inconstant,—never pursuing one train of thinking,—nor ever regular."

Morris, who spoke more often than any other delegate to the Convention, seemed exotic there, with his wit and arrogance, his reputation for gallantry, and his wooden leg. It was whispered in Philadelphia that he had lost his leg in a leap from a balcony to escape an angry husband. There were no amorous balconies in Philadelphia, and nobody now knows the names of the ladies who may have loved Morris in that prim city to which he had come from New York and which he was soon to leave for Paris. A more dependable story about his accident is more revealing about his character. He had been thrown from his carriage seven years before, and his left leg so badly broken that, as surgeons then thought, it had to be amputated. One of his friends came to offer him consolation "on an event so melancholy." Such a trial would have a good effect on his morals, since it would reduce his impulses towards "the pleasures and dissipations of life, into which young men are too apt to be led. 'My good Sir,' replied Mr. Morris, 'you argue the matter so handsomely, and point out so clearly the advantages of beings without legs, that I am almost tempted to part with the other.'"

Armed sentries outside the State House, and in the corridor before the closed door of the chamber where the Convention sat, served to enforce its rule of secrecy. Pierce in his notes tells of something that might have made a very important secret public. The delegates were permitted to have copies of the Virginia plan, apparently taken by each in his own handwriting. One day in June a delegate dropped his copy, which was found by Mifflin outside the chamber and turned over to Washington. He kept it in his pocket till the end of the session, and the motion to adjourn. Then, before putting the motion, Washington rose from his chair and spoke sternly, as Pierce remembered the incident:

" 'Gentlemen, I am sorry to find that some one Member of this Body, has been so neglectful to the secrets of the Convention as to drop in the State House a copy of their proceedings, which by accident was picked up and delivered to me this Morning. I must entreat Gentlemen to be more careful, least our Transactions get into the News Papers, and disturb the public repose by premature speculations. I know not whose Paper it is, but there it is (throwing it down on the table), let him who owns it take it.' At the same time he bowed, picked up his Hat, and quitted the room with a dignity so severe that every Person seemed alarmed."

Pierce was extremely alarmed, when he felt in his pocket for his own copy and found it missing; but the copy on the table turned out to be in the handwriting of another. "When I went to my lodgings in the Indian Queen, I found my copy in a coat pocket which I had pulled off that Morning. It is something remarkable that no Person ever owned the Paper." Yet surely not to be wondered at that no man would admit he had been careless in a matter on which they were unanimously and scrupulously agreed.

II

Resolved again into a committee of the whole, the delegates on May 31 once more took up their exploratory work along the lines laid down by the Virginia plan. Apparently without debate or dissent they agreed that the national legislature ought to consist of two branches. It was known that Franklin preferred a legislature of a single house, like that of Pennsylvania, but he did not speak, and the others saw no objection to the dual form to which Americans had been long accustomed under the British government and in most of the separate states both before and after independence.

The next resolution, the fourth in the Virginia plan, was that "the members of the first branch of the national legislature ought to be elected by the people of the several States."

To this there was prompt opposition from New England. Sherman of Connecticut thought the election should be by the state legislatures. The people, he declared, should have "as little to do as may be about the Government." They lacked information and were constantly liable to be misled. Sherman had himself come from the people, but he had for more than thirty years been an official in a state which was strongly under the influence of learned ministers and conservative magistrates, joined in a kind of republican theocracy. The ministers saw the people as in need of being informed, and the magistrates as in need of being led.

Gerry of Massachusetts had, he thought, even better reason to distrust the people. The severe depression which followed the war had forced many people in that state to demand relief from the legislature and, when this was not granted, had driven them in 1786 to armed interference with the state supreme court at Worcester and an attempt to capture the United States Arsenal at Springfield. Though the Shays insurrection had been put down by the militia the past February, Massachusetts was still unquiet. Men of property like Gerry were in no mood to look favorably on giving fresh powers to the people. "The people do not want virtue," he now said to the Convention; "but they are the dupes of pretended patriots." The misguided people of Massachusetts —many of them debtors in distress—had protested against the high salaries paid to the governor and other officials. "It would seem to be the maxim of democracy to starve the public servants." Gerry had been, he believed, "too republican heretofore: he was still however republican, but had been taught by experience the danger of the levelling spirit."

Both Sherman and Gerry here confirmed the impression which Mason of Virginia had early formed about the sentiments of the New England delegates. Mason's reply to them was clear and uncompromising. The popular branch of the national legislature, he held, "was to be the grand depository of the democratic principle of the Government. It was, so to speak, to be our House of Commons—It ought to know & sympathise with every part of the community; and ought therefore to be taken not only from different parts of the whole republic, but also from different districts of the larger members of it." In Virginia, for instance, certain districts differed from others in productions and habits, and so naturally differed in "interests and views." "He admitted that we had been too democratic but was afraid we should incautiously run into the opposite extreme."

Probably no delegate present thought of Mason as correcting

Gerry when he changed Gerry's "too republican" to "too democratic," or as contradicting himself when he could agree that
Americans had been too democratic and yet could argue that
the national legislature ought to be "the grand depository of the
democratic principle." The terms "democracy" and "democratic"
had in 1787 not acquired their later honorable meanings in common usage, but still carried with them the implication of that
unreasoning turbulence which had often characterized the voting
populace in ancient Athens. Even thoughtful Americans could in
1787 still use "democratic" and "republican" interchangeably
without particular discomfort, as they could sometimes say
"nation" when they meant "federation," or "federation" when
they meant "confederation." While most of these terms came to
be more precisely defined as the Convention went on, neither the
delegates nor the public ever arrived at a general acceptance of
an accurate terminology. The best they could do was to draw
together in a sentiment and program which finally prevailed.

They would, that is, give up the confederation which they
had, but would not make themselves over into a nation with a
consolidated government. They would stop midway between
confederation and nation, and become a federation of states
which could continue to be self-governing in local affairs while
giving to a federal government the authority to legislate, judge,
and administer in affairs common to all the states and their
people. The new federal government would be democratically
founded on the consent of the people, as expressed in their votes,
but it would take the form of a republic in which representatives
chosen by the people would actually make the laws and put them
into effect.

All this was in Mason's mind, whatever terms he used. And
there was no possibility of misunderstanding his further remarks,
as reported by Madison. "We ought to attend," Mason said, "to
the rights of every class of the people." He had often wondered
that the "superior classes of society" could be indifferent "to
this dictate of humanity & policy." No matter how affluent their
circumstances might be, or how elevated their stations, "the
course of a few years, not only might but certainly would, distribute their posterity throughout the lowest classes of Society.
Every selfish motive therefore, every family attachment, ought to
recommend such a system of policy" as would provide for the

rights and the happiness of all orders of citizens without respect to their temporary rank. Mason might think of himself as republican, but his words were democratic.

So were the words of Wilson of Pennsylvania, who "contended strenuously for drawing the most numerous branch of the Legislature immediately from the people." He was for "raising the federal pyramid to a considerable altitude," by which he meant granting the federal government extensive powers, "and for that reason wished to give it as broad a basis as possible. No government could long subsist without the confidence of the people. In a republican Government this confidence was peculiarly essential." Wilson thought it "wrong to increase the weight of the State Legislatures by making them the electors of the national Legislature." There had been too much interference between the local and general governments already. And he reminded the Convention that "the opposition of States to federal Measures had proceded more from the Officers of the States, than from the people at large."

Madison, as reported by King of Massachusetts, thought that if the people elected the first branch of the national legislature they would be more likely to feel affection for the general government (as parents feel affection for their offspring) than if the state legislatures should be the electors and so take both the responsibility and the satisfaction from the people. The "great fabric to be raised" would therefore be more "stable and durable . . . than if it should stand merely on the pillars of the Legislatures."

When the resolution came to a motion, six states, including Massachusetts, voted aye, New York and Delaware were divided, and New Jersey and South Carolina voted no. The New Jersey and South Carolina delegates had said little or nothing, but they were opposed to election by the people, on different grounds. New Jersey was a small state, and did not like the prospect of having to give up equal representation in the national legislature. South Carolina, a large state, was represented only by men from Charleston and the low country section, who distrusted the voters of the inland counties.

The committee of the whole went on to the fifth resolution of the Virginia plan, "that the members of the second branch of the national legislature ought to be elected by those of the first." There was disagreement on various points, and seven states voted against the motion.

Leaving the problem of the second branch for future consideration, the committee took up the detailed clauses in the sixth Virginia resolution and unanimously agreed "that each branch ought to possess the right of originating acts," and "that the national legislature ought to be empowered to enjoy the legislative rights vested in Congress by the confederation." Connecticut was divided on the vague clause providing that the national legislature should be empowered "to legislate in all cases, to which the separate States are incompetent, or in which the harmony of the united States may be interrupted by the exercise of individual legislation," but nine states approved it.

Then came the extraordinary clause giving the proposed new Congress the power "to negative all laws, passed by the several States, contravening, in the opinion of the national legislature, the articles of union." Franklin moved that the clause be further strengthened by the added words at the end: "or any Treaties subsisting under the authority of the union." The delegates were just now in such harmonious, not to say enthusiastic, agreement on their plans for a national legislature that they accepted the amended clause without debate.

Nothing they had so far done more clearly revealed their general attitude toward the defects of the Articles of Confederation. All the delegates were aware that the history of the Confederation had been full of encroachments by individual states upon the central government. Even Virginia had insisted on separately ratifying the treaty of peace with Great Britain, as if the ratification by Congress were not enough, and had refused to carry out the treaty's stipulations in regard to the treatment of loyalists and the debts owed by Virginians to their British creditors. Several states had borrowed, or tried to borrow, money abroad as if they were sovereign republics. Nine of the states, from Massachusetts to South Carolina, had organized navies of their own, and all of them regarded their militia forces as state armies.

Congress, though it was supposed to have the sole right to regulate coinage, had done nothing. There were no American coins of any kind. Where hard money was used, it had to be a confusion of English sovereigns, French louis d'or, Spanish pistoles or dollars, Portuguese moidores or johanneses, ducats or caroluses from different countries, smaller coins like shillings that had found their way to America in the course of trade—all of varying and shifting values which were difficult and tedious to calculate. The paper money issued by the various states was not uniform in value. Delegates coming to Philadelphia from other sections had to adjust their money to Pennsylvania pounds and shillings, in which most Revolutionary and Confederation accounts had been reckoned. In spite of Congress, there had been irresponsible issues of paper money in some of the states: particularly in Rhode Island, where the two houses of the legislature were in such conflict that they had not bothered to concur on the selection of delegates to the Federal Convention.

Congress had tried in vain to raise money for its purposes by a five per cent duty on imported goods, and had been blocked by New York, which had its own customs system, aimed chiefly at the neighboring states of Connecticut and New Jersey. In violation of the provisions of the Articles, there had been separate agreements between individual states, and retaliatory legislation in one state against another. Individuals in the more recalcitrant or more distant states occasionally referred to the Confederation as a foreign government. William Houstoun, sent in 1785 to Congress from Georgia, thought of himself as leaving his "country" to go to "a strange land amongst Strangers." John Adams had come to the unavoidable conclusion that Congress under the Articles was "not a legislative assembly, nor a representative assembly, but only a diplomatic assembly." Its very nature denied it any authority or force, and it could not be expected to resist encroachments by the states.

Aware of all these things, the Convention delegates had no doubt that the proposed national legislature must be paramount to the state legislatures, and they decided to give it the power to negative state legislation which might affect the whole union. Because at this stage of the discussion they were thinking rather of a national government in general than of the parts of it, they were willing to put the power into the hands of the national legislature, the only part of the projected government which had yet been discussed.

But they were not yet willing to go as far as they might in this direction. On June 8 Charles Pinckney and Madison moved to reconsider and give the national legislature the power to negative *all* state laws "which shall seem to them improper," without specifying in advance what would be regarded as improper. Pinckney insisted that "this universal negative was in fact the corner stone of an efficient national Government." Madison said that "this prerogative of the General Government is the great pervading principle that must controul the centrifugal tendency of the States; which, without it, will continually fly out of their proper orbits and destroy the order & harmony of the political system." Wilson pointed out that individuals are not bound by some laws and left free to judge whether or not they will obey others. So with states. "Federal liberty is to States, what civil liberty is to private individuals. And States are not more unwilling to purchase it, by the necessary concession of their political sovereignty, than the savage is to purchase Civil liberty by the surrender of the personal sovereignty which he enjoys in a State of nature. A definition of the cases in which the Negative should be exercised, is impracticable. A discretion must be left on one side or the other. Will it not be most safely lodged on the side of the National Government?"

Here were some of the strongest statements yet advanced in favor of a general government to which the separate states would yield their sovereignty in respect to legislation. Only the three largest states—Massachusetts, Pennsylvania, and Virginia—voted aye. Delaware was divided, and all the others voted no.

It seemed, on May 31, well enough to agree that the national legislature must be paramount to the state legislatures, in specified cases, but how could its supremacy be made effective? The final clause in the sixth resolution faced the issue and empowered the national legislature "to call forth the force of the union against any member of the union, failing to fulfil it's duty under the articles thereof."

The proposal was so remote from American experience that it is no wonder it was hardly discussed. Gerry of Massachusetts foolishly suggested that the clause ought to be expressed in language which the people could not understand, to save them from alarm. His idea, according to Pierce, was "rejected on account of its *artifice*." Madison, recurring to Mason's arguments of the day before, again pointed out that there is no way to apply force "collectively and not individually." The use of force against a state "would look more like a declaration of war, than an infliction of punishment, and would probably be considered by the party attacked as a dissolution of all previous compacts by which it might be bound." He moved that the clause be postponed, and everybody agreed. The house adjourned without further discussion of the matter, which in fact was never put to a vote in any committee of the whole or in the Convention itself. The delegates realized from the first that coercion, as applied to a state, must be not only impossible but also senseless. Since all the citizens of the state could not have offended, it must be unjust to punish all of them. Fortunately, it was also unnecessary. If individuals were bound by federal laws in federal affairs, as they were bound by state laws in local affairs, there need be no trouble. Just as law-abiding citizens did not object to the state punishment of offenders against state laws, so they would not object to the federal punishment of offenders against federal laws. And the state government would feel no more obligation to intervene in cases like treason or counterfeiting than the federal government would feel in cases like larceny or murder.

III

Naturally the Convention could not go straight ahead, logical step by logical step, from the first branch of the federal legislature to the second, then to the executive, and finally to the judiciary. They were not setting up a row of independent monuments, but constructing an edifice which must have an organic unity if it was to survive. Some of the delegates hesitated to approve the election of the lower house of the legislature by the people without the assurance that the upper house would be elected by some less popular method. Other delegates wished to be sure, before putting so much power in the hands of the popular representatives, that the new executive would have power to restrain extravagant legislation by some kind of veto. All the delegates more or less clearly held, with Montesquieu and Blackstone, that in any government the powers of the legislative, executive, and judicial departments should be separate, so that the whole could be kept in order by a system of checks and balances. John Adams, American envoy to Great Britain, had just published in London *A Defence of the Constitutions of Government of the United States of America,* which vigorously applied to America the doctrine of the separation of powers, and argued in favor of a legislature of two houses as a form of control in the legislative branch. His book, speedily reprinted in Boston, New York, and Philadelphia, had its effect both on the Convention delegates and on the general public.

The doctrine of checks and balances appeared in the discussions of June 1 to June 5, on the executive and the judiciary, neither of which could be considered without reference to the others. Then on the 6th Charles Pinckney of South Carolina, given leave to interrupt the program, moved to reconsider the election of the first house of the legislature by the people—and to go back to the alternative plan of election by the state legislatures.

All the South Carolina delegates were agreed. Rutledge seconded the motion. Charles Pinckney argued that if the state legislatures should be excluded from the election they would be less likely to promote the adoption of the new government. Charles Cotesworth Pinckney believed that in a state so sparsely settled as theirs it would be impossible to bring more than four or five thousand voters together in any election, which could consequently not represent the will of the people. The legislature would be more truly representative, as well as more reliable. The legislature was against the issue of paper money, the people probably for it. General Pinckney was here speaking for all the low-country men, who insisted on a sound currency. Butler went still further in this direction. He was opposed to determining the mode of election until some ratio of representation had been fixed. If that should be based "on a principle favorable to wealth as well as numbers of Free Inhabitants," then he should be willing to see the state legislatures abolished altogether and one consolidated nation take the place of a confederation of republics.

Sherman of Connecticut agreed that if the state governments were to be abolished, the people ought to elect the legislature. But if the states were to be preserved, as he held they must be, the state legislatures should elect the national legislature, and should limit the central government to a few definite purposes: defense against foreign enemies, defense against internal dispute and a resort to force, the making of treaties with other countries, the regulation of foreign commerce and the revenue to be derived from it. In all other matters, the states should govern themselves.

People were happier, he thought, in small states than in large. Rhode Island was perhaps too small, and it was subject to faction. Some states were perhaps so large, though Sherman did not name any, that the powers of government were not "able to pervade them." He evidently believed that Connecticut was the best size, neither too small nor too large.

Wilson of Pennsylvania and Mason of Virginia repeated and reinforced their earlier arguments, and Madison in a remarkable speech on the whole problem made a specific answer to Sherman. Sherman had admitted that in a very small state faction and oppression might prevail. "It was to be inferred then that wherever these prevailed the State was too small. Had they not prevailed in the largest as well as the smallest tho' less than in the smallest; and were we not thence admonished to enlarge the sphere as far as the nature of Government would admit? This was the only defence against the inconveniences of democracy consistent with the democratic form of Government." There were bound to be factions and interests in any state. But if the state were large enough, then no one interest would be likely at any given time to form itself into a majority against the interest of the whole people or of any particular minority. It was therefore incumbent on the Convention delegates to try "to frame a republican system on such a scale & in such a form as will controul all the evils which have been experienced."

When the vote was taken, Connecticut, New Jersey, and South Carolina were in favor of election by the state legislatures, but eight states stood firmly by their original decision. New York and Delaware were not divided, as before, and Maryland was now represented.

After that there was no further discussion of the matter till it was reported by the committee of the whole to the Convention on June 21 for final settlement. New Jersey was still opposed to election by the people, and Maryland was now divided. But South Carolina, having raised a few objections, voted aye, and with it eight more states.

This was the greatest victory for popular government in the entire Convention. It should be noted that the delegates who were from the outset most favorable to a stronger central government were those who had the most faith in the people. They were not mystical in this, but practical. Mason, Wilson, and Madison all knew that democratic or republican governments had often shown themselves unstable and dissentious. But this, Madison was convinced, would be less likely in large states or nations than in small ones. Something was involved that had to do with the very nature of government, no matter what kind it might be. He had summed it up the past April in a paragraph of his *Notes on the Confederacy:*

"The great desideratum in Government is such a modification of the sovereignty as will render it sufficiently neutral between the different interests and factions to controul one part of the society from invading the rights of another, and, at the same time, sufficiently controuled itself from setting up an interest adverse to that of the whole society. In absolute Monarchies the prince is sufficiently neutral towards his subjects, but frequently sacrifices their happiness to his ambition or avarice. In small Republics, the sovereign will is sufficiently controuled from such a sacrifice of the entire Society, but is not sufficiently neutral towards the parts composing it. As a limited monarchy tempers the evils of an absolute one, so an extensive Republic meliorates the administration of a small Republic."

5

THE VIRGINIA PLAN

"The revolt from Great Britain and the formations of our new governments at that time, were nothing compared to the great business now before us; there was then a certain degree of enthusiasm, which inspired and supported the mind; but to view, through the calm, sedate medium of reason the influence which the establishment now proposed may have upon the happiness or misery of millions yet unborn, is an object of such magnitude, as absorbs, and in a manner suspends the operations of the human understanding." *George Mason to George Mason, Jr., June 1, 1787.*

"What is government itself, but the greatest of all reflections on human nature? If men were angels, no government would be necessary. If angels were to govern men, neither external nor internal controls on government would be necessary. In framing a government which is to be administered by men over men, the great difficulty lies in this: you must first enable the government to control the governed; and in the next place oblige it to control itself. A dependence on the people, is, no doubt, the primary control on the government; but experience has taught mankind the necessity of auxiliary precautions." *James Madison, The Federalist No. 51, February 8, 1788.*

THROUGHOUT the first two weeks of June the Convention was guided by the Virginia plan, though not in the order of the original resolutions. On the 4th the hour of meeting was changed from ten to eleven, and the sessions—daily except for Sunday—were continuous for five, six, or even seven hours. Each morning the house resolved itself into a committee of the whole "to consider of the state of the american Union," Washington sitting silent with the Virginia delegation but voting with them, and Gorham of Massachusetts in the "Chair of the Committee." This was a parliamentary device, then familiar to all American deliberative bodies, for keeping discussions as informal as possible and for leaving certain decisions still subject to review by the Convention, even when as here the committee and the Convention were in fact the same. While the delegates seem to have been regular in attendance, not all of them had yet arrived, and it is probable that more than thirty were seldom present on the same day.

They were not always the same thirty. On June 1 the obscure William Houstoun first attended for Georgia, and McHenry of Maryland was called back to Baltimore by the dangerous illness of his brother. The next day Daniel of St. Thomas Jenifer (whose unusual name is unexplained) of Maryland took his seat in the Convention. He was a steadfast bachelor, who according to Pierce spoke "warmly of the Ladies notwithstanding," a "Gentleman of fortune" who had served his state in various capacities at home and in Congress. Also on the 2nd John Lansing, former member of Congress and now mayor of Albany, joined Hamilton and Yates of the New York delegation; and William Samuel Johnson completed the delegation from Connecticut. Johnson, now member of Congress and president of Columbia College, had been suspected of loyalty to Great Britain during the Revolution, but had since then been restored to public favor in his state. He was a scholar, a lawyer with an honorary degree from Oxford, and an orator of reputation, though Pierce found "something in the tone of his voice not pleasing to the ear."

On June 4 Wythe of Virginia was called away by his duties as judge of the High Court of Chancery and professor at William and Mary, and he resigned from the Convention twelve days later, though approving the Virginia plan. On June 5 "William Livingston Esquire, Governor, Captain General and Commander in Chief in and over the State of New Jersey and Territories thereunto belonging" (to give him his full title as set forth in his commission, signed by himself) arrived in Philadelphia. He was a member of the powerful family of his name in New York, where he had begun his career as official and satiric wit. In New Jersey he had been a farmer, brigadier general of militia in the Revolution, governor for the past eleven years, and poet whose *Philosophic Solitude* had forty years before become one of the mild American classics of the century.

On or soon after June 7 Gouverneur Morris was obliged to leave the Convention for nearly a month spent in arranging the affairs of his estate at Morrisania, which since the death of his loyalist mother he had bought from his loyalist brother who was a major general in the British Army and married to the Duchess of Gordon. On the 9th Luther Martin of Maryland, first attorney general of the state, former member of Congress, put in his appearance. At once disturbed by the Virginia plan, he was not long in becoming energetic in the opposition to it: "so extremely prolix," Pierce thought him, "that he never speaks without tiring the patience of all who hear him." On the 11th Abraham Baldwin, who had been brigade chaplain in the Continental Army and was now president in title of the University of Georgia, which was still to be established, appeared as the last of the Georgia delegates.

Every state was fully, or at least legally, represented during June except New Hampshire, which did not even name its delegates till the 27th, and Rhode Island, which never named or sent any.

II

Still postponing consideration of the second branch of the legislature, the committee of the whole on June 1 took up the seventh Virginia resolution, which was concerned with the executive. The resolution proposed that "a national executive be instituted"; to be elected by the national legislature; to serve for a term of years left blank in the proposal; to receive a fixed compensation, which should not be changed during the executive's term of office; to be ineligible "a second time"; and "besides a general authority to execute the national laws, it ought to enjoy the executive rights vested in Congress by the confederation."

At once Wilson moved that the executive consist of a single person, and Charles Pinckney seconded the motion. "A considerable pause ensuing," Madison notes, "and the Chairman asking if he should put the question, Doctor Franklin observed that it was a point of great importance and wished that the gentlemen would deliver their sentiments on it before the question was put."

The gentlemen had been slow to speak because it was hard for any one of them to think of a single executive without thinking of a king. The Revolution had been fought as much against the British Parliament as against the British Crown, but George III had become the symbol of the rule which the Americans had thrown off. Some of the delegates were old enough to remember days of peace and happiness under the former government. Others were learned and dispassionate enough to know that monarchy had advantages as well as disadvantages. Yet not a single delegate in the Convention believed that it would be possible for them to return to monarchy or that a constitution providing for it would have the slightest chance of being adopted by the American people as a whole. Might the people not object as much to a single executive, even though elected, as to a king? And might not a single executive, once in office, somehow find it possible to seize power and make himself into a king, with that or some other name? If there was anything which these republicans in Independence Hall dreaded as much as anarchy in the states, it was a single tyrant ruling over them. The history of republics, they all knew, was full of instances of disorder ending in despotism.

Rutledge began the discussion by saying that, as he understood it, the delegates were free to disclose their present sentiments without being later bound by them. For himself, he was in favor of a single executive, "tho' he was not for giving him the power of war and peace." Sherman saw the "Executive magistracy" as nothing more than the agent and servant of the national legislature. The legislature, which ought in his opinion to appoint the executive, "should be at liberty to appoint one or more as experience might dictate." Wilson preferred "a single magistrate," as giving most energy, dispatch, and responsibility to the office. Certain powers possessed by the British monarch, such as that of war and peace, were legislative and would not be granted to the American executive under the Virginia plan. Gerry "favored the policy of annexing a Council (to the Executive) in order to give weight & inspire confidence."

Randolph "strongly opposed a unity in the Executive magistracy. He regarded it as the fœtus of monarchy. We had he said no motive to be governed by the British Government as our prototype. He did not mean however to throw censure on that Excellent fabric. If we were in a situation to copy it he did not know that he should be opposed to it; but the fixt genius of the people of America required a different form of Government." He thought the American executive department ought to be composed of more than one person, possibly three.

The committee of the whole, not yet ready to decide between

a single and a plural executive, agreed only that a national executive should be instituted. They turned then to the powers to be granted to the executive. Madison pointed out that as some powers were "in their nature Executive," and would have to be held by the executive whether one person or more, "a definition of their extent would assist the judgment in determining how far they might be safely entrusted to a single officer." That day the delegates could agree only that the executive should have power "to carry into execution the national laws" and "to appoint to offices in cases not otherwise provided for."

They postponed consideration of the method of election in order to discuss the length of the executive's term in office. Wilson preferred three years, provided a good executive might be re-elected. Sherman, still insisting that the executive ought to be chosen by the national legislature, agreed with Wilson as to three years and possible re-election. Mason spoke strongly in favor of a term of seven years with no re-election permitted. In that case the legislature would be careful whom it chose, and the executive would never be tempted "to intrigue with the Legislature for a reappointment." Bedford of Delaware protested vigorously against so long a term. Suppose the electors should make an unwise first choice and then find they had an incompetent magistrate "saddled on" them for seven years.

It is probable that a good many of the Convention delegates were favorable to so long a term, and to several of the powers later granted to the executive, because they already believed that the election would be sure to fall to Washington. And it is ironical that he, who desired this so little, should have been obliged on June 1 to decide what the opinion of the house was. When the motion for a term of seven years came to a vote, five states voted aye, four no, and Massachusetts was divided. "A question was asked whether a majority had voted in the affirmative. The President decided that it was an affirmative vote."

When they proceeded next to the "mode of appointing" the executive, Wilson urged that this be election by the people, as with the national legislature. Mason thought it desirable, but impracticable, yet he wished that Wilson might have time to prepare fuller arguments. The next day (June 2) Wilson came forward with a scheme for enabling the people to choose the executive without intervention either by the states or by the national legislature. Let the states be divided into districts, and let the voters qualified to vote for the members of the first branch of the national legislature, in each district choose persons to serve as electors of the national executive. Then let all the electors meet and elect by ballot, but not out of their own number, the executive, whether single or plural.

Here was the first outline of a method which was in time to prevail, but on this day Wilson's motion was lost by a vote of eight to two. The Convention was not ready to approve the election of the executive by the people, and perhaps did not see much difference between electors who should be chosen specifically for the purpose and the state legislatures which were the people's representatives in general. Not only did the Convention reject Wilson's scheme, but it straightway proceeded to vote, eight to two, in favor of the election of the national executive by the national legislature, for a term of seven years.

When the matter of compensation for the executive came up, Franklin moved that the executive department have necessary expenses defrayed but receive no salary, stipend, fee, or reward. He had written out his observations, which he asked leave to read. Wilson, aware that it was painful for Franklin to stand, courteously offered to read the paper.

Franklin, speaking through Wilson, said that from the first reading of the Virginia plan, he had "borne a good will to it, and in general wished it success," but he could not agree as to salaries to the executive. "Sir, there are two passions which have a powerful influence on the affairs of men. They are ambition and avarice; the love of power, and the love of money. Separately each of these has a great force in prompting men to action; but when united in view of the same object, they have in many minds the most violent effects." The vast number of posts of honor which were also places of profit in England had, Franklin knew from his long experience there, been the cause of fierce contentions in the British government. If such a system should be introduced into the United States, public office would not attract "the wise and moderate, the lovers of peace and good order, the men best fitted for the trust," but instead "the bold and the violent, the men of strong passions and indefatigable activity in their selfish pursuits." Even suppose the new government should set out with moderate salaries, reasons would be found for augmenting them. "There will always be a party for giving more to the rulers, that the rulers may be able in return to give more to them."

It was true, Franklin said, that the Americans did not propose to establish kings. "But there is a natural inclination in mankind to Kingly Government. . . . I am apprehensive therefore, perhaps too apprehensive, that the Government of these States, may in future times, end in a Monarchy. But this Catastrophe I think may be long delayed, if in our proposed system we do not sow the seeds of contention, faction & tumult, by making our posts of honor, places of profit. If we do, I fear that tho' we do employ at first a number, and not a single person, the number will in time be set aside, it will only nourish the fœtus of a King, as the honorable gentleman from Virginia very aptly expressed it, and a King will the sooner be set over us."

Some of the delegates might imagine it was "an Utopian Idea" that men would be found to serve the country in the executive department without being well paid. "I conceive this to be a mistake." Franklin cited high offices in France and England which were expensive rather than profitable to the holders, and yet were well executed. He cited the practice among the Quakers, who for more than a hundred years had served their communities in certain laborious functions without salaries, fees, or perquisites.

"To bring the matter nearer home, have we not seen the great and most important of our offices, that of General of our armies"—here many eyes must have turned to Washington—"executed for eight years together without the smallest salary, by a Patriot whom I will not now offend by any other praise; and this through fatigues and distresses in common with the other brave men his military friends & companions, and the constant anxieties peculiar to his station? And shall we doubt finding three or four men in all the United States, with public spirit enough to bear sitting in peaceful Council for perhaps an equal term, merely to preside over our civil concerns, and see that our laws are duly executed? Sir, I have a better opinion of our country. I think we shall never be without a sufficient number of wise and good men to undertake and execute well and faithfully the Office in question.

"Sir, The saving of the salaries that may at first be proposed

is not an object with me. The subsequent mischiefs of proposing
them are what I apprehend. And therefore it is that I move the
amendment. If it is not seconded or accepted I must be con-
tented with the satisfaction of having delivered my opinion
frankly and done my duty."

All the delegates present knew that Washington had served
as commander in chief without pay, and some of them knew that
Franklin accepted his statutory salary as president of Pennsylvania only to give it away to various philanthropies; just as he
had refused to patent his lightning rod and the Franklin stove
because he did not wish to profit at the expense of others who
might be benefited by his inventions. There was no question
about Washington's and Franklin's freedom from self-interest.
But the delegates did think Franklin's belief about executive
salaries was "an Utopian Idea," and they probably thought he
had shown himself an old-fashioned philosopher, not a modern
politician. Madison, who copied the whole of Franklin's speech
out in his notes, described the reception of the motion in a quiet
paragraph which brings tellingly to light the place of Franklin
in the Convention: the respect shown to him, the independent
judgment as to his proposals.

"The motion was seconded by Col. Hamilton with the view he
said merely of bringing so respectable a proposition before the
Committee, and which was besides enforced by arguments that
had a certain degree of weight. No debate ensued, and the proposition was postponed for the consideration of the members. It
was treated with great respect, but rather for the author of it,
than for any apparent conviction of its expediency or practicability."

The committee, postponing the whole question of compensation, had now agreed that the national executive should be
elected by the national legislature for a term of seven years. But
there must also be some provision for removing the executive
from office in case of incompetency or misconduct. Dickinson of
Delaware proposed that the executive be removable on the request of a majority of the legislatures of the individual states.
Madison and Wilson both opposed bringing the states into what
was an essentially national concern. Dickinson replied at length
about the danger of such an executive as the Virginia plan con-

templated. It was not, he thought, republican at all: "a firm Executive could only exist in a limited monarchy. . . . A limited Monarchy he considered as *one* of the best Governments in the world. It was not *certain* that the same blessings were derivable from any other form. It was certain that equal blessings had never yet been derived from any of the republican form. A limited monarchy however was out of the question. The spirit of the times—the state of our affairs, forbade the experiment, if it were desireable. . . . But though a form the most perfect *perhaps* in itself be unattainable, we must not despair. If antient republics have been found to flourish for a moment only & then vanish forever, it only proves that they were badly constituted; and that we ought to seek for every remedy for their diseases."

Far from believing, with Madison and Wilson, that an extensive republic could have about the same virtues as a limited monarchy, Dickinson was sure that "the accidental lucky division of this country into distinct States" gave it the best security for the future. He hoped the division would be preserved, and that the states would have equal votes in at least one branch of the national legislature. Here he had struck out an idea which was later to be fruitful, but no particular notice of it seems to have been taken on that day. Everybody knew that Dickinson was a spokesman for Delaware, determined—and indeed obliged by instructions—to insist on the sovereign rights of the small states, with respect to the national executive as well as to the legislature. When the vote was taken on Dickinson's motion, only Delaware was for it.

Without much debate the committee further decided that the executive should be ineligible after seven years, and "be removable on impeachment and conviction of mal-practice or neglect of duty." But when Rutledge moved, with Charles Pinckney seconding, that the executive be one person, Randolph opposed it, and said he thought he always would. "He urged 1. that the permanent temper of the people was adverse to the very semblance of monarchy. 2. that a unity was unnecessary, a plurality being equally competent to all the objects of the department. 3. that the necessary confidence would never be reposed in a single Magistrate. 4. that the appointment would generally be in favor of some inhabitant near the center of the Community, and consequently the remote parts would not be on an equal footing." He preferred an executive department of three persons, "drawn from different portions of the Country."

The debate went over to Monday, June 4, when Wilson replied to Randolph. The gentleman from Virginia, Wilson observed, had argued less about the measure itself than about its chances for popularity. Wilson believed that the people, who all knew that "a single magistrate is not a King," would not find in a single executive any semblance of monarchy. Each of the thirteen states, though agreeing in almost nothing else in their constitutions, had a single head, as governor or president. "The idea of three heads has taken place in none." If there should be three heads in the national executive, there could be neither vigor nor tranquillity.

When the vote was taken, New York, Delaware, and Maryland voted no. This meant that Yates and Lansing outnumbered Hamilton in the New York delegation; that Delaware was keeping to its line of resistance to anything that seemed to threaten small states; and that Jenifer of Maryland, the only delegate present from that state, was a quorum of one. All the other seven states represented were in favor of a single executive.

But the Virginia delegation was divided within itself. Randolph, Blair, and Mason, who was just then out of the chamber though he had left his adverse vote, were opposed. Washington, Madison, and McClurg were present and favorable, and Wythe before he departed for Virginia had left his vote on their side. Since Wythe was not to return, and would not vote after today, the six delegates remaining might continue to be divided in such a way as to make their agreement impossible. This would cost their delegation the advantage it had so far had, and might imperil the success of the Virginia plan.

The first clause of the eighth Virginia resolution, which the committee took up next, was "that the national executive and a convenient number of the national judiciary ought to compose a Council of revision" with authority to pass on all the acts of the national legislature. In the debate that followed, the committee could not agree to join the judiciary with the executive in this veto power, and the matter was postponed for later consideration. Wilson and Hamilton were for giving the executive "an absolute negative on the laws." The vote against them was ten to none. Butler of South Carolina moved, and Franklin seconded, that the executive have the power to suspend any legislative act for a period of years. The vote was unanimously against the motion. On a motion by Gerry, modified during the debate, it was finally agreed to give the executive the right to negative any legislative act "which shall not be afterwards passed unless by two thirds parts of each branch of the national legislature." Only Connecticut and Maryland were opposed.

But Mason, who had rejoined the committee, was vigorously in dissent. "We are, Mr. Chairman," he said, "going very far in this business. We are not indeed constituting a British Government, but a more dangerous monarchy, an elective one. . . . Do gentlemen mean to pave the way to hereditary Monarchy? Do they flatter themselves that the people will ever consent to such an innovation? If they do I venture to tell them, they are mistaken. The people will never consent. And do gentlemen consider the danger of delay, and the still greater danger of the rejection not for a moment but forever, of the plan which shall be proposed to them? Notwithstanding the oppressions & injustice experienced among us from democracy; the genius of the people is in favor of it, and the genius of the people must be consulted." He looked upon the Confederation as in effect dissolved by the appointment of this Convention. There would be a "dangerous interval between the extinction of an old, and the establishment of a new Government." This was no time to undertake something like a monarchy. He never could, Mason said, "agree to give up all the rights of the people to a single Magistrate." If the executive were to have such rights, then the executive should be more than one person.

Mason was speaking in the language of a classic republicanism, fundamentally opposed to monarchy, and slow to believe that any strong executive would not in time become a king. Generally speaking, the older men in the Convention were of the same opinion. The younger men, again generally speaking, in face of the weakness and disorder of the Confederation were willing to risk a strong executive, and confident the executive could be controlled by the will of the people as well as in any limited monarchy. In this, Washington sided with the younger men. There is no record of what he was thinking while he sat silent during the June debates, or later when the executive was given further powers, including the right to be re-elected to office. But the following April, Washington made his position clear in a letter to Lafayette, who felt with Jefferson that the president under the new constitution might be a danger to the republic. "There cannot, in my judgment," Washington wrote, "be the least danger that the President will by any practicable intrigue ever be able to continue himself one moment in office, much less perpetuate himself in it; but in the last stage of corrupted morals and political depravity: and even then there is as much danger that any other species of domination would prevail. Though, when a people shall have become incapable of governing themselves and fit for a master, it is of little consequence from what quarter he comes."

Over the whole Convention still hung the dread of future tyranny as well as of immediate anarchy. The delegates were sure that unless anarchy could be avoided, an early despot was certain to appear, as in the classic pattern of republican failure. They believed that anarchy could be at least postponed by the establishment of an adequate central government, but they could only guess what powers would make it neither too weak for security nor too strong for liberty.

It may seem strange that they were willing to give the executive the power to veto legislative acts. The state assemblies under the Crown had bitterly resented the veto of their acts by the royal governors. The Declaration of Independence had made its first charge against George III that he had "refused his Assent to Laws, the most wholesome and necessary for the public good." But under the various state constitutions since independence there had been a rush of hasty and uncurbed legislation by the states. More laws had been put on the statute books, according to Madison, in the past eleven years than in a century before. The legislatures had passed laws which were encroachments on the executive powers of the Continental Congress. The Virginia plan, in a clause already accepted by the committee of the whole, gave the national legislature the power to negative state laws "contravening . . . the articles of union or any treaties subsisting under the union." The national executive now being instituted must be given power to resist similar encroachments on the part of the national legislature. This was, as Wilson had expressed it, "raising the federal pyramid to a considerable altitude." And eight out of ten of the Convention delegations were in favor of it.

III

Postponing consideration of the clause in the Virginia plan which would associate the judiciary with the executive in the revision of legislative acts, the committee of the whole on June 4, proceeding to the ninth resolution, voted with little debate that "a national judiciary be established, to consist of One supreme tribunal, and of one or more inferior tribunals." But on the 5th the program on the judiciary was so much interrupted by disagreements that the committee went ahead to later resolutions in the Virginia plan. They agreed on the tenth resolution: "that provision ought to be made for the admission of States lawfully arising within the limits of the United States, whether from a voluntary junction of government and territory or otherwise." The delegates were of course thinking of Vermont, which had declared its independence of New York ten years before but had not yet been admitted to the Union; of Tennessee, which in 1784 had set itself up as the independent State of Franklin but had so far obtained recognition from neither North Carolina nor Congress; of Kentucky, to the independence of which Virginia had already consented; and of all the Western territories which it was supposed would be incorporated in time into the United States. The committee of the whole agreed on the twelfth resolution: "that provision ought to be made for the continuance of a Congress and their authorities and privileges, until a given day, after the reform of the articles of union shall be adopted, and for the completion of all their engagements." The committee was evidently assuming, with Mason, that the appointment of the Convention had in effect dissolved the Confederation, and that there must be some interim government till a new one could be put in operation. Consideration of the 11th, 13th, 14th, and 15th Virginia resolutions was postponed.

As to the judiciary, the first matter discussed on the 5th was the method of appointment. The Virginia plan proposed that this be by the national legislature. Wilson opposed it. "Experience shewed," he said, "the impropriety of such appointments by numerous bodies. Intrigue, partiality, and concealment were the necessary consequences." He preferred to see the national judiciary appointed by a single, responsible executive. Rutledge was for appointment by the legislature. He "was by no means disposed to grant so great a power to any single person. The people will think we are leaning too much towards Monarchy." Nor did Rutledge favor establishing any national tribunal except a single supreme one. The state courts were better fitted to decide in "all cases in the first instance."

Franklin, whose humor was irrepressible in the gravest company, observed that only two modes of selection had been mentioned: by the legislature and by the executive. He wished the gentlemen of the committee might suggest such other modes as might occur to them; "it being a point of great moment." He would himself mention one which he understood prevailed in Scotland. There, where the judges were nominated by the lawyers, the lawyers simply selected the ablest of the profession, "in order to get rid of him and share his practice among themselves." Perhaps in America some method might be found for making it to the interest of the electors to select the best possible men for the judiciary.

The gentlemen of the committee, so many of them lawyers and judges, were amused by Franklin's cheerful suggestion, and Madison hinted, though only hinted, at a third method of selection, which might be by the "senatorial branch" of the national legislature. This would be "not so numerous as to be governed by the motives of the other branch," and "sufficiently stable and independent to follow their deliberate judgments." But Madison's motion, seconded by Wilson, was merely that the committee for the present give up selection of the judiciary by the national legislature and leave the choice of some better method to be settled "on maturer reflection." Nine states voted aye, only Connecticut and South Carolina no.

The committee readily agreed also that the members of the national judiciary should hold their offices "during good behaviour" and receive "a fixed compensation" for their services.

Rutledge of South Carolina and Sherman of Connecticut now moved to reconsider the establishment of inferior tribunals. Sherman spoke chiefly of "the supposed expensiveness of having a new set of Courts when the existing State Courts would answer the same purpose." Rutledge still believed that the creation of inferior courts would be an encroachment on the rights of the states and would raise opposition to the whole new system of government. Let the state courts decide in the first instance, and then let the appeals be carried to the supreme tribunal.

Madison insisted that "unless inferior tribunals were dispersed throughout the Republic with *final* jurisdiction in *many* cases, appeals would be multiplied to a most oppressive degree; that besides, an appeal would not in many cases be a remedy." If the fault in the original verdict came from "the biassed directions of a dependent Judge, or the local prejudices of an undirected jury," it would do no good for the supreme tribunal to remand the cause for a new trial, which would presumably end in no better verdict. "To order a new trial at the supreme bar would oblige the parties to bring up their witnesses, tho' ever so distant from the seat of the Court." An effective judiciary was as important as an effective executive. "A government without a proper Executive & Judiciary would be a mere trunk of a body without arms or legs to act or move." Wilson argued that admiralty jurisdiction ought to be given wholly to the national judiciary, and King of Massachusetts sensibly remarked that inferior tribunals "would cost infinitely less than the appeals that would be prevented by them."

But when the motion was put, the committee voted by a narrow margin against the establishment of inferior national tribunals. The most Wilson and Madison could do, on their following motion, was to get the committee's consent to giving the national legislature the power to institute such tribunals, if it should so choose. Butler of South Carolina was sure the states would "revolt at such encroachments. Supposing such an establishment to be useful, we must not venture on it. We must follow the example of Solon who gave the Athenians not the best Government he could devise; but the best they would receive."

On June 6 Wilson and Madison moved that the committee reconsider the vote excluding the judiciary from a share in the revision of the laws. It seemed to Madison, he said, that the nature of a republican government made it difficult for an executive under it to have competent powers. He could not have the "settled pre-eminence in the eyes of the rest" that belonged to "an hereditary magistrate," nor a king's special interest in the state as if it were in a sense his property. A republican executive would have to owe his election to his personal merit, which could but rarely be so great as to make everybody accept his administration. He would be envied and assailed by disappointed competitors. Therefore he should be supported. He would not be so rich or so secure as to be "out of the reach of foreign corruption." Therefore he should be controlled. Madison believed the executive could be best supported and controlled by being joined with the judiciary in revising the acts of the legislature. The objection to this among the delegates was that it did not preserve the desired separation of the executive and the judiciary. But, Madison argued, the reason for the separation of powers was to provide checks and balances among them. The legislature, all the delegates were agreed, must be prevented from encroachment on the co-ordinate departments and on the rights of the people. This could be best prevented by adding to the power of the executive the wisdom and weight of the judiciary.

But the committee of the whole voted eight to three against the motion. The delegates, apprehensive as they were of encroachments by the legislature, were not willing to put the veto power into the hands of two departments combined.

Nor did the committee during the following week's discussion of the Virginia plan make further progress with the national judiciary: on inferior tribunals, on the method of selecting the judges, on the jurisdiction of the courts. These matters were either postponed or never brought up till the committee of the whole on June 13 was filling the last gaps in its report to the house. On that day the committee resolved that the judges should be appointed by the second branch of the legislature, and that the jurisdiction of the national judiciary—still only one supreme tribunal—should extend to "cases which respect the collection of the national revenue, impeachments of any national officers, and questions which involve the national peace and harmony." The delegates were already sure that, in view of the difficulty of collecting any national revenue under the Confederation, there should be legal methods for deciding this. If national officers were to be impeached, this must be put within the jurisdiction of national courts. And there should be a final court to which appeals could be taken on questions, still vaguely described in advance, which might disturb the peace and harmony of the whole country but could not be settled by the individual states.

IV

When the committee of the whole on June 7 once more took up the consideration of the second branch of the national legislature, it was evident that the delegates were most of them expecting the Senate, as they already called it, to restrain the first branch, and therefore desiring it to be relatively independent of popular opinion. Dickinson, moving that the members of the second branch ought to be chosen by the "individual Legislatures," gave two reasons for his motion. One was that this would "more intimately connect the state governments with the national legislature" than would be possible if the people voted directly for the senators. The other reason was that "he wished the Senate to consist of the most distinguished characters, distinguished for their rank in life and their weight of property, and bearing as strong a likeness to the British House of Lords as possible; and he thought such characters more likely to be selected by the State Legislatures, than by any mode." He thought the Senate should be large in number rather than small, because if it were small it could not "balance" the popular branch.

Sherman of Connecticut, seconding the motion, agreed that this mode of election would promote harmony between the "two Governments," state and national. "He admitted that the two ought to have separate and distinct jurisdictions, but they ought to have a mutual interest in supporting each other." Wilson of Pennsylvania, dissenting from the motion, believed that both branches of the national legislature ought to be elected by the people. "If one branch of it should be chosen by the Legislatures and the other by the people, the two branches will rest on different foundations, and dissentions will naturally arise between them." He wished to see the Senate elected in districts formed for that purpose such as he had in vain proposed for the election of the executive. He moved to postpone Dickinson's motion and vote first on his own. In this he was seconded by Gouverneur Morris of Pennsylvania, who had that day not yet left the Convention for his visit to New York.

Both motions remained before the house while the discussion went on. Read of Delaware, who had now come to believe that the states ought to be absorbed into one consolidated national government, thought the state legislatures should nominate a number of persons for the Senate and then leave it to the national executive to appoint those he preferred. Nobody seconded or supported Read's motion.

Madison of Virginia argued that if the legislatures chose the Senators, and if representation were proportional, then the Senate would have to be very large. (Delaware delegates had been saying from the first that on a proportional basis, the national legislature would have to number at least eighty for Delaware to be entitled to even one member.) Now "the use of the Senate," according to Madison, "is to consist in its proceeding with more coolness, with more system, & with more wisdom, than the popular branch. Enlarge their number and you communicate to them the vices which they are meant to correct." The Senate would not automatically become more weighty by being made more numerous. "When the weight of a set of men depends merely on their personal characters, the greater the number the greater the weight. When it depends on the degree of political authority lodged in them the smaller the number the greater the weight."

Gerry of Massachusetts, summing up the reasoning so far, brought in a franker statement of economic interest than had yet appeared in the whole course of the Convention. The first mode of election, by the popular house, "would create a dependence contrary to the end proposed." The second mode, by the national executive, was "a stride towards monarchy that few will think of." As to the third mode, by the people: "the people have two great interests, the landed interest, and the commercial including the stockholders." (By the landed interest Gerry meant small farmers no less than large landowners; by "stockholders" he meant all holders of securities of any kind, commercial or public.) To "draw both branches from the people will leave no security to the latter"—the commercial—"interest; the people being chiefly composed of the landed interest, and erroneously supposing that the other interests are adverse to it." The fourth mode of election, that by the state legislatures, Gerry thought the best. "The elections being carried thro' this refinement, will be most likely to provide some check in favor of the commercial interest against the landed; without which oppression will take place, and no free Government can last long when that is the case."

As Gerry was clearly representing the commercial interest, so

Dickinson, when he replied, was representing the interest of the small states. He was in effect a lawyer, and Delaware his client. It was indispensable, he argued, to maintain the states in something like their present influence. "It will produce that collision between the different authorities which should be wished for in order to check each other." Certain of the delegates hearing him must have thought that "collision" was a strong synonym for checks and balances. Yates of New York, to judge by his notes on what Dickinson said, heard him with sympathy and admiration. The two branches of the national legislature, in Yates's version, "like the British house of lords and commons, whose powers flow from different sources," would be mutual checks on each other, and would thus "promote the real happiness and security of the country—a government thus established would harmonize the whole, and like the planetary system, the national council like the sun, would illuminate the whole—the planets revolving round it in perfect order; or like the union of several small streams, would at last form a respectable river, gently flowing to the sea." Madison, reporting what Dickinson said, had him carry this figure of the river further, and declare that if the people elected all the members of the national legislature, in both branches, then "the national Government would move in the same direction as the State Governments now do, and would run into all the same mischiefs. The reform would only unite the 13 small streams into one great current pursuing the same course without any opposition whatever."

Wilson insisted that the British government could not be "our model. Our manners, our laws, the abolition of entails and primogeniture, the whole genius of the people are opposed to it. He did not see the danger of the States being devoured by the National Government. On the contrary, he wished to keep them from devouring the National Government." Nor could he comprehend how the legislatures, which according to Gerry sacrificed the commercial to the landed interest, could be expected to choose men for the Senate who would be more friendly to the commercial interest in national affairs than they were at home. Wilson was still for election of the Senate by the people in large districts.

Madison could as little comprehend why anybody felt sure that election by the legislatures would put more salutary checks on the Senate than election by the people. One of the complaints of the commercial interest was that the legislatures had "run into schemes of paper money &c, whenever solicited by the people, & sometimes without even the sanction of the people. Their influence then, instead of checking a like propensity in the National Legislature, may be expected to promote it. Nothing can be more contradictory than to say that the National Legislature without a proper check will follow the example of the State Legislatures, & in the same breath, that the State Legislatures are the only proper check."

There were further scattering remarks, but Wilson's motion for postponing Dickinson's was lost, with only Pennsylvania voting for it. The overwhelming majority of the delegations was in favor of election by the legislatures, as a method of representing the states as states in the national government. The delegates both from former habit and present reasons preferred a federated republic to a consolidated nation.

Before Dickinson's motion was put to a vote, Mason of Virginia for the first time entered this debate. He had heard it said today that this or that ancient confederation was "dissolved by the overgrown power and unreasonable ambition" of one of its members, and had heard it therefore argued that the new American government ought to guard against similar dangers. He did not believe that America was fully like any earlier confederation. The states of the union were now "substantially and in reality distinct, sovereign and independent," but they had not always been, and he doubted that they would insist on remaining so. It seemed to him that if the national legislature was to have a negative on the state legislatures, this would sufficiently protect the national government against state encroachment. How should they protect the states against national encroachment? He thought this should be done by letting the state legislatures elect the Senate. Every state delegation agreed with him, and the motion was carried unanimously.

In the conflict over equitable representation in the national legislature which arose on June 9 and lasted through Monday the 11th, and on the 12th and 13th, which were given up largely to filling the blanks left in the Virginia plan, the matter of the Senate was not discussed at much length. The committee of the whole on various motions agreed that suffrage in the Senate ought to be according to the proportional ratio established for the first branch; that senators ought to be at least thirty years old; to hold their offices "for a term sufficient to ensure their independency, namely seven years"; to receive fixed stipends paid out of the national treasury; and (like members of the first branch) to be ineligible to state or other national offices during their term of service, and to any national office for a year after the expiration of a term in the national legislature.

The term of seven years for senators "to ensure their independency" caused some debate. Sherman thought five years would be better: halfway between the three years of the first branch and the seven of the executive. If the Senators "did their duty well, they would be re-elected. And if they acted amiss, an earlier opportunity should be allowed for getting rid of them." Pierce of Georgia preferred three years. Seven years would "raise an alarm," because it would remind Americans of the seven-year duration of British Parliaments. Randolph favored seven years as likely to strengthen the Senate against the encroachments not only of the first branch but also of the executive, "who will be apt to form combinations with the demagogues of the popular branch."

Madison, who so often had the final words in these discussions, "lamented" that the delegates had so little experience to guide them. What was needed was a true stability in the government, a stability which "the enemies of the Republican form alleged to be inconsistent with its nature." In most of the states, under their individual constitutions, the upper legislative branches, elected for four years, had been found to be "no check whatever" on legislative instabilities. The Maryland Senate, elected for five years and by a less popular method, had it seemed to Madison a better record. "He conceived it to be of great importance that a stable & firm Government organized in the republican form" should be offered to the American people for their approval. If this were not done, he feared they might judge the republican "species" of government by the defective systems under which they now lived, and sooner or later in "universal disgust . . . renounce the blessings which they have purchased at so dear a rate, and be ready for any change that may be proposed to them."

On the vote, Massachusetts and New York were divided, Connecticut opposed, all the others favorable. Some of the delegates during the discussions had hoped the Senate would be made up of men of family and fortune, but there was nothing to secure this in the Virginia plan, as proposed or revised. The senators were to be chosen by the state legislatures in order to let states be represented in the national legislature. The senators were to serve terms as long as the executive's, for the sake of stability. But this was to be a stability consistent with republican government. The state legislatures were elected by the people. These legislatures would elect men presumably not unlike themselves to serve in the Senate. The senators would be chosen at least indirectly by the people, and they would owe their extended term of office to the people who consented, if they should consent, to this new constitution. The office of senator would not be permanent, privileged, or hereditary. A senator would have to owe his election to the belief that he had enough virtue and judgment to deserve it. But he would be expected to exercise republican virtue and republican judgment.

There is a pleasant anecdote, traditional but not improbable, which represents the attitude of most of the delegates toward the Senate. Jefferson, the story runs, after his return from France once asked Washington at breakfast why he had agreed to a second chamber in Congress. Washington asked him: "Why did you pour that coffee into your saucer?" "To cool it," Jefferson said. "Even so," said Washington, "we pour legislation into the senatorial saucer to cool it."

v

On June 9 Paterson of New Jersey, who had been almost voiceless in the Convention since the opening day, moved to consider the rule of suffrage in the national legislature. He was a very short, acute man, an experienced lawyer, and a speaker who, according to Pierce, was "very happy in the choice of time and manner of engaging in a debate." Paterson now skillfully chose his time to attack the Virginia plan at its most controversial point. The resolution on the subject which had come nearest to winning approval had been in the form proposed by Madison on May 30: "that the equality of suffrage established by the articles of Confederation ought not to prevail in the national Legislature, and that an equitable ratio of representation ought to be substituted." On that day, a vote had been postponed chiefly because the delegates from Delaware thought they were obliged by their instructions to withdraw from the Convention if the matter of representation was even discussed. But now Paterson, in effect taking all the smaller states for his clients, declared that most of the delegates were enjoined by their instructions from altering the established rule of suffrage.

Brearley of New Jersey, who seconded the motion, spoke first. He believed that unless each "sovereign State" had had an equal vote under the Articles, the smaller states would have been destroyed before this. He admitted that a ratio of representation seemed fair on the face of it, but "on a deeper examination" it was unfair and unjust. Given proportional representation, Virginia, Massachusetts, and Pennsylvania would "carry everything before them." The small states would have to "throw themselves constantly into the scale of some large one, in order to have any weight at all." Still—and here Brearley changed sides again—was it just for Georgia to have an equal vote with Virginia? He could not say it was. What then was the remedy? "One only, that a map of the United States be spread out, and that all the existing boundaries be erased, and that a new partition of the whole be made into 13 equal parts."

There was less of such mathematical fantasy in what Paterson had to say. He called for the instructions of the Massachusetts delegation and had them read. They unquestionably authorized those delegates to attend the Convention "for the sole and express purpose of revising the Articles of Confederation." So did most of the state instructions. The delegates in general must keep within the lawful limits of their duties or else "be charged by our constituents with usurpation." Their commissions were the measure of the delegates' power. They also represented the sentiments of the states. "We have no power to go beyond the federal scheme, and if we had the people are not ripe for any other. We must follow the people; the people will not follow us."

Here Paterson, saying "federal" when he meant "confederate" scheme, was also distrusting the people's capacity to think of themselves as Americans, not merely as citizens of individual states. "A confederacy," he went on, "supposes sovereignty in the members composing it & sovereignty supposes equality." It had been proposed in the Virginia resolution that the votes of the states might be on the basis of their contributions to the federal expenses. Paterson insisted that there was no more reason for a rich state to have more votes than a poor state than for a rich citizen to have more votes than a poor citizen. He refused to accept the argument that the national government ought to operate directly on the people and that the people should therefore elect the national legislature. He thought it much better, as under the Articles of Confederation, for the people to elect their state legislatures, and for the state legislatures to elect "their federal representatives." Nothing else was needed but "to mark the orbits of the States with due precision, and provide for the use of coercion, which was the great point." But he did not say what mode of coercion he had in mind.

Wilson had hinted, Paterson said, that if the smaller states would not unite with the others on a federal basis of representation, then the larger might be reduced to "confederating among themselves." Wilson had hinted this on the 5th, possibly to put pressure on New Jersey and Delaware; and had hoped that if such a "partial union" had to be formed, it would leave "a door open" for the others to come in when they saw the wisdom of it. Nothing had been said in reply to Wilson at the time, but Paterson had remembered it. Now he threw out his peroratory defiance. "Let them unite if they please, but let them remember that they have no authority to compel the others to unite. New Jersey will never confederate on the plan before the Committee. She would be swallowed up. He had rather submit to a monarch, to a despot, than to such a fate. He would not only oppose the plan here but on his return home do everything in his power to defeat it there."

These were the most heated words that had yet been spoken in the Convention. Wilson was as warm in his rejoinder. A majority of the states, he said, or even a minority, had a right to form a union, and the rest might do as they pleased. If all authority was derived from the people, then equal numbers of people ought to have equal representation, different numbers different representation. This principle had been violated in the Confederation, "owing to the urgent circumstances of the time." That was no excuse for making the violation perpetual. "We have been told that each State being sovereign, all are equal. So each man is naturally a sovereign over himself, and all men are therefore naturally equal. Can he retain this equality when he becomes a member of civil Government? He cannot. As little can a sovereign State, when it becomes a member of a federal Government." Pennsylvania from its numbers would have a right to twelve votes in the national legislature as against New Jersey's five. "Shall New Jersey have the same right or influence in the councils of the nation with Pennsylvania? I say no. It is unjust —I never will confederate on this plan. The gentleman from New-Jersey is candid in declaring his opinion—I commend him for it—I am equally so. I say again I never will confederate on his principles. If no state will part with any of its sovereignty, it is in vain to talk of a national government. . . . If however, we depart from the principle of representation in proportion to numbers, we will lose the object of our meeting."

It must be remembered that the words here quoted are only those taken down by Madison or others in their notes, and that they are only the gist of what Paterson and Wilson said. But there is fire in their brevity, sharp conflict in their counter-defiances. There was a new excitement in the room when the question was postponed and the house adjourned till Monday the 11th.

On Monday morning Sherman opened the discussion by proposing a compromise motion: "that the proportion of suffrage in the 1st branch should be according to the respective numbers of free inhabitants; and that in the second branch or Senate, each State should have one vote and no more. He said as the States would remain possessed of certain individual rights, each State ought to be able to protect itself: otherwise a few large States will rule the rest. The House of Lords in England he observed had certain particular rights under the Constitution, and hence they have an equal vote with the House of Commons that they may be able to defend their rights." Dickinson had before this suggested that the states might have equality of representation in one branch or other of the national legislature, but it was Sherman who first proposed that this be the Senate.

Rutledge and Butler of South Carolina thought the proportion of suffrage in the first branch should be according to the contributions of the various states to the support of the federal government. "Money was power," Butler bluntly said, "and the States ought to have weight in the Government, in proportion to their wealth." It may be pointed out that South Carolina had perhaps 11,000 more inhabitants than Connecticut, but that in South Carolina more than 100,000 of the inhabitants were slaves. This would make the number of free inhabitants in Connecticut, which had few slaves, greater than in South Carolina, and would give Connecticut more votes in the popular branch of the national legislature.

King of Massachusetts, seconded by Wilson, proposed a trial motion to the effect that suffrage in the first branch ought to be "according to some equitable ratio of representation," without yet deciding what particular ratio would be equitable or desirable. They ought, King said, to establish first the principle on which they were to construct the new government. If it was to remain "federal" (he meant confederate), then the states should continue to have equal votes. If it was to become "national" (he here could mean either "national" or "federal"), then representation would have to be on some equitable basis.

Just before the motion was put, Franklin said that "he had thrown his ideas on the matter" into a paper which Wilson would read. Again Franklin began as a philosopher, not as a politician. He who could be so merry could also be pacific, pouring oil on troubled water as he had done in one of his famous experiments.

"It has given me a great pleasure to observe that till this point, the proportion of representation, came before us, our debates were carried on with great coolness & [good] temper. If any thing of a contrary kind, has on this occasion appeared, I hope it will not be repeated; for we are sent here to *consult* not to *contend,* with each other; and declarations of a fixed opinion, and of determined resolution, never to change it, neither enlighten nor convince us. Positiveness and warmth on one side, naturally beget their like on the other; and tend to create and augment discord & division in a great concern, wherein harmony & Union are extremely necessary to give weight to our Councils, and render them effectual in promoting & securing the common good.

"I must own that I was originally of opinion it would be better if every member of Congress, or our national Council, were to consider himself rather a representative of the whole, than as an Agent for the interests of a particular State; in which case the proportion of members for each State would be of less consequence, & it would not be very material whether they voted by States or individually. But as I find this is not to be expected, I now think the number of representatives should bear some proportion to the number of the Represented; and that the decisions should be by the majority of members, not by the majority of States. This is objected to from an apprehension that the greater States would then swallow up the smaller. I do not at present see what advantage the greater States could propose to themselves by swallowing the smaller, and therefore do not apprehend they would attempt it. I recollect that in the beginning of this Century, when the Union was proposed of the two Kingdoms, England & Scotland, the Scotch Patriots were full of fears, that unless they had an equal number of Representatives in Parliament, they should be ruined by the superiority of the English. . . . And yet to this day I do not recollect that anything has been done in the Parliament of Great Britain to the prejudice of Scotland; and whoever looks over the lists of public officers, Civil & military, of that nation will find I believe that the North Britons enjoy at least their full proportion of emolument."

A good many of those now listening to Franklin must have smiled at his mild way of saying, what was commonly believed and was partly true, that the Scots had invaded London and got more than their proportion of offices. Four of the delegates here present—Sherman, Robert Morris, Wilson, and Read—had been in the Second Continental Congress with Franklin in August 1776 and may there have heard him say the same thing more pointedly. The smaller states at that time were opposed to any Confederation. Franklin had said that "at the time of the union of England and Scotland, the Duke of Argyle was most violently opposed to that measure, and among other things predicted that, as the whale had swallowed Jonah, so Scotland would be swallowed up by England. However, when Lord Bute came into the government, he soon brought into its administration so many of his countrymen, that it was found in event that Jonah swallowed the whale." This little story, according to Jefferson who heard it, "produced a *general* laugh, and restored good humor," so that Congress could resume its work.

And now in June 1787 the Convention delegates seem likewise to have been amused and mollified, whether or not they realized that when Franklin sounded most philosophical he might be actually most politic. The complex scheme of requisitions on the states which he mentioned as a possible way of obtaining revenue was unimportant in comparison with his effect on the passions of the wrangling debaters.

At any rate, the committee of the whole promptly agreed, by a vote of seven to three (New York, New Jersey, Delaware) and one divided (Maryland), that there ought to be "some equitable ratio of representation." Rutledge and Butler moved that the ratio be "according to the quotas of contributions." This was postponed on the motion of Wilson of Pennsylvania and Charles Pinckney of South Carolina, who themselves moved a compromise. It was that the ratio be "in proportion to the whole number of white and other free Citizens and inhabitants of every age, sex, and condition, including those bound to servitude for a term of years, and three fifths of all other persons not comprehended in the foregoing description, except Indians, not paying taxes in each State."

The terms of this ratio were familiar to all the delegates. Congress in April 1783 had proposed it to the states as a method of determining what individual states should contribute to the Confederation government. The Southern states held it was not equitable for them to be charged for slaves as much as for so many free inhabitants. The Northern states held it was not equitable for slaves to be omitted from the estimate of a state's population, since their labor was productive of wealth in proportion to their numbers. The three-fifths ratio had been accepted by eleven of the states already, in the matter of contributions. It would probably be acceptable to them again, in the matter of representation.

Gerry insisted that slaves in the South were property as much as cattle and horses were in the North, and he saw no reason why the one kind of property should be counted as population any more than the other. But nine of the delegations voted aye on the motion, with only New Jersey and Delaware opposed.

Sherman moved, Ellsworth of Connecticut seconding, that each state should have one vote in the second branch of the legislature. The smaller states, he said, would never agree "to any other principle" than an equality of suffrage in this branch. The motion was lost by a vote of six to five. Wilson and Hamilton moved that the vote in the second branch be the same as that in the first. This vote was won by six to five.

The delegations unanimously agreed to a reworded form of the eleventh Virginia resolution, "that a republican Constitution, and its existing laws, ought to be guaranteed to each State by the United States." They unanimously agreed to the thirteenth resolution: "that provision ought to be made for the amendment of the articles of Union, whensoever it shall seem necessary"; but they postponed decision on the clause saying that amendments would not require the consent of the national legislature.

There was more disagreement over the fourteenth Virginia resolution: "that the legislative, executive, and judiciary powers within the several States ought to be bound by oath to support the articles of union." Sherman thought the motion unnecessarily intruded "into the State jurisdictions." Gerry thought there was as much need of asking the national officers to take oaths of fidelity to the several states as vice versa. Randolph was sure that the national authority "needs every support we can give it." The vote was carried by the same six states (Massachusetts, Pennsylvania, Virginia, the Carolinas, Georgia) against the same five (Connecticut, New York, New Jersey, Delaware, Maryland).

The conflict, it will be observed, was not merely between large and small states. Georgia, one of the smallest in population, voted with the large, because she claimed all the territory west of her to the Mississippi and expected to be large herself. New York, the fifth largest, voted with the small states because Yates and Lansing were opposed to extensive changes in the Confederation, and outvoted their colleague Hamilton. Maryland, the sixth largest, now had Luther Martin in attendance, who had begun to overpower the amiable Daniel of St. Thomas Jenifer.

On June 12 and in part of the session of the 13th the committee of the whole moved steadily through a series of decisions clause by clause on matters of detail in the Virginia plan which had been left unsettled. Most of the votes were not so close as six to five, and the conflict of large and small states was not invariably in evidence.

It was decided that the provisions for ineligibility to office should be alike in both branches of the national legislature; and that the members of both branches ought to be paid out of the

national treasury. Madison and Mason urged that payment ought
not to be left to the states. Some of them might exert undue
pressure on their representatives. Some might be so parsimonious
that they would find themselves represented by the most willing
rather than the ablest men. The Virginia plan had originally
spoken of "liberal" compensation for the legislators. Madison
urged that this be "liberal and fixed," to avoid uncertainty and
reckless changing. Franklin enlivened the discussion by his
reasons for suggesting that the word "liberal" be struck out, as
it was. The word could at any time be reinterpreted, and there
was always a "tendency of abuses . . . to grow of themselves
when once begun." Only "gratuitous provision" had been originally made for the support of the Apostles; but out of that had
developed the whole papal system.

On the length of the term of office in the first branch of the
national legislature, Gerry of Massachusetts insisted that this
must be a single year, as provided by the Articles of Confederation and practiced in the New England states. "The people of
New England," he declared, "will never give up the point of
annual elections. They know of the transition made in England
[in 1716] from triennial to Septennial elections, and will consider
such an innovation here as a prelude to a like usurpation. He
considered annual elections as the only defence of the people
against tyranny. He was as much against a triennial House as
against a hereditary Executive." Gerry was sure the Convention
must consider the feelings of the people, as was "the policy of
all Legislators," and he was sure he knew what the feelings of
the New England people were.

Madison's reply admirably summed up the position taken by
the most enlightened and courageous delegates. "No member of
the Convention could say what the opinions of his Constituents
were at this time; much less could he say what they would think
if possessed of the information & lights possessed by the members
here; & still less what would be their way of thinking 6 or 12
months hence. We ought to consider what was right & necessary
in itself for the attainment of a proper Government." Let such
a plan be offered to the people, and the most intelligent and
influential citizens would be its powerful advocates. But they
could be enlisted in its support only if the plan offered were as
right and necessary as the Convention knew how to make it.

Some inferior, compromising plan would turn them against it, and would probably have no better fortunes with the "unreflecting multitude."

On the 12th the committee of the whole agreed on the fifteenth and last of the original Virginia resolutions, which was that the plan proposed by the Convention should be submitted for ratification to assemblies called for the special purpose in the various states. The text of the resolution as now adopted called the new plan "amendments" to the Articles of Confederation, made them subject to the "approbation" of Congress, and provided that the state ratifying conventions should be recommended by the state legislatures. But there could be no question that the projected constitution looked to the people for its acceptance, not to Congress or the state legislatures.

On the 13th the committee of the whole presented its report, now renumbered as nineteen resolutions,[1] to the house. Randolph moved to postpone further consideration till the next day. On the 14th Paterson moved that consideration of the report be postponed one day more. Several of the delegations, he explained, particularly that of New Jersey, wished to put forward an alternative plan which was not yet ready to be offered. Again the Convention adjourned, to Friday, June 15. Every delegate must have been aware that a new chapter of their deliberations was to begin.

VI

The people of America knew nothing about the progress of the Convention. Benjamin Rush in Philadelphia believed on June 2 that everything was harmonious in Independence Hall. Franklin had said, Rush wrote to a friend in England, that this was "the most august and respectable Assembly he ever was in in his life," and that he thought they would "soon finish their business, as there are no prejudices to oppose, nor errors to refute in any of the body." Dickinson had told Rush that the delegates "were all *united* in their object and he expects they will be equally united in the means of attaining them." William Grayson, member of Congress from Virginia, wrote from New York on May 29 to James Monroe that probably not "much good" would come of

[1] See Appendix 4.

the Convention. "The weight of Genl. Washington as you justly observe is very great in America, but I hardly think it is sufficient to induce the people to pay money or part with power." Stephen Mix Mitchell, member of Congress from Connecticut, on June 6 wrote a hitherto unpublished letter[1] from Wethersfield which singularly reveals the hopes some people were already building for a new American world.

". . . If any interesting particulars have transpired from the Convention, I wish you to communicate them to me.—

"We are at such a Distance from the present Head-Quarters of Politicks, that we know very little of the great things in Contemplation at Philadelphia.—

"I find the Expectations of Politicians from the Wisdom & Magnanimity of the Convention are much raised; all our Difficulties are at once to be removed, and we are to have almost a new Earth.— The Clergymen begin to omit poor old Congress in their prayers and substitute instead thereof, the Convention. You know many of our political ideas in New England, have their birth in the pulpit.—

"Time alone will discover whether a Convention or Congress is to govern in this Country, we are impatient to know which."

[1] Gratz Autograph Collection, Historical Society of Pennsylvania.

6

SMALL AND LARGE STATES

"Was, then, the American Revolution effected, was the American Confederacy formed, was the precious blood of thousands spilt, and the hard-earned substance of millions lavished, not that the people of America should enjoy peace, liberty, and safety, but that the government of the individual States, that particular municipal establishments, might enjoy a certain extent of power, and be arrayed with certain dignities and attributes of sovereignty?" *James Madison, The Federalist No. 45, January 25, 1788.*

"A sovereignty over sovereigns, a government over governments, a legislation for communities as contradistinguished from individuals, as it is a solecism in theory, so in practice it is subversive of the order and ends of civil polity, by substituting *violence* in place of *law,* or the destructive *coercion* of the *sword* in place of the mild and salutary *coercion* of the *magistracy.*" *Alexander Hamilton, The Federalist No. 20, December 11, 1787.*

WHAT seems to have been a sudden revolt of the minority against the Virginia plan was not so surprising as it may appear in the record. The delegates in general were convinced that the government of the Confederation, under the Articles, was insecure and might be headed towards collapse. All of them had come to Philadelphia, at whatever sacrifice of time and convenience, in the belief that extensive changes must be made. A good many of them thought of themselves as representatives of the whole people rather than as agents of their particular states, so far as they were capable of thinking that. Only some of them could help having local prejudices and sharing local interests. The Confederation was too new and weak to compel their loyalties or capture their imaginations. They were "inhabitants"—and the term they commonly used is revealing—of this or that state rather than citizens of the United States. Those who had been members of the Continental Congress, particularly since the end of the war, were not notably less sectional than the others. For Congress had been, as John Adams called it, a diplomatic assembly, to which the members went as delegates charged with safeguarding the rights of the separate sovereign governments that sent them. Like ambassadors, they owed their first duty to their sovereigns. The Confederation was a league of sovereigns, not quite a sovereign itself.

Coming to Philadelphia, the majority of the delegates had encountered in the foremost men of the Convention a set of political ideas for which they were unprepared by experience or reflection. Franklin, who had in effect represented the whole of America so many years in Europe, felt himself a citizen of the whole United States, as indeed of the world, though he had been born in Boston and now lived in Philadelphia. Washington, during his years as leader of the allied American armies, had learned to think of himself as primarily an American who happened to be a Virginian, and as "a Citizen of the great republic of humanity at large." Wilson had lived for twenty-three years in Scotland before he came to Pennsylvania, and Hamilton fifteen in the Leeward Islands before he came to New York. Neither of them had developed exclusive affections for the state in which he lived as an American. Madison, born and bred a Virginian, had begun his studies in history and government during his years at Princeton, had confirmed his reading by experience in the Virginia assembly and in Congress, and had brought all his learning and observation to bear on the political circumstances of the entire country, especially the defects of the Confederation. The venerable Franklin, the massive Washington, the brilliant and speculative Wilson, Hamilton, and Madison, joined with several others of foresight and courage, had been bound to have an effect on the body of the delegates. The Virginia plan, ready for discussion when the Convention met, had furnished powerful guidance during the fateful first two weeks of their deliberations.

But as the days went on, the more sectional delegates were increasingly alarmed by the threat of the Virginia plan to the separate interests of the individual states. Though they were unable to stop its march, they managed to modify some of its provisions. The one thing to which they were most vigorously opposed, proportional representation in the Senate as well as in the first branch of the national legislature, was carried against them. In this the delegates from the dissenting states saw a threat so alarming that they gathered their forces and struck back with the New Jersey plan, which Paterson offered on Friday, June 15.

The motives of the states in opposition were not all the same. Delaware had been a state only since 1776. Before that it had been in turn a Dutch, Swedish, or English colony until its incorporation into Pennsylvania as the Three Lower Counties, with its own assembly but under the administration of Pennsylvania's governor. Being so new to statehood, Delaware was determined to survive as a state. Being so small, it was afraid of being swallowed up. In the Confederation it had, if not in fact an equal influence, at least in law an equal vote with any other state, no matter how large or populous. Its delegates to the Convention, positively instructed against any yielding on the right of suffrage, were handicapped even in debate. Read was willing to see the United States made into a consolidated nation, which would do away with all the states. In that case, Delaware would have the same chances as any three counties anywhere. Dickinson, believing this impossible, insisted that the division into states must be maintained as a check on the central government. The most eminent of the Delaware delegates, he was the principal spokesman for their state in the Convention.

New Jersey was a relatively small state between the much larger Pennsylvania and New York. By reason of its geographical situation it had suffered heavily during the war, and had been left damaged and impoverished. The debtors among the people had forced an issue of paper money, which neither New York City nor Philadelphia would accept. The money had promptly depreciated, leaving New Jersey finances as badly off as before. There was a special resentment in New Jersey against New York. A great deal of produce from New Jersey farms and forests went to New York City to be consumed there. New York required that such goods pay entrance fees and obtain clearances at the New York custom house as if they were from a foreign country. New Jersey in angry retaliation put a preposterous tax on the small plot of ground on Sandy Hook which New York had bought for a lighthouse it had to have. Since Congress under the Confederation had no power to regulate interstate trade, New Jersey had no recourse but to petty retaliations in her own behalf. Yet instead of desiring to help create a central government which might prevent such local injustices and irritations, the New Jersey delegates had come to the Convention with an obstinate, almost a perverse, will to preserve the Confederation substantially as it was, with New Jersey still a state with an equal voice in Confederation affairs.

Governor Livingston for some reason took little part in the debates. He seemed to Pierce of Georgia "rather to indulge a sportiveness of wit, than a strength of thinking." The leadership fell to Paterson, who chose to be guided by the strictest obedience to the delegation's instructions from their legislature.

Though New York was not so populous as Virginia, Massachusetts, Pennsylvania, or North Carolina, it expected to surpass them all in time. A large part of its present territory had been held, down to the Revolution, by the Six Nations of the Iroquois. The state still was hardly settled outside of New York City, the New York islands, strips nowhere more than a single county wide on either side of the Hudson and along Lake Ticonderoga, and narrower strips along the lower Mohawk. But the rich unsettled interior, and those inland waterways leading to and from the great port at the mouth of the Hudson, made New York confident of its future. If it did not take its stand with the other large states, this was for special local reasons. Its chief city and the adjacent islands had been occupied by the British during seven years of the war. Many of the inhabitants had been pro-British. Afterward, the victorious patriots were vengefully, fiercely eager to restore their state to an independent footing.

George Clinton, governor during the war and for a dozen years after, was convinced that New York would lose more than it could gain by a closer union with the other states. It laid duties on imported goods and collected them for itself. Since many of the goods imported for use in New Jersey, Connecticut, western Massachusetts, and Vermont had to come in through New York harbor, New York enjoyed a handsome revenue at the expense of its neighbors, and did not wish to lose the revenue by putting all imposts in the hands of Congress. Moreover, Clinton had built up such a system of patronage in New York, with such a political machine, that the state was virtually his barony. Neither he nor his henchmen could be friendly to any change in the Confederation which would reduce their consequence and perquisites. Better be first in New York than anything less than first in the union. The legislature, under the influence of Clinton, had chosen two delegates—Yates and Lansing—who could be counted on to support the separate interests of their state. Hamilton would be in a minority with his dangerous views about centralized government.

Connecticut had as much cause for grievance as New Jersey against New York, though it seems not to have been specially affected by this in its opposition to the Virginia plan. The state was prosperous, but it was provincial, and even among the New England states it had always kept up an independence that was really self-sufficiency. In 1785 it had passed a law giving foreign merchants and manufacturers an advantage over Americans in the adjoining states, at a time when Congress was pleading that it be granted power to regulate all American trade. Whereas New York objected to the Virginia plan out of ambition, Connecticut objected to it chiefly out of caution. Its delegates to the Convention were restricted to the discussion of amendments "agreeable to the general principles of Republican Government." The delegates were disposed to think that republics were best when not too large, and that consequently the smaller individual states must lose some of their republican quality if they were absorbed into a national union. Sherman, as the oldest of the Connecticut delegates, was more or less their leader, but all three were generally in agreement.

The opposition of Maryland to the Virginia plan was primarily Luther Martin's private quarrel with what he thought its threat to the individual states. If McHenry had not been called home, he and Jenifer of the Maryland delegation would probably have supported most of the Virginia provisions. With McHenry absent, Maryland could be no better than divided on any vote. It generally was divided during the contest between the Virginia and New Jersey plans.

Martin, who took his seat in the Convention on Saturday, June 9, listened that day to the clashing arguments of Paterson and Wilson over proportional representation. In this conflict Martin instantly sided with Paterson. He provided himself with a copy of the Virginia plan. On Sunday the secretary of the Convention "was so polite," Martin afterward wrote, "as, at my request, to wait upon me at the State House . . . and there gave me an opportunity of examining the Journals and making myself acquainted with the little that had been done before my arrival. I was not a little surprised at the system brought forward, and was solicitous to learn the reasons which had been assigned to its support; for this purpose the Journals could be of no service; I therefore conversed on the subject with different members of the Convention, and was favored with minutes of the debates which had taken place before my arrival." All that Martin learned strengthened him in opposition. Short, burly, slovenly, rough-voiced, gifted, learned if pedantic, a torrent in speech, a lover of brandy and taverns, he was at once a conspicuous figure in the Convention and outside it. Welcomed as a new recruit to the opposition, he probably joined with Paterson and other New Jersey delegates in drawing up the New Jersey plan, along with the delegations or unidentified members of the delegations from Connecticut, New York, and Delaware.

II

The New Jersey plan,[1] offered by Paterson on Friday, June 15, was explicitly a revision of the Articles of Confederation, and proposed few changes that could affect the sovereignty of the separate states. It would grant to Congress certain additional powers: to levy import duties and stamp taxes for confederation purposes; "to make rules & regulations for the collection thereof"; to regulate trade with foreign nations and between the states, but leave offenders to be tried in the courts of the states where the offenses had been committed, with the right of appeal to the judiciary of the United States. Requisitions were to be made, not on the value of land in the different states as under the Articles, but in proportion to the number of free inhabitants and three-fifths of all others; if the requisitions were not complied with, then Congress should have power to collect them, but only with the consent of a number of the states which was to be specified on further deliberation. There should be a Confederation executive of more than one person chosen by Congress, removable on application of a majority of the executives of the several states, to be ineligible a second time, and to direct all military operations though in no case to take command of troops in the field. There should be a Confederation judiciary of one supreme tribunal, the judges to be appointed by the executive and to hold office during good behavior, with jurisdiction in the first in-

1 See Appendix 5.

stance over impeachments, and final authority on appeals from
state courts in various specified cases including admiralty matters, litigation with foreigners, the regulation of trade, and
the collection of Confederation revenues. All the acts of the
United States in Congress assembled and all treaties made by
them were to be the supreme law of the respective states, so far
as those acts or treaties related to the states or their citizens; and
the executive should have the right to call forth the power of
"the Confederated States" against any offending state or "any
body of men in any state." Provisions should be made for the
admission of new states. The rule for naturalization ought to be
the same in every state.

Lansing of New York observed that this was truly a plan for
amending the Confederation, while the Virginia plan aimed to
replace it with a national government. He urged that further
consideration be postponed to the next day, to give the friends
of the New Jersey plan more time in which to prepare their
supporting arguments, and all the delegates the chance to take
copies for their own use. The house agreed and adjourned.

On Saturday, Lansing first briefly, and Paterson later at length,
presented their arguments in support of the New Jersey plan.
They both held that the delegates had no authority to go beyond
amendment of the Articles, and that the people would not accept
anything so revolutionary as the Virginia plan. "The Scheme
itself is totally novel," Lansing said. "There is no parallel to it
to be found." Paterson asked: "Can we, as representatives of
independent states, annihilate the essential powers of independency?" They could not do that without violating the fundamental
principle of confederated governments. "When independent societies confederate for mutual defence, they do so in their collective capacity; and then each state for those purposes must be
considered as *one* of the contracting parties. Destroy this balance
of equality, and you endanger the rights of the *lesser* societies
by the danger of usurpation in the *greater*." It might be right in
principle to say that, since all power is derived from the people,
therefore the people ought to participate in their government
in proportion to their numbers, but this could apply only if state
distinctions were wholly abolished. The Virginia plan did not
propose that. Certain state distinctions for certain purposes were
to be continued. Quotas of contributions, Paterson assumed,

would still be levied on states as states. Surely it would be unjust for Georgia, when such quotas were being apportioned, to have only one vote as against Virginia's sixteen. And of course Paterson argued that the Virginia plan would greatly increase the cost of government.

Both Lansing and Paterson confined themselves largely to objecting to the Virginia plan on secondary grounds: that the Convention had no authority to propose it; that the people would not accept it; that it would be difficult to put in operation. Wilson, and other supporters of the plan, insisted on carrying the argument back to primary ground.

As to the powers of the Convention, Wilson said he believed it was "authorized to *conclude nothing,* but to be at liberty to *propose anything.*" As to the sentiments of the people, he did not profess to know what they actually were. "Those of the particular circle in which one moved, were commonly taken for the general voice." He doubted that the state governments were so precious to the people, or a national government so obnoxious, as some of the delegates appeared to believe. Why should a national government be unpopular? "Has it less dignity? will each Citizen enjoy under it less liberty or protection? Will a Citizen of *Delaware* be degraded by becoming a Citizen of the *United States?*"

Randolph boldly declared that when "the salvation of the Republic was at stake, it would be treason to our trust not to propose what we found necessary." The delegates were authorized to propose measures which in their judgment would "render the Federal Constitution adequate to the exigencies of Government, and the preservation of the Union." The New Jersey plan proposed nothing stronger than a limited right in Congress to employ force on uncomplying states. This was not even a full power of coercion. Coercion at best was "*impracticable, expensive, cruel to individuals.*" The Virginia plan proposed to strengthen the general government by "real legislation . . . national *Legislation over individuals.*" Randolph had no doubt which method was better. Congress, by the New Jersey plan, would continue to be a "mere diplomatic body," its members "always obsequious to the views of the States." Nor could Congress, elected according to the New Jersey plan, be safely entrusted with the powers it would need. Nothing short of a national government, Randolph concluded, would "answer the purpose; and he begged it to be considered that the present is the last moment for establishing it. After this select experiment, the people will yield to despair."

On the first day of the discussion the supporters of the New Jersey plan made it clear that they laid more stress on revising and altering the Articles, as such, than on discovering measures which would make the general government adequate to the higher purposes stated in the delegates' instructions. The supporters of the Virginia plan thought less about the methods suggested than about the final aim of the Convention, which was the preservation of the union. The supporters of the New Jersey plan, strict in their interpretation of the instructions, found arguments in the sovereign rights of the separate states. The supporters of the Virginia plan, creative in their interpretation, found arguments in the rights of all the American people to a general government which could furnish them the peace, liberty, and security they had not found under the Confederation. The New Jersey plan was in the interests of the separate states. The Virginia plan was in the interests of the united people.

On Monday the 18th Alexander Hamilton for the first time spoke at length, for five or six hours. Pierce thought Hamilton, because of his quiet voice, "rather a convincing Speaker, than a blazing Orator. . . . He enquires into every part of his subject with the searchings of phylosophy, and when he comes forward he comes highly charged with interesting matter, there is no skimming over the surface of a subject with him, he must sink to the bottom to see what foundation it rests on.— His language is not always equal, sometimes didactic like Bolingbroke's at others light and tripping like Stern[e]'s. . . . He is . . . of small stature, and lean. His manners are tinctured with stiffness, and sometimes with a degree of vanity that is highly disagreeable."

Hamilton had heretofore been silent, he explained, partly because of his youth, partly because of his respect for delegates of more ability and experience with whom he could not agree, and partly because he was not in accord with his colleagues in the New York delegation. But the crisis was now too serious for him to shirk the "duty imposed on every man to contribute his efforts to the public safety & happiness. He was obliged therefore to declare himself unfriendly" to both the Virginia and the New

Jersey plans. No amendment of the Articles, he thought, "leaving the States in possession of their sovereignty could possibly answer the purpose." On the other hand, the "amazing extent" of the United States discouraged him from thinking that any "general sovereignty" could be substituted.

At present the natural impulses in men which everywhere maintain governments were more favorable in America to the states than to the general government. The states had an active and constant interest in maintaining themselves and in increasing their power. Demagogues in the states hated the control of the central government, and the citizens felt less anxiety over dangers to the government of the whole country than over dangers to their own states. Suppose the central government collapsed, there would still be the state governments to which the citizens were accustomed. The whole force of habitual attachment in the overwhelming number of the people was to the states, not to the Confederation. Many men had an interest in honors and emoluments they could obtain from the individual states, but there was nothing of the sort to be expected from the United States. "All the passions then we see, of avarice, ambition, interest, which govern most individuals, and all public bodies, fall into the current of the States, and do not flow in the stream of the General Government." This had always been true in confederacies, and must be true in America so long as the states continued to exist.

"How then are all these evils to be avoided? Only by such a compleat sovereignty in the general government as will turn all the strong principles & passions above mentioned on its side." The New Jersey plan would not serve. It set up what amounted to rival sovereignties. "The general power whatever be its form if it preserves itself, must swallow up the State powers, otherwise it will be swallowed up by them." Hamilton was himself for going further than either the New Jersey or the Virginia plan, and doing away with the states altogether. "He did not mean however to shock the public opinion by proposing such a measure." He assumed, like all the delegates, that the people would not accept it.

The one obstacle he saw to a truly national, a consolidated, government was the size of the United States. What would induce men of fortune and ability to leave their houses and business and "come 600 miles to a national legislature?" No one but a "demagogue or middling politician" would accept election "for the sake of a small stipend and the hopes of advancement." Possibly no republican government could be made to operate over so large a territory. Although Hamilton knew it would be unwise to propose any other form for the United States, he did not hesitate to give it as his private opinion that the British government was "the best in the world; and that he doubted much whether any thing short of it would do for America." It was the only government in the world "which unites public strength with individual security." The House of Lords was, he thought, "a most noble institution." Its members had "nothing to hope for by a change," and had enough property to make them identify their interests with the national interest. "They form a permanent barrier against every pernicious innovation, whether attempted on the part of the Crown or of the Commons." Mere senators elected for a time could never be expected to have such firmness. Nor could, he thought, any good executive ever be established "on Republican principles." There could not be a good government without a good executive. "The English model was the only good one" in this respect. The hereditary monarch, with his great wealth, was above corruption from abroad, and was "both sufficiently independent and sufficiently controuled, to answer the purpose of the institution at home."

"What is the inference from all these observations? That we ought to go as far in order to attain stability and permanency, as republican principles will admit." A single executive chosen for life and a Senate for life or at least during good behavior might serve nearly as well as a monarch and nobles. It might be asked whether the people would accept any such plan. He asked in return whether they would accept any other, such as the Virginia plan, which lessened the power of the states but still preserved them? Hamilton had a plan which he would offer, not as a proposal to the committee, but as an indication of his opinions and of the amendments which he would probably offer to the Virginia plan as they deliberated on it.

His plan left almost no powers in the states except over local affairs. The states would elect the popular branch of the national legislature, but that branch would be definitely inferior to the Senate. The Senate, its members elected during good behavior, would have the sole power of declaring war and would be closely joined with the executive in making treaties and appointing national officers. The single executive, chosen also during good behavior, would have virtually monarchical powers, including a negative on all laws "about to be passed." The governors of the separate states would be appointed by the "General Government" and would have the power to negative all laws in their respective states.

Having read the outline of his plan, Hamilton went over the suggestions point by point with "explanatory observations," and then concluded, according to Yates's notes, with a fling at the other plans before the Convention. "I confess that this plan and that from Virginia are very remote from the idea of the people. Perhaps the Jersey plan is nearest their expectation. But the people are gradually ripening in their opinions of government —they begin to be tired of an excess of democracy—and what is even the Virginia plan, but *pork still, with a little change of the sauce?*"

Hamilton's proposals, so energetic, so Hamiltonian, were supported by no other delegate, and were not even discussed. The next day, June 19, Madison spoke on the New Jersey plan with theoretical acuteness and practical good sense. In particular he reminded the small states that "their pertinacious adherence to an inadmissable plan" might prevent the adoption of any plan. Then if the union were dissolved, and they became independent republics, would they not be in more danger from aggressive neighbors than from any general government? And if they entered into any of the regional confederacies likely to be formed, could they expect that their larger neighbors would confederate with them on terms more favorable than those proposed by the Virginia plan?

When it came to a vote deciding in effect between the Virginia and the New Jersey plans, Connecticut voted with the Virginia supporters. New York, New Jersey, and Delaware were still opposed, and Maryland was divided. The committee of the whole then rose and reported itself to the Convention as in favor of the Virginia plan, which was therefore resubmitted.

Before it was taken up again for consideration, several interesting remarks were made in the house about the sovereignty of the states. King of Massachusetts said that the terms "states," "sovereignty," "national," "federal" had been used "inaccurately & delusively"—as indeed they had. He did not point out that the delegates repeatedly said "federal" when they meant "confederate," and "national" when they meant only "federal." But he insisted that the states "were not 'sovereigns' in the sense contended for by some. They did not possess the peculiar features of sovereignty. They could not make war, nor peace, nor alliances, nor treaties. Considering them as political Beings, they were dumb, for they could not speak to any foreign sovereign whatever. They were deaf, for they could not hear any propositions from such Sovereign. They had not even the organs or faculties of defence or offence, for they could not of themselves raise troops, or equip vessels, for war." If the "Union of the States" had had the right to establish a confederation, it must have the right also to effect a consolidation. While the states retained "some portion" of their sovereignty, they had "certainly divested themselves of essential portions of it" when they joined the Confederation. "He doubted much the practicability of annihilating the States; but thought that much of their power ought to be taken from them."

Martin of Maryland argued on the basis of an entirely different theory. "The separation from Great Britain," he declared, "placed the 13 States in a state of nature towards each other." They would have remained in that state of nature "till this time, but for the confederation." They had entered into the Confederation "on a footing of equality," and in his opinion they had now "met to amend it on the same footing." That is, the states, on the calling of the Convention, had reverted to their pre-Confederation status, and were now making a new central government as if none had existed and as if nothing had happened to the United States during the period of union. "He could never accede to a plan that would introduce an inequality and lay 10 states at the mercy of Virginia, Massachusetts and Pennsylvania."

Wilson could not admit that the Revolution had thrown the states into a state of nature. He read the original resolution of Congress, June 7, 1776, on the right of the United Colonies to independence, "observing thereon that the *United Colonies* were declared to be free & independent States; and inferring that they were independent, not *Individually* but *Unitedly*, and that they were confederated as they were independent, States."

Hamilton agreed with Wilson that the states had not been thrown into a state of nature. He admitted that the states met now on an equal footing, but he could see no reason why they might not change the system of representation. Practically, there could be no special danger from Massachusetts, Pennsylvania, and Virginia. They were separated by intervening states, and by the difference of their interests. In a federation of states ranging in size from Delaware to Virginia there would naturally be conflicts of interests and combinations of state voting with state for their joint interests in the federal legislature. But "the more close the Union of the States, and the more compleat the authority of the whole; the less opportunity will be allowed the stronger States to injure the weaker."

These theoretical distinctions between states acting individually and states acting collectively were important to the delegates. Some of them had speculative minds; all of them were altering, or were being asked to alter, their conceptions of the states and of the Confederation as they went forward in the work of shaping a new kind of government on a scale never before attempted. Their political conceptions of the whole country were involved in their imaginations, their memories, their attachments, their prejudices. The freer minds among them moved more rapidly than most of the others, who followed with effort, objections, and often with strong resistance.

From June 20 to July 2, in very hot weather and with rising tempers, the Convention considered the Virginia plan as submitted by the committee of the whole. On the motion of Ellsworth of Connecticut on June 20 it was unanimously agreed to change the words "national government" in the first Virginia resolution to "government of the United States." The dissenting states did not like the word "national." The others did not mind so long as the central government, however named, was not affected. The same change was made wherever necessary in all the later resolutions. This was a step in the direction of a more correct terminology. The men who were later to call themselves "federalists" had hitherto spoken of the federal government they desired as "national." The men who were later to be called "antifederalists" now considered themselves "federalists"—meaning that they supported the Confederation. But though there was confusion in the terms, there was no confusion in the understanding of the delegates. The conflict was not between terms, but between the new idea of a federal government operating directly on the citizens and the old idea of a confederate government operating on the states. Madison long afterward pointed out that the government formed by the Convention, "being a novelty & a compound, had no technical terms or phrases appropriate to it; and that old terms were to be used in new senses, explained by the context or the facts of the case."

Day after day the Convention worked, clause by clause, word by word, over the provisions of the Virginia plan for the federal legislature. The dissenting states contested every step. They were able to get the term of office of members of the first branch of the legislature reduced from three to two years, and of senators from seven to six, one third of the number to go out biennially. They insisted that the legislators of both houses be paid by the states, not out of the federal treasury, and prevented any clear decision on the point. But the contention over these and other details was slight compared with that which rose when, on June 27, the Convention came again to the problem of proportional representation.

In the meantime, William Blount of North Carolina took his seat on the 20th and Jonathan Dayton of New Jersey on the 21st. Blount came from New York, where he was representing his state in Congress. He had been paymaster in a North Carolina regiment, and since then almost continually in public office. Taking no part in the debates, he seemed to Pierce to have none of "those talents that make men shine;—he is plain, honest, and sincere." Dayton, a captain in the Continental Army at nineteen, was not yet twenty-seven, the youngest member of the Convention. He and Pierce had served as aides to General John Sullivan in the campaign against the Six Nations in 1779 and were well acquainted. According to Pierce, Dayton had "an impetuosity in his temper that is injurious to him," but also an "honest rectitude." Dayton came late because he had been appointed late, after two other New Jersey delegates had failed to attend and his own father, Colonel Elias Dayton, had declined an appointment in his son's favor.

On June 25 Charles Pinckney enlarged the discussion, which was usually close and technical, with some general observations of great courage and independence. It was a mistake, he thought, to try to make the American Senate correspond to the British House of Lords, as some of the delegates appeared to wish. The institution of nobility in Great Britain, as elsewhere, was ancient. The House of Lords had become, through a long course of history, "a Legislative balance between the inordinate power of the Executive and the people." America had no such institution, and no need to create it. Among Americans there were "fewer distinctions of fortune & less of rank, than among the inhabitants of any other country." Probably not a hundred men in all the Continent were rich enough to be "esteemed rich in Europe." Large fortunes could not be kept together by the right of primogeniture. Relative equality of wealth among the people promised to continue for a long time. So with equality of civil rights. "Every member of the Society almost, will enjoy an equal power of arriving at the supreme office & consequently of directing the strength & sentiments of the whole Community."

The British constitution might be, as Pinckney said he believed it was, "the best constitution in existence," but it would not and could not be "introduced into this Country, for many centuries. . . . Our true situation appears to me to be this.—a new extensive Country containing within itself the materials for forming a Government capable of extending to its citizens all the blessings of civil & religious liberty—capable of making them happy at home. This is the great end of Republican Establishments." In Great Britain there were three elements to be considered in the constitution: the king, the peers, and the people. In America there were only the people. "Our government must be made suitable to the people, and we are perhaps the only people in the world who ever had sense enough to appoint delegates to establish a general government."

III

On June 27 the Virginia provision for the right of suffrage in the first branch of the national legislature came again before the Convention. At once Martin of Maryland was on his feet, to speak that day till he was exhausted—and the bored house adjourned—and then to continue the day after. He spoke, according to Madison, "with much diffuseness and considerable vehemence"; according to Ellsworth, with "eternal volubility." Both

Madison and Yates found it difficult to take notes on the wandering discourse.

Martin contended that the general government was meant merely to preserve the state governments, not to govern individuals. Its powers therefore ought to be kept within narrow limits. If too little were given now, more might be added later; whereas if too much were granted, it could never be taken back. To resort to the people for their sanction of the proposed government would be throwing them into a state of nature. It would dissolve the states. The people had no right to decide in such matters, because they had delegated the necessary powers to the men charged with governing the states. Through the tongues of those men only could the people speak, through the ears of those men only could the people hear. The states had failed to comply with the acts of Congress for want of ability, in the hard times following the war. "An equal vote in each state was essential to the federal idea, and was founded in justice & freedom, not merely in policy." As individuals in a state of nature were equally sovereign and free, so were states in the same condition. Martin read long passages from Locke, Vattel, Somers, Priestley, and Samuel Rutherford to prove his point. The states, being equal, could not confederate to give up an equality of votes without thereby giving up their liberty. The Virginia plan, if adopted, would mean the slavery of ten of the states in the union. Certain of the smaller states might join into one for self-protection, but he thought it would be better to divide some of the larger. It had been urged that the larger states, having the same interests as the smaller, would not injure them if the right of suffrage were in proportion to numbers. If there was no conflict of interest, why then should the larger states not allow the small an equal vote? It would be useless to offer any plan "offensive to the rulers of the States, whose influence over the people will certainly prevent their adopting it." The large states, he argued, were really weak in proportion to their extent, and could be formidable only by the weight of their votes. If the union should be broken up, and the three large states league themselves together, then the smaller ten could do the same thing, and have nothing to fear. Martin said he would rather see the states rearranged in "partial Confederacies" than united on the terms of the Virginia plan.

When Martin had at last ended, Lansing of New York and Dayton of New Jersey moved that the Convention reverse its former vote and go back to equal votes for the states in the first branch of the national legislature, as under the Articles of Confederation. The debate began again.

Madison patiently, temperately explained that when sovereign states made treaties binding each other to the performance of specified duties, and so were entitled to equal votes, it was not at all the same as when states entered into a "compact by which an authority was created paramount to the parties, & making laws for the government of them." In this second case, the different states had the same right to be represented according to population as different counties in a state. Large counties did not combine against small. Neither would large states, merely on account of their numbers. Any combination would be on the basis of common interests. The interest of Massachusetts was predominantly in fish, of Pennsylvania in flour, of Virginia in tobacco. There was here no reason for conflict. And if causes for it should arise, the smaller states, neighbors to the large, would be worse off if the central government were weak than if it were strong enough to control any state, large as well as small. Wilson said there was no more reason for small states to have the same vote as large than for certain obscure old boroughs in England to have the same vote as large modern cities, or even more votes. Sherman countered with the argument that a rich man is not entitled to more votes than a poor man.

The delegates were repeating former arguments, as must so often be done in the slow course of political agreement.

At this juncture Franklin asked if he might be heard. This time he himself read his brief speech, in his low, soft, hesitant voice, addressing his words directly to Washington in the Chair, almost as if this matter were between the two.

"The small progress we have made after 4 or 5 weeks close attendance & continual reasonings with each other—our different sentiments on almost every question, several of the last producing as many noes as ays, is methinks a melancholy proof of the imperfection of the Human Understanding. We indeed seem to feel our own want of political wisdom, since we have been running about in search of it. We have gone back to ancient history for models of government, and examined the different forms of those Republics which having been formed with the seeds of their own dissolution now no longer exist. And we have viewed Modern States all round Europe, but find none of their Constitutions suitable to our circumstances.

"In this situation of the Assembly, groping as it were in the dark to find political truth, and scarce able to distinguish it when presented to us, how has it happened, Sir, that we have not hitherto once thought of humbly applying to the Father of lights to illuminate our understandings? In the beginning of the Contest with Great Britain, when we were sensible of danger we had daily prayer in this room for the divine protection.—Our prayers, Sir, were heard, and they were graciously answered. All of us who were engaged in the struggle must have observed frequent instances of a Superintending providence in our favor. To that kind of providence we owe this happy opportunity of consulting in peace on the means of establishing our future national felicity. And have we now forgotten that powerful friend? or do we imagine that we no longer need his assistance? I have lived, Sir, a long time, and the longer I live, the more convincing proofs I see of this truth—*that God governs in the affairs of men.* And if a sparrow cannot fall to the ground without his notice, is it probable that an empire can rise without his aid? We have been assured, Sir, that 'except the Lord build the House they labour in vain that build it.' I firmly believe this; and I also believe that without his concurring aid we shall succeed in this political building no better than the Builders of Babel: We shall be divided by our little partial local interests; our projects will be confounded, and we ourselves shall become a reproach and bye word down to future ages. And what is worse, mankind may hereafter from this unfortunate instance, despair of establishing Governments by Human Wisdom and leave it to chance, war and conquest.

"I therefore beg leave to move—that henceforth prayers imploring the assistance of Heaven, and its blessings on our deliberations, be held in this Assembly every morning before we proceed to business, and that one or more of the Clergy of the City be requested to officiate in that service."

An unsupported legend has grown up about Franklin's proposal and its effect on the Convention. The facts appear to be simple. Sherman seconded the motion. Hamilton and several others expressed a variety of opinions. To begin prayers now, so late in the session, might cause talk, and lead the public to suspect that there was trouble behind the closed doors. It was not the Quaker custom to have prayers at political gatherings, and this was Philadelphia. Among the delegates were members of various Protestant denominations—Quaker, Episcopalian, Presbyterian, Methodist, Baptist—and Roman Catholics. Williamson of North Carolina pointed out that the Convention had no money to pay a chaplain or chaplains. The motion was never put to a vote, and the meeting adjourned. This religious discussion may have cooled the debate for the time being, but the next day, the 29th, the conflict went on with little change of temper.

Johnson of Connecticut thought that since the states were to continue to exist, then both the people and the states ought to be represented in the federal legislature: the people in one branch and the states in the other, as Sherman of his state had already proposed. Gorham of Massachusetts insisted that the smaller states would be better off if they were closely united with all the others than if they forced a separation and had to make their way alone. If they should force a separation, as he implied they were threatening to do, he was willing to remain here as long as any other state was willing to confederate with Massachusetts, in the hope of working out some plan that could be recommended to the people.

Madison also faced the possibility that if the dissenting states refused to join with the others, the states might become totally separate or re-form themselves into partial confederacies. In either event, "the same causes which have rendered the old world the Theatre of incessant wars, & have banished liberty from the face of it, would soon produce the same effects here."

Hamilton said there was another danger to be expected if the union should be dissolved. The separate states, or partial confederacies, would naturally form alliances with European nations that had dominions on this continent. Those nations were much concerned over the course America would take and were anxiously awaiting the outcome of the Convention. The United States must have a government strong and tranquil enough to be respected abroad. "This was the critical moment for forming such a government. We should run every risk in trusting to future amendments. As yet we retain the habit of union. We are weak & sensible of our weakness. Henceforward the motives will become feebler, and the difficulties greater. It is a miracle that we were now here exercising our tranquil & free deliberations on the subject. It would be madness to trust to future miracles."

Pierce of Georgia said that though he was from a small state, he felt himself a citizen of the United States. Gerry "lamented that instead of coming here like a band of brothers, belonging to the same family, we seemed to have brought with us the spirit of political negotiators."

But in the following votes the four states of Connecticut, New York, New Jersey, and Delaware, with Maryland divided, steadily opposed proportional representation in the first branch of the national legislature. The motion was carried against them.

The debate then moved on to the right of suffrage in the Senate. Ellsworth doubted that any state north of Pennsylvania, except Massachusetts, would consent to a plan which deprived the states as states of equal representation in both branches. An attempt to deprive the Northern states of their right would, he supposed, cut the union in two. Wilson on the 30th replied that if the minority of the people of American refused to "coalesce with the majority on just and proper principles, if a separation must take place, it could never happen on better grounds. . . . Can we forget for whom we are forming a Government? Is it for *men*, or for the imaginary beings called *States?*"

Madison at last spoke out on a matter which had not yet been clearly brought into the open. The great division of interests in the United States, he said, did not lie between the large and small states but between the Southern and Northern: between those which had or did not have slaves. He had thought of a compromise that might be suitable to both groups. Instead of basing the vote in both branches on the number of the inhabitants in each state, computing the slaves in the ratio of five to three, the states might be represented in one branch by the number of free inhabitants only and in the other by the whole number, counting the slaves as if free. "By this arrangement the Southern States would have the advantage in one House, and the Northern in the other."

Franklin proposed still another compromise. "The diversity of opinions," he said, "turns on two points. If a proportional representation takes place, the small States contend that their liberties will be in danger. If an equality of votes is to be put in its place, the large States say their money will be in danger. When a broad table is to be made"—the sage spoke in the plain language of a craftsman—"and the edges of planks do not fit, the artist takes a little from both, and makes a good joint. In like manner here both sides must part with some of their demands, in order that they both join in some accomodating proposition." He suggested that the states have equal numbers of senators. Then let the senators vote equally by states in matters affecting state sovereignty, but in money matters "have suffrage in proportion to the sums their respective States do actually contribute to the treasury." When a ship had many owners, Franklin observed, "this was the rule of deciding on her expedition. He had been one of the ministers from this Country to France during the joint war and would have been very glad if allowed a vote in distributing the money to carry it on."

But the dissenting delegates were obdurate to any compromise. Young Captain Dayton declared that assertions were not proof, and that terror was not argument. Mere eloquence could not move him. "He considered this system on the table"—the Virginia plan —"as a novelty, an amphibious monster"; and was sure it would never be received by the people. Martin would never confederate if it could not be done on just principles. Gunning Bedford of Delaware, whom Pierce described as "precipitate in his judgment . . . and very corpulant," spoke with an anger and accusation that had not heretofore been heard in the Convention.

The larger states were acting out of interest, Bedford charged, but pretending not to. "Georgia has an eye to her future wealth and greatness—South Carolina, puffed up with the possession of her wealth and negroes, and North Carolina, are all, from different views, united with the great states. . . . Pretences to support ambition are never wanting. Their cry is, where is the danger? and they insist that altho' the powers of the general government will be increased, yet it will be for the good of the whole; and although the three great states form nearly a majority of the people of America, they never will hurt or injure the lesser states. *I do not, gentlemen, trust you.* . . . The small states never can agree to the Virginia plan; and why then is it still urged?" The delegates knew what the states had instructed them to do in the way of amendments. "As their ambassadors, can we not clearly grant those powers?" It was the small states that were really willing to confederate. The large states were refusing to do so, and insisting on a plan that would destroy the Confederation. "Then the fault will be yours, and all the nations of the earth will justify us. But what is to become of our public debts if we dissolve the union? Where is your plighted faith? Will you crush the smaller states, or must they be left unmolested? Sooner than be ruined, there are *foreign powers who will take us by the hand.*"

Bedford, who must have felt a stir in the room when he made this threat of foreign alliances, quickly went on to say that he did not mean to "intimidate or alarm." He was only reminding the large states of the consequences of their behavior. But King regretted that "the honorable gentleman from Delaware . . . with a vehemence unprecedented in this House, had declared himself ready to turn his hopes from our common Country, and court the protection of some foreign land."

On this clanging note the Convention adjourned till Monday, July 2. Washington, always silent in debate, on Sunday expressed himself in a letter to a friend in Virginia. "Every body wishes, every body expects something from the convention; but what will be the final result of its deliberation, the book of fate must disclose. Persuaded I am, that the primary cause of all our disorders lies in the different State governments, and in the tenacity of that power, which pervades the whole of their systems. Whilst independent sovereignty is so ardently contended for, whilst the local views of each State, and separate interests, by which they are too much governed, will not yield to a more enlarged scale of politics, incompatibility in the laws of the different States, and disrespect to those of the general government, must render this great country weak, inefficient and disgraceful. Weak at home and disregarded abroad is our present condition, and contemptible enough it is.

". . . I have had no wish more ardent, through the whole progress of this business, than that of knowing what kind of government is best calculated for us to live under. No doubt there will be a diversity of sentiments on this important subject; and to inform the judgment, it is necessary to hear all the arguments that can be advanced. To please all is impossible, and to attempt it would be in vain. The only way, therefore, is, under all the views in which it can be placed, and with a due consideration to circumstances, habits, &c., &c., to form such a government as will bear the scrutinizing eye of criticism, and trust to the good sense and patriotisms of the people to carry it into effect. Demagogues, men who are unwilling to lose any of their State consequence, and interested characters in each, will oppose any general government. But let these be regarded lightly, and justice, it is to be hoped, will at length prevail."

On Monday the Convention began its business with a vote on Ellsworth's motion that each state have one vote in the Senate. Connecticut, New York, New Jersey, Delaware, and Maryland voted aye; Massachusetts, Pennsylvania, Virginia, and the two Carolinas voted no. Georgia was divided. This was a tie vote, which did not actually represent the sense of the whole house. Maryland would have been divided if Jenifer had not that morning been late in attending. In his absence, Martin alone cast Maryland's vote, as any of its delegates was authorized to do. Georgia was divided because Pierce and Few had left the day before to go back to Congress in New York. In their absence the two Georgia delegates remaining could not agree. It was said at the time that one of them voted less out of conviction than out of despair that any general agreement could be arrived at. In any case, with Georgia divided and Maryland not divided, more or less by accident, there was no decision.

Just after the result of the vote was announced from the Chair, Jenifer came in, no doubt breathless and apologetic. King asked that the vote be taken again. This was manifestly against the Convention rules, and was not allowed. Even if it had been, there would still have been an inflexible minority of four delegations, who might withdraw from the Convention rather than agree to the Virginia plan.

Sherman said they appeared to be "at a full stop," but he supposed nobody meant they should break up the Convention without proposing something. General Pinckney proposed that a committee be appointed, made up of one member from each state, to "devise and report some compromise." During the discussion, Gouverneur Morris, who had that day resumed his seat, made a flamboyant speech urging that the members of the Senate be appointed by the executive, and for life, in order to give the United States the benefits of an aristocracy. The delegates heard him, in that republican gathering, without any recorded comment. Then by a large majority they voted to resort to a committee in their crisis. They elected Gerry of Massachusetts, Ellsworth of Connecticut, Yates of New York, Paterson of New Jersey, Franklin of Pennsylvania, Bedford of Delaware, Martin of Maryland, Mason of Virginia, Davie of North Carolina, Rutledge of South Carolina, Baldwin of Georgia. To give the committee time to prepare a report, and to permit the delegates, if they chose, to attend the celebration of the Fourth of July, the Convention then adjourned to Thursday the 5th.

The "Gentlemen of the Convention at the Indian Queen" had invited Washington and Franklin, and probably the other delegates, to dine with them at half-past three in their quarters at the tavern. It may be supposed that for the time being they put aside their altercations, but hardly that they avoided discussion of the subject which absorbed them all. From dinner Washington went for tea to William Bingham's, and "walked afterwards in the State house yard," according to the tantalizing entry in his diary.

IV

The Fourth of July at Trenton was celebrated that year, officially known in New Jersey as "the Year of our Lord One thousand seven hundred and Eighty seven and of our Sovereignty and Independence the Twelfth," by the Society of the Cincinnati, which as one of its toasts drank to "The Grand Convention—may they form a Constitution for an eternal Republic." Elsewhere in the country orators, preachers, and convivial men drinking the thirteen toasts then customary on such patriotic occasions, wished the Convention well and had high hopes for it. At Philadelphia, the traditional if unofficial capital, there were entertainments at taverns from The Lilliput on the New Jersey side of the Delaware to Gray's Ferry on the Schuylkill, and public ceremonies for everybody to attend or witness. Early in the morning the City Cavalry, the Light Infantry, a train of artillery, and a battalion of militia assembled on the Commons south of the State House. They performed various evolutions, dressed in line, and fired a *feu de joie:* each man, that is, firing a blank charge from his rifle or musket in rapid order from right to left. The artillery fired the salute of the United States, three times thirteen rounds. The officers of the volunteer corps and of the militia then proceeded to the State House, where the Cincinnati had met, and accompanied them, with martial music and to the sound of ringing bells along the way, to the Reformed Calvinist Church (Lutheran) in Race Street. Washington, president general of the Society of Cincinnati as well as president of the Convention, and many, perhaps most, of the delegates there heard an oration delivered by James Campbell, who addressed them as "Illustrious Senate."

"To you," the orator said, "your country looks with anxious expectations, on your decisions she rests, convinced that men who cut the cords of foreign legislation are competent to framing a system of government which will embrace all interests, call forth our interests, and establish our credit. But in every plan for improvement or reformation, may an attachment to the principles of our present Government be the characteristic of an American, and may every proposition to add kingly power to our Federal system be regarded as treason to the liberties of our country."

Here was evidence, if any of the delegates needed it, that the public sentiment was instinctively anti-monarchical, invincibly republican. The various state constitutions, the orator went on to say, had been made "upon the spur of the occasion, with a bayonet at our breasts," and could hardly have been expected to be perfect. But since then Americans had gained new political knowledge and skill, which must now be employed in the great new undertaking. "How fallen would be the character we have acquired in the establishment of our liberties, if we discover inability to form a suitable Government to preserve them! Is the science of Government so difficult that we have not men among us capable of unfolding its mysteries and binding our States together by mutual interests and obligations?" Some of the listening delegates must have reflected that while these were general statements, not easy to put into a working system, nevertheless they were some further indication of what Americans expected.

Hamilton had left Philadelphia on June 29, aware that the Convention would not recommend so strong a central government as he had in mind, and that his vote in the New York delegation would be of no use against the two votes of Yates and Lansing. But on his journey to New York, and after he arrived there, he talked with numerous persons who, he said in a letter to Washington of July 3, were afraid the Convention, "from a fear of shocking the popular opinion, will not go far enough. . . . Men in office are indeed taking all possible pains to give an unfavourable opinion of the Convention; but the current seems to be running strongly the other way." Hamilton was convinced that the delegates must not worry too much over the "supposed repugnancy of the people to an efficient constitution." If they did, they might "let slip the golden opportunity of rescuing the American empire from disunion, anarchy and misery. No motley or feeble measure can answer the end or will finally receive the public support." But of course Hamilton thought of the New Jersey plan as feeble and the Virginia plan as motley.

7

THE FEDERAL COMPROMISE

"To frame a government for a single city or State, is a business both in its importance and facility, widely different from the task entrusted to the Federal Convention, whose prospects were extended not only to thirteen independent and sovereign States, some of which in territorial jurisdiction, population, and resource, equal the most respectable nations of Europe, but likewise to innumerable States yet unformed, and to myriads of citizens who in future ages shall inhabit the vast uncultivated regions of the continent. The duties of that body therefore, were not limited to local or partial considerations, but to the formation of a plan commensurate with a great and valuable portion of the globe." *James Wilson, speech before the Pennsylvania convention, November 24, 1787.*

"Would it be wonderful if, under the pressure of all these difficulties, the Convention should have been forced into some deviations from that artificial structure and regular symmetry which an abstract view of the subject might lead an ingenious theorist to bestow on a constitution planned in his closet or in his imagination?" *James Madison, The Federalist No. 37, January 11, 1788.*

E ARLY in the morning of July 3 Washington began sitting for his portrait by Charles Willson Peale, who wished to make the mezzotint soon to appear with the title lettered round the margin: "His Excel: G: Washington Esq: LLD. Late Commander in Chief of the Armies of the U. S. of America & President of the Convention of 1787." Washington was painted in a close-fitting wig and his famous uniform of blue and buff (taken over from the First Virginia Regiment which he had commanded when he was a soldier of the Crown) with three gold stars on his epaulets. That day, and perhaps other days, he went to the State House in uniform, general as well as president. Although this day's session was only a meeting of the grand committee of the states, of which Washington was not a member, he attended along with other delegates who were there as observers not debaters.

With Gerry as chairman, the committee took up the problem of conciliating the opposed views which were the same in the committee as they had been in the Convention. The majority favored proportional representation in both houses of the legislature of the United States; the minority favored equal representation in both. Sherman had earlier proposed that the states have proportional representation in the popular branch, but equal votes in the Senate. Franklin had proposed that the states be equally represented in the Senate, but that in money matters the Senate votes be based on the amount of contributions from the separate states. Now in the committee Sherman, who had taken the place of Ellsworth, offered a new compromise: that the states should have an equal vote in the Senate but that no decision could be final unless the states voting for it should comprise a majority of the inhabitants of the United States. None of these compromises suited the committee. At last, after debates of which there is no record, Franklin made the motion which, with "some modifications," was agreed to. As modified, it proposed that in the first branch each state be allowed one member for every 40,000 of its inhabitants (counting three-fifths of the slaves) and that any state with less than that number of inhabitants have one member; that all bills for raising or apportioning money and for paying salaries to federal officers originate in the first branch, without alteration or amendment by the Senate; and that in the Senate each state have an equal vote.

This compromise combined and redefined Sherman's proposed compromise on different modes of representation in the two houses, and Franklin's on a special mode for allowing more votes to the states which paid more money for federal expenses. It was satisfactory to a majority of the members of the grand committee, though the large states were now in dissent because of the equal vote granted to all states in the Senate. The committee agreed to report their compromise to the Convention, with the condition that the provisions relating to both houses must be "generally adopted" together.

On Thursday July 5 Gerry reported for the committee to the Convention. Madison vigorously opposed the concession to the small states of equality in the Senate. It was, he thought, the surrender of a fundamental principle on the mere ground of expediency. It was conciliating a minority, by doing an injustice to the majority of the people of the United States. "It was in vain to purchase concord in the Convention on terms which would perpetuate discord among their constituents." He did not believe that Delaware "would brave the consequences of seeking her fortunes apart from the other States" or "pursue the rash policy of courting foreign support"; or that New Jersey "would choose rather to stand on its own legs, and bid defiance to events," than to accept a government which was absolutely necessary to protect the state from its overshadowing neighbors. "Harmony in the Convention was no doubt much to be desired. Satisfaction to all the States" from the first would be still more desirable. "But if the principal States comprehending a majority of the people of the United States should concur in a just & judicious plan, he had the firmest hopes that all the other States would by degrees accede to it."

Gouverneur Morris was rhetorical. "He came here as a Representative of America; he flattered himself he came here in some degree as a Representative of the whole human race; for the whole human race will be affected by the proceedings of this Convention." But it seemed to him, from some things he had heard, "that we were assembled to truck and bargain for our particular States." He believed that "this Country must be united. If persuasion does not unite it, the sword will." He spoke of the horrors of civil war. "The stronger party will then make traytors of the weaker; and the Gallows & Halter will finish the work of the sword." In the compromise report from the grand committee he saw prospects of confusion and conflict. "State attachments, and State importance have been the bane of this Country. We cannot annihilate; but we can perhaps take out the teeth of the serpents"—the jealousies of the states.

Bedford, who had let slip the unfortunate hint that the smaller states might turn to foreign alliances, again protested that he had not meant what he had said; that he had been speaking as a lawyer, for whom "warmth was natural & sometimes necessary." But no man could foresee "to what extremities the small States may be driven by oppression." Paterson thought the talk about the sword and the gallows was "little calculated to produce conviction." Both he and Bedford resented the treatment the small states had endured from the large in the Convention. Paterson was not entirely satisfied with the grand committee's compromise plan, but he agreed with Bedford that something must be done for the United States. "Better that a defective plan should be adopted," Bedford said, "than that none should be recommended." Defects might be remedied by later meetings.

Gerry had objections to the new plan, but he insisted that the United States were "in a peculiar situation. We were neither the same Nation nor different Nations. We ought not therefore to pursue the one or the other of these ideas too closely." If that were done, some of the states might secede from the Convention, and from the union. "If we do not come to some agreement among ourselves some foreign sword will probably do the work for us." Mason thought there must be an accommodation between the opposing sides in the conflict. "It could not be more inconvenient to any gentleman to remain absent from his private affairs, than it was for him; but he would bury his bones in this city rather than expose his Country to the Consequences of a dissolution of the Convention without anything being done."

Both Gouverneur Morris and Rutledge objected to basing representation in the lower house purely on numbers, one member for each 40,000 inhabitants. Life and liberty might be the first considerations of savages, Morris said, but in civilized conditions "property was the main object of Society." Property, Rutledge agreed, "was certainly the principal object of Society." Here Rutledge was speaking for the slave-owners of South Carolina and Morris for the large land-owners of New York. Moreover, they were both thinking of the new states in the Western territory which might in time be admitted to the union. Any one of these, according to the grand committee's plan, might be entitled to one member even though it had less than 40,000 inhabitants. Some arrangement must be made to protect the rich maritime states from the lean voters of the backwoods.

Nothing was decided that day, and the debate went over to Friday the 6th. On Friday the Convention readily agreed that the proposal of one member in the lower house for each 40,000 inhabitants called for further detailed study. The matter was referred to a smaller committee made up of Gouverneur Morris, Gorham, Randolph, Rutledge, and King. Then the debate continued on the clause providing that all money bills should originate in the popular branch of the federal legislature.

The delegates from the small states were silent. They had

won what they wanted in the proposal that the states be equally represented in the Senate, and were willing to let the larger states, with more votes in the lower house, have some advantage in raising revenues and fixing apportionments. The delegates from the large states failed to see that the small had made any real concession. What was the difference, Wilson asked, which house had the right to originate bills, since the other must concur? Mason explained that the committee had desired to put the voting of money as directly as possible into the hands of the people. If the members of the Senate should have "the power of giving away the people's money, they might soon forget the Source from whence they received it. We might soon have an aristocracy." He had been disturbed by certain aristocratic principles advanced in the Convention, but he was glad to find they did not prevail among the members.

Gouverneur Morris, to whom Mason had obviously referred, declared that he was sure "there never was, nor ever will be a civilized society without an Aristocracy. His endeavour was to keep it as much as possible from doing mischief." He assumed that the American aristocracy would dominate the Senate. If the sole right to originate money bills lay in the popular house, the country would lose the benefit of the superior abilities of the Senate in devising such bills; and the Senate, having no responsibility, would fall into disputes with the originating house, as in the British Parliament. Morris believed that the proposed restriction would be "either useless or pernicious."

Franklin summed up the argument with a clarity which enabled Madison, taking down the slow words, to make them sound almost like one of Franklin's written speeches. "It had been asked," the philosopher said, "what would be the use of restraining the second branch from medling with money bills. He could not but remark that it was always of importance that the people should know who had disposed of their money, & how it had been disposed of. It was a maxim that those who feel, can best judge." (It was a maxim of Franklin's own. He had used it as far back as February 1766 in his examination before the House of Commons, when he said: "Those that feel can judge best.") "This end would, he thought, be best attained, if money affairs were to be confined to the immediate representatives of the people. This was his inducement to concur in the report. As to the danger or difficulty that might arise from a negative in the second [branch] where the people would not be proportionally represented, it might easily be got over by declaring that there should be no such Negative; or if that will not do, by declaring that there shall be no such branch at all"— which was what Franklin preferred in any case.

In the vote which followed, the Convention agreed by a narrow margin to let the clause relating to money bills stand for the present in the report. Connecticut, New Jersey, Delaware, Maryland, and North Carolina were now in the affirmative, with only Pennsylvania, Virginia, and South Carolina in the negative; and Massachusetts, New York, and Georgia divided.

If the popular branch of the legislature was to have the sole right to originate money bills, then the representation in that branch was bound to be of the greatest importance. On Saturday the 7th the Convention agreed that each state should "have an equal vote" in the Senate. There was some lively discussion, but the vote was not too close. Several of the delegates voted aye because they realized that this was only a part of the grand committee's report, and that another vote would later be taken on the whole of it. Before that could be done, there must be some settlement as to the actual number of representatives the people of the respective states would have to speak for them in the disposition of their money.

II

Gouverneur Morris, for the smaller committee, reported on Monday the 9th. His committee had been handicapped by lack of knowledge as to what the population of the states was. For want of better information, they had gone back to the estimates of 1774 with some guesses as to changes since then. They now proposed that at the first meeting of the lower house it should consist of fifty-six members, divided as follows: New Hampshire 2, Massachusetts 7, Rhode Island 1, Connecticut 4, New York 5, New Jersey 3, Pennsylvania 8, Delaware 1, Maryland 4, Virginia 9, North Carolina 5, South Carolina 5, Georgia 2. These figures were to be temporary. The legislature of the United States should be authorized "from time to time" to augment the number of representatives. "In case any of the States shall hereafter be divided, or any two or more States united, or any new State created within the limits of the United States," the legislature should have authority to regulate the number of the representatives of the new states "upon the principles of their wealth and number of inhabitants."

There had been talk in the Convention of the possible division of some of the larger states and the possible union of some of the smaller. The committee had provided for either possibility. But the proposal that new states should be granted representation according to their wealth as well as to their population roused fresh debate. Gorham, a member of the committee, explained the report. One member of the popular house to every 40,000 inhabitants, the committee thought, would make the house unworkably large as the population increased. Moreover, there was danger that new Western states, if admitted on those terms, might soon "out-vote the Atlantic." But if the Atlantic states kept the "Government in their own hands," they could take care of their own interest "by dealing out the right of Representation in safe proportions to the Western States. These were the views of the Committee."

Those were the views of several of the delegates who thought wealth no less than numbers should be represented in all the states. Butler of South Carolina "urged warmly the justice & necessity" of taking wealth into account. King of Massachusetts said that, as the Southern states were the richest, they must naturally hesitate to "league themselves with the Northern unless some respect were paid to their superior wealth." But the Northern states, which looked for commercial advantages from the union, had already consented to the representation of Southern wealth, which was slaves, by agreeing that three-fifths of them might be reckoned as inhabitants.

Nine states now agreed (New York and New Jersey dissenting) that the legislature of the United States should have authority in the future to regulate the representation of all the states "upon the principles of their wealth and number of inhabitants." As to the number of representatives for the present, that matter was referred to another committee of the states. The members were King, Sherman, Yates, Brearley, Gouverneur Morris, Read, Daniel Carroll (who had just taken his seat for Maryland), Madison, Williamson, Rutledge, and Houstoun.

They came in on July 10 with a proposal that the lower house begin with sixty-five members: New Hampshire 3, Massachusetts 8, Rhode Island 1, Connecticut 5, New York 6, New Jersey 4, Pennsylvania 8, Delaware 1, Maryland 6, Virginia 10, North Carolina 5, South Carolina 5, Georgia 3.

At once there was a scuffle of arguments over these figures. Butler and General Pinckney of South Carolina moved that New Hampshire be reduced from three representatives to two. "Her numbers did not entitle her to 3 and it was a poor State." King of Massachusetts, supporting the claim of New Hampshire to three members, made it plain that he was thinking less of New Hampshire in particular than of the Northern states in general. He had been willing to yield something to the Southern states for their security, but "no principle would justify giving them a majority." General Pinckney replied that the Southern states did not expect to have a majority, but he wished them "to have something like an equality." Otherwise, they would be "nothing more than overseers for the Northern states," since the regulation of trade would be in the hands of the central government. He was glad that one member had been added to Virginia, "as he considered her a Southern state. He was glad also that the members of Georgia were increased"—and he did not object to her being given a larger number than her population then entitled her to.

The motion to reduce New Hampshire from three to two members was lost by a vote of eight to two. Motions made by Southern delegates to increase the number of members for the Carolinas and Georgia by one each were lost by decisive votes.

Madison moved that the number of members be doubled, "A *majority* of a *Quorum of 65* members was too small a number to represent the whole inhabitants of the United States." Ellsworth and Sherman of Connecticut objected on the grounds of expense. Read of Delaware approved because the change would give Delaware two votes. Rutledge thought the state legislatures were at present too numerous, and the national legislature should not follow that bad example. The members would be forced by the interests of their states to attend regularly. He supposed "the General Legislature would not sit more than 6 or 8 weeks in the year."

Only two states, Delaware and Virginia, favored doubling the number of members. The number as fixed by the report of the committee of the states was approved by a vote of nine to two: only South Carolina and Georgia opposed.

Washington in the Chair, entertaining motions, putting questions, announcing votes, was troubled by the persistent conflicts. They were, he wrote that day to Hamilton in New York, worse than ever. "I *almost* despair of seeing a favourable issue to the proceedings of our Convention, and do therefore repent having had any agency in the business. The Men who oppose a strong and energetic government are, in my opinion, narrow minded politicians, or are under the influence of local views. The apprehension expressed by them that the *people* will not accede to the form proposed is the *ostensible,* not the *real* cause of the opposition. ... . I am sorry you went away. I wish you were back. The crisis is equally important and alarming, and no opposition under such circumstances should discourage exertions till the signature is fixed." Hamilton returned to the Convention three days later. His colleagues Yates and Lansing left it on the day Washington wrote.

The conflicts which troubled Washington went on for a week in a tangle of motions and motives. Randolph on the 10th moved that "in order to ascertain alterations in the population & wealth of the States the Legislature of the United States be required to cause a proper census and estimate to be taken" at regular intervals which were to be agreed on. Williamson of North Carolina on the 11th proposed an amendment to the effect that in the census enumeration the "free white inhabitants" be counted and three-fifths of "those of other descriptions"—that is, slaves. Butler and Charles Cotesworth Pinckney of South Carolina at once insisted that "blacks be included . . . equally with the Whites," and made a motion to that effect. The labor of a slave in South Carolina, Butler said, was as productive and valuable as that of a free man in Massachusetts. Wealth was the "great means of defence and utility to the Nation." Consequently wealth ought to be considered equal to numbers of free men "in a Government which was instituted principally for the protection of property, and was itself to be supported by property."

Mason of Virginia said that this principle of representation, however favorable it might be to Virginia, was unjust, and he could not vote for it. But since slaves by their labor raised the

value of land, increased imports and exports and therefore revenues, "would supply the means of feeding & supporting an
army, and might in cases of emergency become themselves sol-
diers," he believed they should not be wholly excluded from the
estimates of population. He would be satisfied if three-fifths of
them were counted. Like other Virginia delegates, Mason was
opposed to slavery on principle, regretted the existence of it
in their state, and desired to see slavery abolished if this could
be done without destroying the economy of a society which had
inherited its slaves as it had inherited its land and its laws.

Only three states, South Carolina, Georgia, and (for some
reason) Delaware, voted to count slaves and free citizens equally
in representation. The strength of the vote led the Convention
to reconsider its earlier decision to reckon three-fifths of the
slaves as inhabitants. Wilson did not see on what principle they
could be so counted. "Are they admitted as Citizens? Then why
are they not admitted on an equality with White Citizens? Are
they admitted as property? Then why is not other property
admitted into the computation?" Nevertheless he was willing to
see them included as a necessary compromise. Gouverneur Morris said he found himself in the "dilemma of doing injustice to
the Southern States or to human nature," and must decide in
favor of human nature. To count slaves, in any ratio, as part of
the population must encourage the slave trade, since the importing of slaves would increase not only the wealth but also the
representation of the slave-holding states. He could not concur
in that, even if the Southern states should refuse to "confederate" without it. On the question, six states voted against counting slaves at all in the estimate of population.

But on the 12th Morris made another motion to the effect that
taxation should be proportioned according to representation. This
naturally changed the position of the Southern states. South
Carolina and Georgia were still willing to pay taxes on all their
slaves if all of them could be counted as inhabitants. But the
other states with large numbers of slaves were unwilling. Davie
of North Carolina demanded, in the name of his state, merely
that three-fifths of the slaves be included. Randolph of Virginia
urged the same ratio. "He lamented that such a species of property existed. But as it did the holders of it would require this
security." On another motion six states now favored the ratio

of five to three, with Massachusetts and South Carolina divided, and only New Jersey and Delaware opposed.

On the 13th Randolph moved to alter the vote of July 9 which had said that representation should be based on wealth and population, by striking out wealth altogether. Gouverneur Morris objected. Suppose the population of the South should increase as it was expected to, and the South should make common cause with the Western states. Then between them they would have a majority which would overwhelm the Northern and Middle states. Butler replied that the South did not expect a majority, only an increase in relation to the other states, since "the people & strength of America are evidently bearing Southwardly & Southwestwardly." But the Southern states did want to feel sure that "their negroes may not be taken from them, which some gentlemen within or without doors have a very good mind to do."

Wilson in one of his ablest speeches carried the house with him. "Conceiving," he said, "that all men wherever placed have equal rights and are equally entitled to confidence, he viewed without apprehension the period when a few States should contain the superior number of people. The majority of the people wherever found ought in all questions to govern the minority." Nor was he troubled by the fear that the "interior Country" might some time contain the majority of the population. If they became the majority, they would have a majority's rights, "whether we will or no." Did the delegates not remember that Great Britain had been jealous and apprehensive over the growth of her American colonies? That had led to rebellion and independence. The Atlantic states must avoid behaving toward the interior as Great Britain had once unwisely behaved toward them. The numbers of people had to be regarded as the proper rule of representation, since no better could be found. Congress in 1783, after long discussion, had been satisfied that "the rule of numbers does not differ much from the combined rule of numbers & wealth. Again he could not agree that property was the sole or the primary object of Government & Society. The cultivation & improvement of the human mind was the most noble object. With respect to this object, as well as to other *personal* rights, numbers were surely the natural & precise measure of Representation. And with respect to property, they could not vary much from the precise measure."

On the question of striking "wealth" out of the clause relating to representation in the popular house, all the states on July 13 voted aye except Delaware, which was divided. One of the most important decisions which ever came here to a vote found the Convention nearly unanimous in agreement.

By a memorable coincidence this decision was made on the very day when Congress in New York at last adopted the Ordinance of 1787 for the government of the Northwest Territory. The Ordinance provided that five new states (eventually named Ohio, Indiana, Illinois, Wisconsin, Michigan) from this Territory might be admitted to the union as soon as any of them should have 60,000 inhabitants, which was about the population of Delaware. Slavery was prohibited, thanks to an earlier suggestion of Jefferson, a bill of rights and freedom of religious worship guaranteed, and laws forbidden which might impair the obligations of private contracts. This was federal legislation over separate states-to-be of the sort contemplated by the constitution which the Convention was now trying to make.

The old Congress and the new Convention were in accord on a matter which was fundamental to the future. While Congress was arranging to admit Western states to the United States, the Convention was arranging that this should be on an equality in law with the original Thirteen. The states themselves had long shown partiality to the cities and counties on the seaboard. The "back counties" of Pennsylvania were now in resentful conflict with Philadelphia and the counties nearest it. In South Carolina the "up country," rebelling against the dominance of the "low country," had in 1786 voted the removal of the capital of the state from Charleston to Columbia, still almost in the primeval forest—though this had not yet been carried out. The seaboard shipowners, merchants, and planters all along the Atlantic had made every effort to protect themselves and their property against the rising demands of the frontier. Various delegates to the Convention, notably Gorham of Massachusetts, Gouverneur Morris of Pennsylvania, and Rutledge of South Carolina, had insisted that the Atlantic states must keep control of the government.

Gerry thought on July 14 that the Convention ought to limit the number of Western states to be admitted, so that there should never be more of them than of the Atlantic states. "There was a rage for emigration from the Eastern States to the Western

Country," he said, "and he did not wish those remaining behind to be at the mercy of the Emigrants" once they had established themselves in new states. Sherman, with an odd mixture of shortsightedness and enlightenment, thought there was no probability that the Western states would ever outnumber the Eastern. "If the event should ever happen, it was too remote to be taken into consideration at this time." For the present, he said, "We are providing for our posterity, for our children & our grand Children, who would be as likely to be citizens of new Western States, as of the old States." They should not be discriminated against as Gerry proposed.

While deciding that wealth (except for three-fifths of the slaves) should not be represented in the legislature of the United States, the Convention decided also that the legislature must not be left free to regulate changes in representation at its own will. "From the nature of man," Mason said on July 11, "we may be sure, that those who have power in their hands will not give it up while they can retain it." He agreed with Randolph that alterations must be according to a regular census called for by a constitutional provision. Sherman, who was at first disposed to leave alterations to the discretion of the legislature of the United States, was convinced, he said, "by the observations of Mr. Randolph & Mr. Mason that the *periods* & the *rule* of revising the Representation ought to be fixt by the Constitution." After much discussion and numerous amendments proposed, it was decided on July 12 that representation ought to be "proportioned according to direct Taxation," and that the necessary revisions should be based on a census to be taken within six years after the first meeting of the legislature of the United States and again every ten years thereafter.

III

On the morning of July 14 Martin of Maryland called for the question on the whole report brought in by the grand committee of the states on the 5th. The Convention had now gone piecemeal through the compromise proposal and had accepted, or amended, its various clauses. Instead of one member in the legislature of the United States for every 40,000 inhabitants of a given state, as proposed, the Convention preferred for the present a fixed number of members for each state, subject to revision according to a decennial census as the population might change in the future. But money bills were to originate in the popular branch, and each state should have an equal vote in the Senate, as the committee had recommended. Since the committee had stipulated that the parts of their proposal were not to be adopted separately, the Convention must now either accept or reject it as a whole.

Some of the delegates were not yet ready to put the matter to a vote. Gerry moved that the new states to be admitted should never be allowed more representatives than the original members of the Confederation. Four states (Massachusetts, Connecticut, Delaware, and Maryland) voted aye, all the others no except Pennsylvania, which was divided. Charles Pinckney moved that instead of equal votes in the Senate the states have fixed numbers of representatives in that branch: New Hampshire 2, Massachusetts 4, Rhode Island 1, Connecticut 3, New York 3, New Jersey 2, Pennsylvania 3, Delaware 1, Maryland 3, Virginia 5, North Carolina 3, South Carolina 3, Georgia 2. Wilson seconded the motion. King approved, because he could see no better reason for equality of representation in one branch of the legislature than in the other. What they proposed to create was "a General and National Government over the people of America. There never will be a case," he said, "in which it will act as a federal Government on the States and not on the individual Citizens." Therefore the citizens through their representatives, and not the states as states, ought to influence the operations of the central authority. He thought that to consent to equality of votes in the Senate would be injustice, and worse than doing nothing. Better "a little more confusion & convulsion" than to submit to such an evil. Strong of Massachusetts believed that unless some accommodation could be agreed on, "the Union itself must soon be dissolved." If, as had been suggested, the principal states were to form and recommend a scheme of government without the others, there was no certainty that the smaller would ever be more likely than now to accede to it, or even that the people of the larger would "embrace and ratify it." Wilson thought nothing "so pernicious as bad first principles." If equality in the Senate were merely "an error that time would correct," he might accept it, being aware "that perfection was unattainable in any plan."

But this was "a fundamental and a perpetual error." An evil in representation, like poison in a first potion, "must be followed by disease, convulsions, and finally death itself."

Charles Pinckney's motion for proportional votes in the Senate "passed in the negative," in the language of the time, with six states opposed. Massachusetts was among them, because Gorham was absent that day, and King was outvoted by Gerry and Strong.

On Monday the 16th the Convention voted on the compromise proposal as a whole. The vote was nearly as close as it could be, and as it had regularly been during all the recent deliberations. Connecticut, New Jersey, Delaware, Maryland, and North Carolina approved; Pennsylvania, Virginia, South Carolina, and Georgia opposed; Massachusetts was divided. Even if Massachusetts had voted with the larger states, the result would have been merely a tie. The Convention was at a standstill.

Randolph, original proposer of the Virginia plan over which they had been working for six weeks, said that the vote had "embarrassed the business extremely." He had come this morning with a series of suggestions which he thought might conciliate the smaller states. His suggestions provided for an enumeration of special cases in which the states might have equal votes in the Senate, proportional votes in all others. But since he now saw that the smaller states persisted in demanding equal votes in every case, he "could not but think we were unprepared to discuss this subject further. It will probably be in vain to come to any final decision with a bare majority on either side. For these reasons he wished the Convention might adjourn, that the large States might consider the steps proper to be taken in the present solemn crisis of the business, and that the small States might also deliberate on the means of conciliation."

Paterson thought it was high time to adjourn. The rule of secrecy ought to be rescinded, and the delegates ought to be free to consult their constituents. But the smaller states, he assured the Convention, would in no circumstances yield their absolute demand for equality in the Senate. If Randolph were willing to move that the Convention adjourn sine die, Paterson would second it "with all his heart." Whether or not Paterson was actually in favor of a permanent adjournment, he seized on this troubled moment to make a suggestion that amounted to a threat.

Randolph "had never entertained the idea of an adjournment

sine die; & was sorry that his meaning had been so readily & strangely interpreted." He had meant merely to adjourn till the next day "in order that some conciliatory experiment might if possible be devised." If the smaller States should continue to hold back, then the larger might take "such measures, he would not say what, as might be necessary." Here Randolph too was hinting a threat.

Paterson seconded the adjournment for a day, since the larger states seemed to wish, as he reversed Randolph's terms to put it, "to deliberate further on conciliatory expedients."

In the following discussion nobody favored an adjournment sine die. Gerry said that Massachusetts was opposed to adjournment even for a day, since there appeared to be no "new ground of compromise," but the state could concur with the majority. Rutledge also thought there was no chance of a compromise, and no need of an adjournment. "The little states were fixt. They had repeatedly & solemnly declared themselves to be so. All that the large States then had to do, was to decide whether they would yield or not. For his part he conceiv'd that altho' we could not do what we thought best, in itself, we ought to do something. Had we not better keep the Government up a little longer, hoping that another Convention will supply our omissions, than abandon everything to hazard? Our Constituents will be very little satisfied with us if we take the latter course."

In such words, on the careful level of parliamentary courtesy, the delegates were saying that the Convention despaired of finding any just design for a government which the two parties could agree on, and doubted whether anything was to be gained by debating further. They had got nowhere in their plans for a new constitution. Perhaps the United States would never have a better constitution than the ineffectual old one. Perhaps there would not long be any United States.

The occasion might seem to call for the dramatic interchange of burning speeches, with angry and unhappy men on both sides, such as were in the Convention. There was more fire in the speeches than appears in Madison's quiet notes, which are the sole record of this crucial episode. But there is no missing, in his record, the essential drama of an immense decision being made by men who did not know how immense the decision was.

Nor is there less drama in his brief account of what happened on the morning of July 17. A number of delegates from the larger states, all unnamed in the record like heroes in masks, met "before the hour of the Convention." They believed that the smaller states were inflexible in their demand for equal representation in the Senate. That was what the delegates from the smaller states had said. Some of them were present at this meeting, and their faces today confirmed their words of yesterday.

The delegates from the larger states talked together. Nobody had a specific proposal. There was no agreement on any general principle. An equal vote in the Senate was anathema to some, to others an injustice, a mistake, or only an inconvenience. Some were willing to break off the Convention rather than yield to the smaller states' demand, but more were by no means sure it worth opposing further. Several insisted that the larger states, which meant a majority of the people of the United States, should make a constitution of their own, recommend it to Congress and any states that would accept it, and let the smaller states go their own way. Others were inclined to yield to the smaller states and to concur in some general plan or other. If there was none on which a large majority could agree, then continue, as lately, with a bare majority of the states and even now and then with only a minority of the people represented in the decisions.

The delegates from the smaller states, listening to this inconclusive discussion, were gradually reassured. There was no danger, they perceived, that their opponents would unite in any roughshod resistance to equal votes in the Senate. This was enough for the smaller states. They talked no more of withdrawing from the Convention. From the time of this morning caucus, this clash of drama without remembered words, they were active in support of the general plan for the new government which was to succeed the Confederation without abolishing the states as entities in one branch of the future legislature.

The Great Compromise, as this settlement is commonly called, or the Connecticut Compromise, was a federal compromise. The small states, by giving up their claim to equal representation in the popular branch of the legislature of the United States, had given up their attachment to a mere confederation. The large states, by giving up their claim to proportional representation in the Senate, had given up any hopes they may have had for a consolidated government. The states would now survive as states in a federal system to which they conceded the right to make, execute, and interpret federal laws, while themselves retaining the right to govern themselves within their own borders. The federal compromise was what Hamilton called a "motley measure," what Madison called a "novelty & a compound." Perhaps not a single delegate in the Convention was fully satisfied with the compromise. It was the creation of the corporate mind of the assemblage, reconciling differences, coming to such general agreement as was possible.

Naturally the desires of the conflicting parties in the Convention, or of the states they represented, were affected by their interests. The Southern states desired to be represented in part by their wealth, which was slaves, neither quite property nor quite population. They had been permitted to count three-fifths of the slaves in the estimate of their numbers. This gave them an anomalous advantage in the lower house of the legislature of the United States. The Northern states, averse to letting slaves be counted, nevertheless could realize that slaves would not be represented in the Senate if the votes of the states were there equal. As there were more Northern states than Southern, the North would have a majority in the Senate, and might look to it for security against the Southern votes in the lower house. These were compromises of interest which went with the compromises of political structure in the proposed government, entirely favorable neither to the several states nor to the United States. The individual states had special interests, as the individual delegates had. But the primary concern of all of them was for preservation of the union, defense against foreign aggression and domestic dissension, and the general prosperity of the American people. With these indispensable things provided for, the delegates believed, by the government they were devising, they could hope according to their interests for the particular blessings they might enjoy in the society which could develop under the guarantee of the new government.

At the end of these wrangling days which saw the federal compromise agreed on, a note appeared in the *Pennsylvania Packet* for July 19 which said: "So great is the unanimity, we hear, that prevails in the Convention, upon all great federal subjects, that it has been proposed to call the room in which they assemble—Unanimity Hall." It has been guessed, on no evidence, that this was deliberately given out by some delegate or delegates for the purpose of contradicting any rumors which might reach the public. The note was widely reprinted in newspapers in various states—there were then no national newspapers —and, while in general misleading, gave many readers a justified confidence that some progress was being made.

IV

On July 12 Manasseh Cutler, Massachusetts clergyman and agent for the Ohio Company which was planning to settle a colony of pioneers in what is now Ohio, arrived in Philadelphia. He had been in New York, lobbying for a grant of desirable land from Congress. Finding himself so near to Philadelphia, he had come to visit the capital, partly to discuss his business with any Convention delegates who might be interested, but chiefly, it appears, out of historical, scientific, and literary curiosity. As soon as he arrived at the Indian Queen he was told that several of the delegates were lodged in the tavern. He sent to Strong asking for a chance to speak to him. Strong had not met Cutler but knew of his activities, and invited him to come to the delegates' Hall. The visitor was introduced to Gorham of their state; to Madison, Mason, and his son of Virginia; Alexander Martin and Williamson of North Carolina; Rutledge and Charles Pinckney of South Carolina; and Hamilton of New York—all of them lodgers. Several other delegates were spending the evening there, and Cutler was invited to join them. "We sat until half after one."

Very early the next morning Cutler and Strong went to breakfast with Gerry, who had taken a house in Spruce Street and lived "in a family style." Gerry, then forty-three, had been married only the past year. "Few old bachelors," Cutler thought, "have been more fortunate in matrimony than Mr. Gerry. His lady is young, very handsome, and exceedingly amiable. . . . I should suppose her not more than 17, and believe he must be turned of 55." They had "a fine son about two months old." The customs of the capital, it seemed to the visitor from rural Massachusetts, were admirably republican. "I was surprised to find how early ladies in Philadelphia can rise in the morning and to see them at breakfast at half past five, when in Boston they can hardly see a breakfast table at nine without falling into hysterics. I observed to Mrs. Gerry that it seemed to be an early hour for ladies to breakfast. She said she always rose early, and found it conducive to her health. She was inured to it from her childhood in New York, and that it was the practice of the best families in Philadelphia."

After breakfast Cutler went on a tour of inspection through the city, hospitably received by various scholars, clergymen, and physicians, including Benjamin Rush, to whom he had brought letters of introduction, and much impressed by Peale's Museum, of which he wrote a graphic account. The State House he thought a "noble building; the architecture is in a richer and grander style than any public building I have before seen." That day the Supreme Court of Pennsylvania was in session in the room opposite Independence Hall, the three judges in red robes, the lawyers in black. Cutler understood that the Convention was sitting, not in Independence Hall but in the room directly above it. This may have been some temporary arrangement, or Cutler may have been in error. All he could see with his own eyes was the sentries "planted without and within—to prevent any person from approaching near—who appear to be very alert in the performance of their duty." He admired the State House Yard, which he called the Mall, and spoke of the building for the American Philosophical Society and the "County Court-house" (later Congress Hall) which were in construction on the east and the west sides of the State House. There must have been noises from the convict workmen, but Cutler mentioned instead the outcries of the inmates of the Walnut Street Prison, shouting insults or begging alms from the passers-by.

At five o'clock Gerry took Cutler to call on Franklin. "We found him in his Garden, sitting upon a grass plat under a very large Mulberry, with several other gentlemen and two or three ladies. There was no curiosity in Philadelphia which I felt so anxious to see as this great man, who has been the wonder of Europe as well as the glory of America. . . . In short, when I entered his house, I felt as if I was going to be introduced to the presence of an European Monarch. But how were my ideas changed, when I saw a short, fat, trunched old man, in a plain Quaker dress, bald pate, and short white locks, sitting without his hat under the tree, and, as Mr. Gerry introduced me, rose from his chair, took me by the hand, expressed his joy to see me, welcomed me to the city, and begged me to seat myself close to him. His voice was low, but his countenance open, frank, and pleasing." Cutler presented his letters of introduction. When Franklin had read them, he introduced his guest, "with the usual compliments" to the other men present, "who were most of them members of the Convention."

When it grew dark, "the tea-table was spread under the tree, and Mrs. Bache, a very gross and rather homely lady, who is the only daughter of the Doctor and lives with him, served it out to the company. She had three of her children about her, over whom she seemed to have no kind of command, but who appeared to be excessively fond of their Grandpapa."

Because Cutler was a scientist of note, and a member of the American Philosophical Society of which Franklin was president, their conversation was principally on scientific matters. Franklin had just been sent a two-headed snake preserved in a phial of spirits. While they were talking about this curious specimen, Franklin remarked that such a creature would be in a predicament if it should be crawling through bushes, and the two heads could not decide on which side of a stem to pass. This reminded him of something which had come up that day in the Convention, "in consequence of his comparing the snake to America. . . . He seemed to forget," Cutler observed, "that every thing in the Convention was to be kept a profound secret. But this secrecy of Convention matters was suggested to him, which stopped him, and deprived me of the story he was going to tell."

Madison's notes make no mention of any word spoken by Franklin on July 13. If he spoke of a snake with two heads it must have been some pleasant reference to what he called elsewhere a "famous political fable"—which was apparently of his own invention. In his fable he compared a legislature of two houses with a snake with two heads. "One head chose to go on the right side of the twig, the other on the left, so that time was spent in the contest; and before the decision was completed the poor snake died with thirst." He may have said something of the sort during the day, and may have remembered it when he was talking with Cutler. It was a slight matter, and soon stopped. But out of this has grown the grotesque legend that some discreet delegate always attended Franklin at convivial dinners to keep him from divulging Convention secrets. It is pure legend. Franklin is not known to have dined in public with anybody but members of the Convention during the whole session, and was in discretion at least the equal of any of his associates in the enterprise.

After tea Franklin took Cutler into what the visitor presumed was "the largest, and by far the best, private library in America." There Cutler saw and admired the letter press Franklin had invented, and his "long arm" for taking books down from high shelves; "and his great armed chair, with rockers, and a large fan placed over it, with which he fans himself, keeps off flies, etc, while he sits reading, with only a small motion of his foot; and many other curiosities, and inventions, all his own." The host "seemed extremely fond, through the course of the visit, of dwelling on Philosophical subjects, and particularly that of natural History, while the other Gentlemen were swallowed up with politics. . . . I was highly delighted with the extensive knowledge he seemed to have of every subject, the brightness of his memory, and clearness and vivacity of all his mental faculties. . . . His manners are perfectly easy, and every thing about him seems to diffuse an unrestrained freedom and happiness. He has an incessant vein of humor, accompanied with an uncommon vivacity, which seems as natural and involuntary as his breathing."

Back at the Indian Queen at ten, Cutler found that "the gentlemen who lodged in the house were just sitting down to supper; a sumptuous table was spread, and the attendance in the style of noblemen." After supper, Strong again invited Cutler to the delegates' Hall, where they talked till midnight.

But the next morning Cutler, after a turn before daylight through the Market, was ready by five to leave with Strong, Martin of North Carolina, Mason and his son, Williamson, Madison, Rutledge, Hamilton, and some other friends, all in their carriages, on an expedition across the Schuylkill to the famous botanic garden of John Bartram, whom they found hoeing in his bare feet, and at first "embarrassed at seeing so large and gay a company so early in the morning." The gentlemen of the Convention had chosen this early hour so they might be back at the State House at eleven.

8

PLANS FOR THE UNITED STATES

"It is obviously impracticable in the fœderal government of these States, to secure all rights of independent sovereignty to each, and yet provide for the interest and safety of all—Individuals entering into society, must give up a share of liberty to preserve the rest. The magnitude of the sacrifice must depend as well on situation and circumstance, as on the object to be obtained. It is at all times difficult to draw with precision the line between those rights which must be surrendered, and those which may be reserved; and on the present occasion this difficulty was encreased by a difference among the several States as to their situation, extent, habits, and particular interests.

"In all our deliberations on this subject we kept steadily in view, that which appears to us the greatest interest of every true American, the consolidation of our Union, in which is involved our prosperity, felicity, safety, perhaps our national existence. This important consideration, seriously and deeply impressed on our minds, led each State in the Convention to be less rigid on points of inferior magnitude, than might have been otherwise expected; and thus the Constitution which we now present, is the result of a spirit of amity, and that of mutual deference and concession which the peculiarity of our political situation rendered indispensable.

"That it will meet the full and entire approbation of every State is not perhaps to be expected; but each will doubtless consider, that had her interest alone been consulted, the consequences might have been particularly disagreeable or injurious to others; that it is liable to as few exceptions as could have been expected, we hope and believe; that it may promote the lasting welfare of that country so dear to us all, and secure her freedom and happiness, is our most ardent wish." *The President of the Federal Convention to the President of the Continental Congress, September 17, 1787.*

O N JULY 18 Madison wrote to Jefferson in Paris that it was impossible to feel any certainty about how long the Convention would sit. "I am led by sundry circumstances to guess that the residue of the work will not be very quickly dispatched."

Because of the rule of secrecy he was not free to speak of the federal compromise that had just been made, nor could he yet be sure that this would, as in fact it did, do away with the main grounds of conflict. But he was thoroughly aware that many tedious and often difficult details must still be debated and agreed upon. Whatever majority of the delegates might favor the large outlines of the plan, there were still special interests to be considered, individual objections to be answered.

The Convention had early resolved to create a new government, not merely revise an old one. It had six weeks later reached a stultifying crisis of uncertainty, then emerged with an effectual compromise agreement. Those were the dramatic decisions. From the middle of July to the middle of September the work went on, in minute revisions of the original creation. These were the necessary drudgery of the undertaking. But the long process of working out the precise forms which the proposed government was to have and which were to make it the particular government it was to be, calls for less attention in this history than the steps the delegates took when they were deciding on a creative action and determining to recommend it to the people of the United States.

There still remained, after the federal compromise, the final adoption of the Virginia plan as reported by the committee of the whole. On July 17, after some discussion, Bedford of Delaware moved that the legislature of the United States should have power "to legislate in all cases for the general interests of the Union, and also in those to which the States are separately incompetent, or in which the harmony of the United States may be interrupted by the exercise of individual legislation." The motion was carried. The Convention then reversed a former decision and voted against giving the national legislature the power to negative state legislation. But it agreed, on the motion of Martin of Maryland, that the legislative acts of the United States made in conformity with the "articles of union"—that is, the proposed constitution—and all treaties should be "the supreme law of the respective States as far as those acts of Treaties shall relate to the said States"; and that the judiciaries of the several states should be "bound thereby in their decisions," no matter what the laws of the states themselves might say. This provision had come almost literally from the New Jersey plan. It was adopted without a dissenting vote. The resolution, later revised, made the Constitution the "supreme law of the land" and bound the judges in every state to support it.

Martin had not intended his motion to go so far, but it is notable that Maryland, New Jersey, and Delaware could now support measures which they would presumably have opposed if they had not known they were to have equal representation in the Senate.

The problem of the executive ran through several days, with digressions. On the 17th it was again agreed that the executive should be one person, be chosen by the national legislature, and have powers to carry into effect the national laws and to appoint officers in cases not otherwise provided for. His term of office was again fixed at seven years, but he was made eligible a second time. On the 19th the term was changed to six years. On the 19th, his election by the legislature was questioned. If he could be re-elected, would he not be so dependent on the legislature as to be unwilling to resist it, and even willing to intrigue with it? Where then would be the division of powers in the departments of the government? Ellsworth of Connecticut moved that the executive be chosen by electors appointed by the state legislatures, which was voted that day. On the 24th the Convention changed its mind and returned to election by the national legislature. This brought up again the matter of re-eligibility. It was generally agreed that if the executive was to be elected by the legislature, he should not be re-eligible. But for the sake of stability, he might be chosen for a longer term: eight, eleven, fifteen, twenty years were mentioned, but no vote was taken. Finally on the 26th the Convention went back to the first Virginia plan for a single term of seven years and no re-election. On the 21st the executive's veto power was confirmed as in the revised Virginia plan reported by the committee of the whole.

During these indecisive days Wilson steadily insisted on the election of the executive by the people, and numerous schemes were proposed without effect. It was generally felt that the citizens of any given state would vote only for local candidates, would indeed not know about able men in other states. As interstate information then went, this was probably true. Though nothing was more important than that the people should elect the President, this could be effectively done only through electors specially chosen for the purpose. The Convention put off, almost to the last days, any decision as to how the electors were to be chosen and how they were to do the electing.

On July 18 the Convention took up the national judiciary. The Virginia plan, as reported by the committee of the whole, had provided for one supreme tribunal but had left inferior tribunals to be instituted or not by the federal legislature, at its own discretion. There was still opposition to federal tribunals which would sit in the separate states. The Convention again left it to the legislature, with the result, it turned out, that such inferior courts are still provided for by Congress. Madison moved that the judges of the supreme tribunal be appointed by the executive with the approval of the Senate. The motion was lost on the 21st, when the Convention voted that the Senate should appoint the judges. (The method proposed by Madison was finally adopted, but not until September 7.) The Convention without dissent agreed on July 18 that the jurisdiction of the supreme tribunal should extend to "cases arising under laws passed by the general Legislature, and to such other as involve the National peace and harmony." This gave the Court even broader jurisdiction than had been recommended by the committee of the whole, but the Convention refused to specify the classes of cases which would fall under the Court's jurisdiction. That was left to a later date. Nothing then or later was explicitly said about giving the Supreme Court the power to pass on the constitutionality of acts of Congress. It was an implied power which did not come into existence until the powers of Congress had been limited, with the implication that there must be some power to enforce the limitations.

Under the Articles of Confederation the states had been permitted to have no less than two, no more than seven, members in the Continental Congress, but the members had voted by states, one vote for each state. Presumably the smaller states, demanding equality in the Senate, had expected this system to continue. On July 23 Gouverneur Morris and King moved that the Senate consist of [*blank*] members from each state and that they vote per capita. Here was a radical alteration of the former system. On the per capita principle, a senator from Delaware might vote with the senators from Virginia, for instance, and leave Delaware, so anxious for equality, with less than the vote she was entitled to. The principle of equality would thereby lose much of its value to any smaller state. But now Ellsworth of Connecticut said he had always "approved of voting in that mode."

Morris thought the number for each state should be three. Gorham preferred two. He expected that peace and war would be vested in the Senate, and if it should, a small Senate would be "most convenient." Moreover, other states would probably soon be added: Kentucky, Vermont, Maine (still a part of Massachusetts), and Franklin (eventually Tennessee). Gorham "presumed also that some of the largest States would be divided." Mason of Virginia thought three senators from each state would be a needless expense; he also preferred two. Williamson of North Carolina thought if the number were too great, distant states would be at a disadvantage. The states near at hand could "more easily send & support their ablest Citizens"—who, he took it for granted, would not serve if the allowances were small. It was unanimously agreed that the number of senators from each state should be two.

Martin of Maryland "was opposed to voting per Capita, as departing from the idea of the *States* being represented in the second branch." Carroll of Maryland saw no particular objection, but he did not wish "so hastily to make so material an innovation." But on the question nine states voted for two senators from a state and per capita voting, with only Maryland opposed. As it cannot be believed that the delegates from the other smaller states did not know what they were doing, it must be believed that since the federal compromise they no longer felt the need of being sticklers for abstract and liberal equality in the Senate.

Also on the 23rd the Convention once more debated whether the new constitution should be submitted for ratification to the legislatures of the states or to state conventions called specially for that purpose. Ellsworth and Paterson preferred ratification by the legislatures. Mason thought ratification by "the authority of the people" was essential. The legislatures, in his opinion, had no power to ratify. "They are the mere creatures of their State Constitutions, and cannot be greater than their creators. . . . Whither then must we resort? To the people with whom all power remains that has not been given up in the Constitutions derived from them." Randolph was sure that opposition in the states was most likely to come from "the local demagogues" who under a federal constitution would lose the importance they had in the states. It was therefore advisable to transfer ratification from the legislatures, "where this class of men have their full influence," to conventions, in which they would be less able to do mischief. Gerry characteristically believed the people would never agree on anything, and would bring only confusion. Gorham pointed out that certain valuable men were excluded from some of the state legislatures, but would not be from state conventions. "Among these may be ranked many of the Clergy who are generally friends to good Government." The legislatures might procrastinate. State conventions would have to meet and act when summoned. He hoped too that some arrangement might be made for putting the new government into effect without having to wait for the unanimous concurrence of the states. New York, prosperous from taxing her neighbors under the Confederation, would probably hesitate to enter into general measures with the whole United States.

Ellsworth observed "that a new sett of ideas seemed to have crept in since the articles of Confederation were established. Conventions of the people, or with power derived expressly from the people, were not then thought of. The Legislatures were considered as competent." They had ratified the Articles of Confederation, and they might with equal right ratify the Constitution. King agreed with Ellsworth that the state legislatures "had a competent authority, the acquiescence of the people of America in the Confederation being equivalent to a formal ratification by the people." But he preferred ratification by conventions. Some members of the legislatures might have scruples because they had taken oaths to support and maintain the existing state constitutions, which the projected federal constitution would do away with.

Madison was masterly. The changes now proposed "would make essential inroads on the State Constitutions, and it would be a novel & dangerous doctrine that a Legislature could change the constitution under which it held its existence. . . . He considered the difference between a system founded on the Legislatures only, and one founded on the people, to be the true difference between a *league* or *treaty*, and a *Constitution*." In treaties, a breach of any one article by any of the parties freed the other parties from all engagements. In a union of people under one constitution, the pact by its nature excluded the conception of parties such as made leagues or treaties. Just as it had seemed better to call this Convention than to look to Congress for a new constitution, so he thought it better to look for ratification to conventions not to legislatures.

When the vote was taken, only Delaware voted in the negative. Neither New York nor New Jersey voted, for want of quorums present, but New Hampshire was represented for the first time that day, by John Langdon and Nicholas Gilman. They were so late because the state had been unable to raise money to pay their expenses. Langdon, a prosperous merchant, paid both his expenses and Gilman's from New York, where they were both serving in Congress. Though they were from a small state, they fell in at once with the majority of the Convention and regularly supported measures for an effective federal government.

On July 26 the Convention, having now reconsidered all the resolutions of the Virginia plan, adjourned to August 6. This was, the newspapers were informed, "to give a committee, appointed for the purpose, time to arrange and systematize the materials which that honorable body have collected." The Committee of Detail, elected by ballot, was composed of Rutledge of South Carolina, Randolph of Virginia, Gorham of Massachusetts, Ellsworth of Connecticut, and Wilson of Pennsylvania. They were to digest and reduce the proceedings to the form of a constitution. The New Jersey plan, which had been considered less desirable than the Virginia plan, and the Charles Pinckney plan, which had not been considered, also were referred to the committee. The Convention so far departed from its rule of secrecy as to permit the committee to have copies of the resolutions to date,[1] but voted against Luther Martin's motion that all the delegates might take copies for themselves.

II

During the ten days of waiting Washington went with Gouverneur Morris, "in his Phaeton with my horses," to the "vicinity of Valley Forge to get Trout." While Morris fished, Washington

[1] See Appendix 6.

rode over to the scene of his army's bitter winter of ten years before. He found all the works in ruins and the grounds uncultivated. Again, he went with Robert Morris and his wife and Gouverneur Morris to Trenton, where Washington fished, "not very successfully" one afternoon, and the next morning "with more success (for perch)." He was seldom permitted to be alone, except when he retired to his room at Robert Morris's house to write letters.

The other delegates diverted themselves in different ways. Some of them used the books which had been made available to the Convention by the Library Company, founded more than fifty years before by Franklin and the young tradesmen of the Junto and now numbering six of the Pennsylvania delegates among its subscribers. Some of the gentlemen of the Convention probably patronized the Opera House, as the New Theatre had lately come to be called. Though theatrical performances had been forbidden in Philadelphia during the Revolution, a company of actors had come over from New York in June of this year, to give plays which were cautiously advertised as concerts or operas. Charles Cotesworth Pinckney made an excursion to Bethlehem, Pennsylvania, first inquiring carefully about the best public houses along the road. Butler visited his family in New York, which he thought healthier in summer than Philadelphia. The New Jersey delegates went home, Paterson to be absent till he came back to sign the finished Constitution in September. Sherman and Johnson went to Connecticut. During the recess McHenry of Maryland, who had been away since June 1, arrived again in Philadelphia. John Francis Mercer, another Maryland delegate, appeared to take his seat on August 6. He had been a soldier in a Virginia regiment during the war, and had later represented Virginia in Congress. But since his marriage to a Maryland heiress in 1785 he had moved to her state. He at once opposed the centralizing tendency which he found among the delegates, and remained only ten days or so.

Meanwhile the Committee of Detail worked on the task of reducing the Convention's proceedings to a systematic draft of a constitution. Special, and probably excessive, claims have been made for the credit of this or that member of the committee. There are no minutes of their meetings. The surviving documents show only that the committee began with a copy, presumably furnished by the Convention's secretary, of the resolutions voted through July 23. Randolph, who had introduced the Virginia plan, made a first draft of a constitution. It has been preserved in his handwriting, with extensive changes in the manuscript made by Rutledge. This seems to mean that Randolph submitted his draft to the committee for discussion, and that as changes were made they were written in by Rutledge, the chairman. There is a continuation of the plan in Wilson's hand, showing Randolph's draft further developed; and a harmonized draft of the two parts worked out by Wilson, in his handwriting, with more changes written in by Rutledge. Then a fair copy of the whole was confided to the Philadelphia printers Dunlap and Claypoole, who printed about sixty copies of a folio pamphlet of seven numbered pages with broad margins for notes by the delegates in their discussions.

When Rutledge on Monday, August 6, reported for the committee and submitted the constitution[1] which had been made "conformable to the Resolutions passed by the Convention," the delegates found it very different from what most of them had probably expected. It incorporated details from the New Jersey and Pinckney plans. Other new details came from a series of recommendations made in Congress six years before for strengthening the Confederation—recommendations made by a committee of which both Randolph and Ellsworth had been members. This constitution gave new names to elements of the government. The "Legislature of the United States" was called "Congress"; the "first branch" had become the "House of Representatives" and the "second branch" the "Senate"; the "Supreme Tribunal" was now the "Supreme Court"; the executive was to be the "President of the United States of America" and his title "His Excellency." Instead of general statements of the broad powers granted to the legislative, executive, and judicial departments there were specific powers granted or withheld, and several specific restrictions laid on the states as states. There was a preamble which said: "We the people of the States of New Hampshire, Massachusetts"—and so on down to—"Georgia, do ordain, declare, and establish the following Constitution for the Government of Ourselves and our Posterity."

The Preamble by itself was enough to startle some of the dele-

[1] See Appendix 7.

gates, who still found it hard to realize that the people, not the states, were to make the new government. Several of the delegates had not yet returned, or at least were absent on that day. As soon as the proposed constitution had been read to the Convention, somebody moved to adjourn to Wednesday the 8th "to give leisure to examine the Report." The motion was lost by five votes to three, but the house at once adjourned to the next day.

McHenry of Maryland, who had missed all the debates on the Virginia and New Jersey plans and the federal compromise, was still in the frame of mind in which many of the delegates had been two months before. He persuaded his Maryland colleagues to meet with him that afternoon at Carroll's lodgings, "to prepare ourselves to act in unison." But he found they were not unanimous in their opinions, and after one further meeting on the 7th the Maryland caucus seems to have been discontinued, with McHenry in time voting generally with the state's majority.

The Convention on the 7th once more took up the long business of going clause by clause through the new version of a constitution, now in twenty-three articles of which seven were further subdivided into forty-one sections. On that day the Preamble and Articles I and II were accepted without debate. The first notable disagreement came over the question who should elect the members of the House of Representatives.

The Committee of Detail proposed that any person might vote who was qualified to vote in a given state for the "most numerous branch" of the state legislature. This was not then so simple as it now sounds. In no state in 1787 could a citizen vote unless he owned property (land in most of the states) or paid taxes. Since something like nine-tenths of the people lived on farms and owned them (that is, were freeholders), real property was widely distributed. Not more than a fifth, it is estimated, of the adult males in New England was disfranchised by the property qualifications for voting; and not more than a third anywhere, except slaves. But the qualifications differed from state to state, and in several states were not the same for the two branches of the legislatures. If the qualifications for voting for the representatives were to be fixed by the different states, according to their own rules in respect to their legislatures, the basis of the election would not be equal throughout the country.

Ellsworth and Wilson, who had helped draw up this provision, thought it was as good as any that could be drawn in the circumstances. The people had formed habits of voting for their own legislatures, and it would be natural for them to vote by the same rule for the federal legislature. Dickinson argued that the vote ought to be restricted to freeholders, who had a stake in the country. They were, he said, "the best guardians of liberty." They could be counted on to resist the "dangerous influence of those multitudes without property & without principle, with which our Country like all others, will in time abound." Gouverneur Morris insisted that unless the vote were restricted to freeholders, rich men would buy up the votes of the poor and dominate the popular House. The Convention must consider the future, when there would be many hired "mechanics & manufacturers" who could not be trusted as freeholders could. Most of the people were now freeholders, and would be pleased with the restriction. Merchants who wished to vote could buy land and obtain the right. "If not, they don't deserve it," Morris said. Mason opposed the freehold qualification. "The true idea in his opinion was that every man having evidence of attachment to & permanent common interest with the Society ought to share in all its rights & privileges." Madison believed that the freehold qualification would be satisfactory to most of the states, since they already had it. This was one reason for making it a part of the Constitution. As to the intrinsic merits of the qualification: "In future times a great majority of the people will not only be without landed, but any other sort of, property." They would either combine in their own interest or else become the "tools of opulence & ambition."

Franklin, the oldest of the delegates but so often the boldest, had the strongest faith in the people, from whom he had sprung. It was of great consequence, he said, "that we should not depress the virtue & public spirit of our common people; of which they displayed a great deal during the war, and which contributed principally to the favorable issue of it." He told of the American seamen who had been taken by the enemy and confined to British prisons. They had patriotically refused "to redeem themselves from misery or to seek their fortunes" by renouncing their country and serving on enemy ships of war; whereas British seamen captured by Americans had seldom hesitated to serve on American ships "on being promised a share of the prizes that might be made out of their own Country." This, he said, was the result of "the different manner in which the common people were treated in America & Great Britain. He did not think that the elected had any right in any case to narrow the privileges of the electors."

On the vote the states were unanimously in favor of the rule of suffrage proposed by the Committee of Detail. This meant that the Convention declined to set up any property qualifications for the electors. It meant also, however, that many of the delegates had, or represented, interests in other property besides land. They did not want to see the suffrage restricted to freeholders, who were many of them small farmers, friends of paper money and other measures threatening to the shipowners, merchants, and owners of securities.

The Convention refused also to set up property qualifications for members of Congress. Most of the states by their constitutions required their legislators to own property of varying amounts: in South Carolina so high as a freehold of two thousand pounds for a state senator. On August 10 Charles Pinckney moved that the members of Congress, and also the executive and the federal judges, be required to take oath that they were possessed of "a clear unincumbered estate" of values respectively to be determined. Rutledge seconded the motion.

Franklin again "expressed his dislike of every thing that tended to debase the spirit of the common people. If honesty was often the companion of wealth, and if poverty was exposed to peculiar temptation, it was not less true that the possession of property increased the desire of more property. Some of the greatest rogues he was ever acquainted with, were the richest rogues. We should remember the character which the Scripture requires in Rulers, that they should be men hating covetousness. This Constitution will be much read and attended to in Europe, and if it should betray a great partiality to the rich—will not only hurt us in the esteem of the most liberal and enlightened men there, but discourage the common people from removing to this country."

After Franklin sat down the majority on his side was so evident that the vote of the states was not even called for. It is interesting to note that the next month Franklin permitted the *American Museum* in Philadelphia to publish his *Information for those who would wish to remove to America,* which had first appeared in Paris three years before and was already known throughout Europe.

The debate wound its long, slow way through August. It was supposed to be the hottest summer in Philadelphia since 1750, and the full-fed, formally dressed gentlemen in Independence Hall were often uncomfortable. On account of their rule of secrecy they had to keep the windows closed or their voices down, though a sentry permitted no outsider to stand or pass close enough to overhear what was being said. On August 13 the delegates continued in session till past five o'clock over the provision requiring that all money bills originate in the House of Representatives, without alteration or amendment by the Senate.

This was a complicated matter. In the federal compromise of July 16 the smaller states had won equal representation in the Senate by conceding to the larger that money bills should originate solely in the House where the representation was proportional. On August 8 the Convention had reversed its former action and had in effect given the Senate equal power over money bills, with New Jersey, Delaware, and Maryland on the side of Pennsylvania, Virginia, South Carolina, and Georgia. Here was a threat to the whole compromise. The smaller states, having won equality in the Senate, were now, it appeared, opposed to paying the price agreed to. Some of the larger states, having never thought the concession important, saw no reason why the Senate should not have a hand in money bills and some right to restrain possible extravagance in the House. On the 13th Randolph moved a modified form of the provision, giving the House the right to originate only certain bills "for the purposes of revenue" and the Senate the right to alter or amend in certain cases. Again there was a long debate. In the end seven states voted against vesting the sole right in the House even on modified terms.

Virginia was now in the minority, because Washington had turned from Madison and Blair to vote with Randolph and Mason. Washington, according to Madison, had hitherto voted against the House's exclusive right to originate money bills, but he "gave up his judgment" since it was "not of very material weight with him & was made an essential point with others, who if disappointed, might be less cordial in other points of real weight." Not till September 8 did the Convention finally agree that bills for raising revenue should originate in the House, but might be amended by the Senate the same as other bills.

On August 18 the Convention unofficially authorized a public statement in the *Pennsylvania Herald* which was speedily reprinted throughout the country. "We are well informed," the statement said, "that many letters have been written to the members of the federal convention from different quarters, respecting the reports idly circulating, that it is intended to establish a monarchical government, to send for the Bishop of Osnaburgh, etc. etc.—to which it has been uniformly answered, 'tho' we cannot, affirmatively, tell you what we are doing; we can, negatively, tell you what we are not doing—we never once thought of a king.'"

If it seems incredible that the Convention was suspected of intending to import a Hanoverian bishop to be king of the United States, it seems even less credible when the Secular Bishop of Osnaburgh in question is given his more familiar name and title of Frederick Augustus, Duke of York, second son of George III. There was no conceivable reason why the Americans should want him for himself, and no conceivable excuse for any American to think of him except for the fact that he was next in line to his elder brother the Prince of Wales, who would be king of England. Yet some never-identified person in Fairfield, Connecticut, seems in July to have issued a circular letter proposing "to send to England" for the Bishop (who was then twenty-three) and "have him crowned King over this continent." The Americans had found, the writer said, that they had not wit enough to govern themselves, and that it was high time for them "to tread back the wayward path" they had taken a dozen years before. The letter had been picked up by newspapers and made the subject of wide and agitated comment.

Two of Washington's former aides, Hamilton and David Humphreys (who was then in Connecticut), investigated the mystery but could come to no conclusion about it. Humphreys believed that the proposal had been "manufactured" by Connecticut loyalists and that the circular letter had certainly been distributed "with avidity" by them. They had reason to be dissatisfied with the government of the independent United States under the Articles of Confederation, and discreetly longed for a reunion with Great Britain and the restoration of monarchy. The circular letter may have been put out with a view to finding what approval it would win. The effect of the letter was rather to prepare the people, who were invincibly republican, to support the efforts of the Convention. Those who opposed it were warned that their opposition might end in another king over America. No wonder that many letters were written to the Convention delegates, asking what the Convention intended; and no wonder that the Convention hastened to make a statement. Not one of the delegates had thought for a moment that anything besides a republican form of government would serve, or could even be proposed with safety to themselves.

They kept republican ideas always in mind while they debated on the powers and duties of the President on various days through August and into September. They made his term of office four years instead of seven, and permitted him to be re-elected. He must be "a natural born Citizen, or a Citizen of the United States, at the time of the Adoption of this Constitution." If he was a naturalized citizen, he must have been "fourteen years a Resident within the United States." He must be at least thirty-five years old when elected. He was to be elected, not as hitherto proposed, by Congress, but by electors chosen for that purpose in the several states. The intricate scheme of electors devised by the Convention had to be amended in 1804, but it in any case provided that the President should be elected by the people, not by another department of the government. He was to be commander in chief of the Army and Navy. He should have power to grant reprieves and pardons for offenses against the United States, except in the case of impeachments. By and with the advice and consent of the Senate, he should have power to make treaties, and to appoint ambassadors, ministers, and consuls, and all other officers of the United States whose appointments were "not here-in otherwise provided for"—and the judges of the Supreme Court.

The Convention voted against giving the President a council to assist him, but assumed there would be heads of the executive departments. Out of this was to grow the Cabinet, never even mentioned in the Constitution. The President's duties were specifically stated, but no restrictions specifically laid upon him. He might be removed from office "on Impeachment for, and Con-

viction of, Treason, Bribery, or other high Crimes and Misdemeanors." There was to be a Vice-President, elected at the same
time, in the same manner, and for the same term of office as the
President, to discharge the powers and duties of the presidency
if the President should be removed from office or should die,
resign, or be incapacitated.

Nothing like the President had existed under the Confederation. The Continental Congress had had some executive powers,
but they were limited by the sovereign rights of the states and
had never been put fully into effect. The President, while in
several of his functions dependent on the Senate, could refuse
assent to acts of Congress unless they were passed over his veto
by a vote of two-thirds of the members of both House and Senate. This gave to him, and to the central government, a power
completely new to the United States since independence.

Congress too under the new plan of government would have
an immense increase of power. Instead of asking for quotas of
contributions from the states, as states, it would lay taxes on the
individual citizens of the United States and have the power to
collect them. Granted a long list of specific powers, it was
granted also the right to "make all Laws which shall be necessary
and proper for carrying into Execution the foregoing powers,
and all other Powers vested by this Constitution in the Government of the United States, or in any Department or Officer
thereof." Specific restrictions were laid on Congress, but others
were laid on the states in the interest of the federal authority.

Under the Articles of Confederation the states had been restricted from entering into treaties with foreign powers, engaging
in war, maintaining troops or ships in time of peace, granting
titles of nobility, entering into compacts with particular states of
the United States, or laying imposts or duties which might interfere with the engagements entered into by "the United States in
Congress assembled." Now the states were forbidden to lay any
duties on imports or exports, to coin money, to issue "bills of
credit" (paper money) without the consent of Congress, or to
make anything but gold and silver coin a legal tender in payment
of debts.

On the matter of paper money the delegates were virtually
unanimous. The Continental Congress, having no funds with
which to support its resistance to the British government, had

issued paper money and insisted that it be a legal medium of exchange in all transactions. Nevertheless it had steadily depreciated to a point where it was worthless. "Not worth a continental" became a proverb—to remain so long after men had forgotten how the term arose. Seven of the states, since the Revolution, had resorted to the same method of supplying themselves with the money they did not have and would not tax their citizens for. There were many debtors, particularly among the small farmers effectively represented in the legislatures, who were hard pressed by creditors under laws which might imprison men for debt and which made few provisions for the temporary relief of unfortunate but honest debtors. Not all debtors were honest. Some of them welcomed the opportunity to pay off debts in currency worth far less than the original obligation. The fluctuating currency made everybody hesitate to enter into long-term contracts. In the uncertainty all commercial operations were attended with debilitating risk. Congress had done almost nothing to pay off the public debts incurred during the Revolution, either to foreign creditors or to the neglected veterans of the Continental Army. The private debts owed by Americans to European creditors were still largely unsettled.

Not a few of the delegates to the Federal Convention were themselves heavily in debt, but they did not think of themselves as belonging to a debtor class. They were convinced on principle as well as out of interest that public and private debts ought to be paid in honest money, and that the states ought to be restricted from passing any further legal tender laws. On the day they voted for this restriction, August 28, they voted also to restrict the states from passing any laws that would impair the obligation of contracts.

And there was the question of the public debt owed by the Confederation. This had not been paid by the Continental Congress, because it had no money and no power to tax the states. The Convention delegates were resolved that the new Congress should have money and should pay the debt. On August 21 it was proposed, by a committee, that Congress should be given power to pay the debts of the United States and also the "debts incurred by the several States during the late war." The Convention did nothing about the debts of the states, which were left to the states to settle. But on the 25th it was agreed that the debts of the United States contracted before the adoption of the Constitution should be as valid against the United States under the Constitution as under the Confederation. This left the position of the public creditors exactly where it had been before, unless the credit of the new government should be better than the old. As Congress was given the power, in the taxing clause, to pay the debts, the credit of the new government would be better. This was the only advantage the public creditors would get from the Constitution. They were not otherwise privileged, as it is often but inaccurately said they were.

III

The Convention delegates were organizing for order, not for Utopia. One of the things the majority of them most desired was an orderly regulation of foreign and interstate trade under the control of the general government. "Most of our political evils may be traced to our commercial ones," Madison had written to Jefferson in March 1786, "as most of our moral may to our political." The report of the Committee of Detail on August 6 provided that Congress be restricted from laying duties on exports. When the restriction was debated on August 16 and 21 it brought up the sharpest conflict of interest in the entire course of the Convention.

On those days the same restriction had not yet been extended to the states, and it was assumed that if the right was withheld from Congress the states would still have it individually. This seemed of the greatest importance to South Carolina and Georgia, and not much less important to North Carolina and Virginia. The Southern states, almost wholly agricultural, produced vast amounts of tobacco, rice, and indigo, which were produced nowhere else in the country. If Congress had the power to tax exports, then the Northern majority in Congress might lay what export taxes it pleased on those crops. Since the Southern states, particularly South Carolina and Georgia, had no manufactures or shipping, but depended almost wholly on the profits of their exports, they might be damaged, if not ruined, by discrimination in Congress with no objection from the states which had no such crops to protect. South Carolina, if left to itself, would lay export duties or not, according to its interest. It was firmly opposed to having Congress lay them for the benefit of the United States.

Williamson of North Carolina said that if Congress should be given power to tax exports, it would do away with the last hope that the Convention could adopt the proposed constitution or the states accept it. Mason of Virginia concurred with the principle, often advanced, "that a majority when interested will oppress the minority." The Northern states were an interested majority, and the Southern states "had therefore good grounds for their suspicion."

Madison and Wilson favored giving Congress the power to tax exports. This might, Madison agreed, have unequal effects on different states, but he insisted that the Convention ought to be "governed by national and permanent views." Since states with different interests could not with justice exercise the right to pay export taxes individually, they should do it collectively: that is, under the regulation of Congress. Wilson pointed out that to give Congress the right to tax imports but not exports was to take from the "Common Government half the regulation of trade." He believed that if Congress had the power over exports this might be more effectual than the power over imports in making favorable commercial treaties with foreign countries.

Three states sided with Madison and Wilson, on grounds of special interest. New Hampshire, obliged to ship its produce through Massachusetts ports, would be taxed by Massachusetts. New Jersey would have to ship through New York and Pennsylvania, Delaware through Pennsylvania; and those shipping states would lay the export duties. Maryland would ship through Pennsylvania and Virginia, and North Carolina through Virginia; but they preferred that to being taxed by Congress. Pennsylvania, though it would profit by shipping for New Jersey, Delaware, and Maryland, yet disregarded its special interest and voted in the larger interest for control of exports by Congress. Madison and Washington voted for control by Congress, but they were outvoted by Mason, Randolph, and Blair. The other Southern states were solidly opposed to letting a majority in Congress regulate their export trade, and Massachusetts and Connecticut voted with them. Finally, on the 28th, the Convention resolved the conflict by deciding by a bare majority to prohibit export taxes laid by the separate states as well as by Congress.

The section in the report of the Committee of Detail which

restricted Congress from taxing exports had further provisions for the protection of Southern interests: the "migration or importation of such persons as the several States shall think proper to admit" was not to be prohibited, nor were such persons to be taxed. The Committee had meant slaves, but had avoided using the word.

Martin of Maryland on August 21, as soon as the vote had gone against permitting Congress to tax exports, proposed that the importation of slaves—he used the word—be taxed. If three-fifths of the slaves were to be counted as population, this must encourage the traffic in slaves. Not only would this increase the votes of the slave states in the House of Representatives, but it would weaken the states themselves, since they would be in danger of slave insurrections, which the United States might have to assist in putting down. Moreover, "it was inconsistent with the principles of the revolution and dishonorable to the American character to have such a feature"—as slavery—"in the Constitution."

Rutledge of South Carolina, according to Major Pierce, was often "too rapid in his public speaking to be denominated an agreeable Orator." But today there was a cold precision in Rutledge's words, at least as noted down by Madison. "Mr. Rutledge did not see how the importation of slaves could be encouraged by this section. He was not apprehensive of insurrections and would readily exempt the other States from the obligation to protect the Southern against them. Religion & humanity had nothing to do with this question.—Interest alone is the governing principle with Nations—The true question at present is whether the Southern States shall or shall not be parties to the Union. If the Northern States consult their interest, they will not oppose the increase of Slaves which will increase the commodities of which they will become the carriers."

Ellsworth of Connecticut, whom Pierce thought "eloquent and connected in public debate," and who represented a state which had already forbidden the importation of slaves within its own borders, agreed with Rutledge. "Mr. Ellsworth was for leaving the clause as it stands. Let every State import what it pleases. The morality or wisdom of slavery are considerations belonging to the States themselves.—What enriches a part enriches the whole, and the States are the best judges of their particular interest. The old confederation had not meddled with this point, and he did not see any greater necessity for bringing it within the policy of the new one."

Charles Pinckney flatly declared: "South Carolina can never receive the plan if it prohibits the slave trade. In every proposed extension of the powers of Congress, that State has expressly & watchfully excepted that of meddling with the importation of negroes." But if the states were "all left at liberty on this subject," South Carolina might "perhaps by degrees" pass her own laws against the importation of slaves, as Virginia and Maryland had already done—and also, though he did not speak of it, New Hampshire, Massachusetts, Rhode Island, Connecticut, New York, and Pennsylvania. Even in South Carolina, Rutledge's own brother, Edward Rutledge, who was a brother-in-law of Charles Cotesworth Pinckney, had in 1785 made a vigorous effort to have the slave trade to their state prohibited for three years.

In all of the states, from the northernmost down through Virginia, slavery had become steadily less profitable, and opposition to it on political and moral grounds was steadily rising. The Quakers had organized the Pennsylvania Society for Promoting the Abolition of Slavery, and the Relief of Free Negroes Unlawfully held in Bondage, with Franklin as president. The Continental Congress had forbidden slavery in the Northwest Territory. But in South Carolina and Georgia the cultivation of the staple crops, particularly rice, called for so many slaves who died so rapidly that it was impossible to depend on the natural increase of their numbers and necessary to import more if the economy of those states was to be maintained. The South Carolina delegates were resolved that it must be, and the Georgia delegates followed their lead. Baldwin of Georgia, born in Connecticut, educated at Yale, and a clergyman, was as firm as any of his Southern colleagues, though he thought that Georgia, "if left to herself," might "probably put a stop to the evil" of slavery.

The most powerful attack on the slave trade came from Mason of Virginia on August 22. He stood up that day like a Commonwealth man of Milton's time, tall, white-haired, his black eyes burning, to condemn "the infernal traffic." It had originated, he said, "in the avarice of British Merchants." Virginia had made many attempts to stop it, always overruled by the British government. "The present question concerns not the importing States alone but the whole Union. . . . Slavery discourages arts & manufactures. The poor despise labor when performed by slaves. They prevent the immigration of Whites, who really enrich & strengthen a Country. They produce the most pernicious effect on manners. Every master of slaves is born a petty tyrant. They bring the judgment of heaven on a Country. As nations can not be rewarded or punished in the next world they must in this. By an inevitable chain of causes & effects providence punishes national sins, by national calamities. He lamented that some of our Eastern brethren had from a lust of gain embarked in this nefarious traffic." He was here referring to the slave traders of New England in New England ships. "As to the States being in possession of the Right to import, this was the case with many other rights, now to be properly given up. He held it essential in every point of view, that the General Government should have power to prevent the increase of slavery."

Ellsworth of Connecticut took the floor before the delegates from South Carolina and Georgia. "As he had never owned a slave," Ellsworth said, he "could not judge of the effects of slavery on character. He said however that if it was to be considered in a moral light we ought to go farther and free those already in the country." In Virginia and Maryland it was cheaper to raise slaves than to import them, but in "the sickly rice swamps" of South Carolina and Georgia "foreign supplies" were necessary. To stop the slave trade would therefore be unjust to the states in the extreme South. "Let us not intermeddle. As population increases; poor laborers will be so plenty as to render slaves useless. Slavery in time will not be a speck in our Country."

Charles Pinckney, young, handsome, perspicuous, replied to Mason that if slavery was wrong, it was nevertheless "justified by the example of all the world." He cited Greece, Rome, and other ancient states. Charles Cotesworth Pinckney, who spoke well, according to Pierce, only when he spoke warmly, declared that South Carolina and Georgia could not do without slaves. "As to Virginia she will gain by stopping importations. Her slaves will rise in value, & she has more than she wants." The importation of slaves would "be for the interest of the whole Union. The more slaves, the more produce to employ the carrying trade; the more consumption also, and the more of this, the more of revenue for the common treasury." He thought it would be reasonable for imported slaves to be taxed, but he repeated that to end the slave trade would be to exclude South Carolina from the United States.

There could be no doubt that the delegates from South Carolina and Georgia meant what they said. Rutledge and Butler made it plain that they were as resolute as the two Pinckneys. King of Massachusetts, who spoke often and brilliantly but with an occasional rudeness in his manner, thought the slave trade should be "considered in a political light only." If the two southernmost states could not agree to the Constitution as proposed, there were others who would object to it without the provisions to which South Carolina and Georgia objected. For instance, there was the exemption of the slaves from import duty, while every other import was taxed. This was "an inequality that could not fail to strike the commercial sagacity of the Northern & middle States." There could be no doubt as to what King was saying. If the Southern states objected to restrictions on the slave trade, then the Northern states would object to exemption of imported slaves from taxation. Gorham, also of Massuchusetts, went further still. He reminded the Convention that "the Eastern States had no motive to Union but a commercial one. They were able to protect themselves. They were not afraid of external danger, and did not need the aid of the Southern States."

Gouverneur Morris, who was himself energetically opposed to slavery, now proposed that the whole matter of exports and the slave trade be referred to a committee, to be considered along with the provision for a navigation act. "These things," he said, "may form a bargain among the Northern & Southern States." Randolph agreed to the proposal. He himself could never consent to an unrestricted slave trade. "He would sooner risk the constitution." The Convention, he said, was in a dilemma. To permit the slave trade to continue would "revolt the Quakers, the Methodists, and many others in the States having no slaves. On the other hand, two States might be lost to the Union" if the slave trade were to be ended. "Let us then, he said, try the chance of a commitment."

By a vote of seven states to three the Convention agreed on a committee, which was composed of Langdon, King, Johnson, Livingston, Clymer, Dickinson, Luther Martin, Madison, Williamson, Charles Cotesworth Pinckney, and Baldwin.

On August 24 Governor Livingston, as chairman of the committee, reported a compromise. The importation of slaves was not to be prohibited before 1800, but a duty might be laid on them "at a rate not exceeding the average of the duties laid on imports." With this, as an essential part of the compromise, no capitation (poll) tax was to be laid unless in proportion to the census provided for in the Constitution, but any navigation act which might be passed by Congress would require only a majority, not the two-thirds vote in both House and Senate as required by the report of the Committee of Detail.

These were the technical details of an involved compromise. The Southern states would be free for the present to import slaves, but would have to pay duty on them. The right to lay direct (capitation or poll) taxes, granted to Congress in order that it might have every power to obtain an adequate revenue, was to be on conditions which would reassure the Southern states. They were apprehensive that Congress, if free to lay direct taxes without reference to the census, might lay such a heavy poll tax on slaves as to force emancipation. (Congress has in fact never imposed a federal poll tax, and even the income tax could not be imposed without an amendment to the Constitution.) But if the Southern states were to be favored by this restriction on direct taxes, they would have to give up the favor shown them in the matter of navigation acts.

It must be remembered that British navigation acts had required, and more or less enforced the requirement, that colonial shipping must be in British-built, British-owned ships. The Southern states, with almost no shipping industries, suspected that the Northern states, having a majority in Congress, might by a majority vote pass an act requiring all American exports and imports to be carried in American ships. The Committee of Detail, as a concession to the South, had recommended that no navigation act should be passed except on a two-thirds vote. But the compromise committee now restored the majority vote.

It seemed to the Southern states that they were conceding more than they were gaining by the present compromise. On August 25, General Pinckney of South Carolina moved that the importation of slaves be permitted to continue till 1808 instead of 1800. Gorham of Massachusetts, which had no slaves but did have ships engaged in the slave trade, seconded the motion. It was carried by a vote of seven Northern and Southern states against the four Middle states of New Jersey, Pennsylvania, Delaware, and Maryland. The import tax on slaves was fixed at not more than ten dollars a head. Then on the 28th all export taxes, either by Congress or the individual states, were given up. That the Southern states were now satisfied appeared from the debates on the 29th.

On that day Charles Pinckney of South Carolina on his own initiative moved that Congress should have no power to pass any act regulating commerce (whether navigation acts or otherwise) unless by a two-thirds vote. This was not, he claimed, merely in the interest of the Southern states. They did not need the protection of the Northern states, and were consenting to the regulation of commerce as a pure concession. But there were five interests to be considered: (1) New England, in fisheries and the West India trade; (2) New York, in free trade everywhere; (3) New Jersey and Pennsylvania, in wheat and flour; (4) Virginia and Maryland, and partly North Carolina, in tobacco; (5) South Carolina and Georgia, in rice and indigo. No one of these sections could protect its interest if a mere majority in Congress had the power to regulate commerce for all the states. Martin of Maryland seconded the motion.

None of the other delegates from South Carolina agreed with Pinckney. His cousin, General Pinckney, was in diplomatic accord with New England. It was to the interest of the Southern states, he said, to have no regulation of commerce. But because the New England delegates had shown themselves so "liberal" about the importation of slaves, he thought it proper to raise no further objection to a majority vote in Congress on commercial acts. "His constituents though prejudiced against the Eastern States, would be reconciled. . . . He had himself, he said, prejudices against the Eastern States before he came here, but would acknowledge that he had found them as liberal and candid as any men whatever." Rutledge and Butler seemed to be of the same opinion.

The New England delegates kept modestly silent in the face of this praise from South Carolina. Gorham merely said he thought it unlikely that the Northern states, with their variety of interests, would ever combine against the special interests of the South; nor did he suppose that foreign ships would be excluded from the American trade, "especially those of nations in treaty with us." A spirit of amity for a moment pervaded the whole Convention. Without any dissent an act was passed providing (as finally phrased) that an indentured servant or a fugitive slave (here called "a person held to Service or Labour in one State, under the laws thereof, escaping into another") in even a free state must be "delivered up on Claim of the Party to whom such Service or Labour may be due."

Madison perceived that the South and New England had arrived at an "understanding," but seemed to accept it as unavoidable. Randolph announced that there were "features so odious" in the Constitution as it now stood that "he doubted whether he should ever be able to agree with it." Mason too saw the "bargain" as a threat to the constitution he himself demanded. This was, he wrote to Jefferson in May 1788, "a Compromise between the Eastern & the two Southern States, to permit the latter to continue the Importation of Slaves for twenty odd years; a more favourite Object with them, than the Liberty and Happiness of the People." In those last days Mason as well as Randolph stood a good deal alone, in the not too satisfactory company of the tempestuous Luther Martin and the fractious Gerry.

The four were intransigent in different degrees and out of different impulses. Martin was like a contentious lawyer, holding a brief for the rights of the states as states. He left Philadelphia in disgust on September 4. Gerry was captious and inconsistent, theoretically a republican but practically full of contempt for the people, in the habit of opposing any proposal in the Convention which he had not made himself. Mason was a republican of the true ancient breed, rigorous and honorable, who believed that if the Convention gave up certain classic principles of republican government the Constitution could not prosper. Randolph was in opposition partly because of his principles and partly because he was an ambitious young politician who hesitated to commit himself to the Constitution for fear it might fail and discredit him along with the other delegates.

The great majority of the delegates all had their individual reservations on various points, but they were generally united in the belief that a new and stronger government must be set up, that the Constitution promised to serve that end, and that it would be better to agree on some compromises than to hold out for abstract perfection and perhaps get nothing. They could not be sure of the future, but they could dare to hope that the best plans they were capable of now might be realizable then. In this spirit they had made political and economic compromises, even compromises that some of them thought immoral and inhumane. It seemed impossible to make the future world perfect. It might be possible to give the future world a safe foundation for its house, and leave it to posterity, if it would, to model that house with justice and adorn it with wisdom and goodness.

IV

In the spirit of compromise and of hope the Convention in its final days worked on rounding out the Constitution. On August 30 they provided for the admission by Congress of new states into the union. The clause did not say that the new states would be on equal terms with the older, but in practice they have been. On that same day the Convention agreed that the United States should guarantee each state a republican form of government and protect it from invasion; protect it also against "domestic Violence," if help were asked by the legislature or by the executive if the legislature could not be convened. In the early days of the Convention few of the delegates would have consented to a scheme for sending federal forces into a state in serious disorder. Now nine states voted for it against Delaware and Maryland.

On August 30 and 31 Carroll and Martin of Maryland insisted that ratification of the Constitution by the states must be unanimous, since ratification would amount to dissolving the Confederation; and the Confederation could not be dissolved without the consent of the thirteen states. But on the vote all the states in the Convention except Maryland agreed that the ratification of nine states would be sufficient "for the Establishment of this Constitution between the States so ratifying the same." This meant that Congress would not be asked to approve, though it had called the Convention. The Constitution would go back to the people for its authority. And the new government, instead of waiting till all the states consented, would be set up by the first nine that did consent, leaving the others to come in or not as they chose. Or rather, it would be set up by the people of those first nine states, who had the same right to adopt the Constitution as some of the states had formerly had to adopt the Articles of Confederation, leaving the others to ratify when they would. Maryland had then taken more than three years to make up its mind.

Here was one of the most revolutionary decisions in the whole Convention, and in the long run one of the most practical.

On September 4 the Convention, afraid of establishing the federal government in any of the states for fear of local influence, unanimously voted to give Congress "exclusive Legislation" over a district "not exceeding ten Miles square" when ceded by "particular States" and accepted by Congress.

On September 7 and 8 there was a complex debate over the treaty-making power. The Committee of Detail on August 6 had provided that treaties should be made by the Senate. There had been various objections to granting this power to a single branch of the legislature, without check by any other parts or departments of the government. In particular the Southern states were afraid that a Northern majority in the Senate might be willing to give up to Spain the freedom of navigation of the Mississippi, which the South and West thought they must have but which was not a primary concern of the Northern states—some of which did not wish to see the development of Western interests to the possible disadvantage of the mercantile, manufacturing, and shipping interests of the Northeast. On September 4 it was recommended, by a committee, that treaties be made by the President "by and with the advice and Consent of the Senate." This was amended, on the 8th, by the provision that two-thirds of the "Senators present" must concur; and was carried by the vote of all the states but three.

On Saturday, September 8, the Convention felt itself to be so close to the end of its work that it appointed a Committee of Style to put into final order the articles so far agreed to.[1] The members were Johnson of Connecticut, Hamilton of New York, Gouverneur Morris of Pennsylvania, Madison of Virginia, and King of Massachusetts. The Convention sat on Monday, but on Tuesday met only to adjourn because the committee was not yet ready to report. On Wednesday, Johnson, as chairman, presented a draft which except for a few slight changes was to be the Constitution of the United States.[2]

Particular credit for the drafting appears to belong to Gouverneur Morris. Long afterward, in December 1814, Morris wrote that the Constitution "was written by the fingers, which write this letter." Madison in April 1831 wrote that "the *finish* given to the style and arrangement of the Constitution fairly belongs to the pen of Mr. Morris." As Madison remembered it, Johnson and the other members of the committee had entrusted the actual writing to Morris, though of course all the rest had to concur. Wilson, in December 1787, was credited by Baldwin of Georgia with having been joined with Morris in "the last arrangement and composition"; and in March 1828, Timothy Pickering said in a letter: "James Wilson once told me that after the Constitution had been finally settled, it was committed to him to be critically examined respecting its style, in order that the instrument might appear with the most perfect precision and accuracy of language." In these accounts there is no essential conflict. Most drafting committees assign the work of the original draft to one member, and then go over it. The choice in this case fell to Gouverneur Morris, the ready speaker and gifted writer. But King, Johnson, and Madison, as well as Wilson, shared the responsibility and had to be satisfied with the final version, probably not without alterations at various points.

The most striking addition made by the Committee of Style was to the Preamble. As drafted by the Committee of Detail, and adopted by the Convention on August 7, this had read: "We the people of the States of New Hampshire," and all the others, including Rhode Island, "do ordain, declare, and establish the following Constitution for the Government of Ourselves and our Posterity." As drafted by the Committee of Style it now read:

[1] See Appendix 8.
[2] See Appendix 9.

"We, the People of the United States, in order to form a more perfect union, to establish justice, insure domestic tranquillity, provide for the common defence, promote the general welfare, and secure the blessings of liberty to ourselves and our posterity, do ordain and establish this Constitution for the United States of America."

The change from "We the people of the States" to "We, the People of the United States" did not have for the delegates who noted it when it was read, quite the implications which are now sometimes found in it. When the earlier version had been adopted it was on the assumption that all the states of the Confederation would have to accept the new government before it could be established. They were therefore named in the Preamble. But since it had been agreed by the Convention that the ratification by nine states would be sufficient, and that as soon as so many ratified, the Constitution would be put into effect, it was no longer possible to name the constituent states in the Preamble, for the reason that nobody could know which nine of them would first ratify it and so, at the outset, make up the United States. The change was primarily in the interests of accuracy. But what had been done for the sake of accuracy had the effect of making it appear that the Constitution was by and for the united people, not by and for the confederated states.

In a sense, the Constitution went back rather to the Declaration of Independence than to the Articles of Confederation. The Articles nowhere referred to the people of the United States but always to the "United States in Congress assembled." The Declaration had spoken of "one people" and "our people" and had acted "by the Authority of the good people of these Colonies."

There is no record of any objection to the Preamble, which was adopted without a change. Washington later said that the delegates were on the whole better pleased, when they saw "the propositions reduced to form and connected together, than they expected." They were all furnished with printed copies of the version of the Constitution submitted by the Committee of Style. On September 12 they went paragraph by paragraph through the letter to Congress which the Committee had drawn up, and agreed to it. But they were now too impatient to be willing to debate again over all the objections that might be raised to matters on which the majority had already agreed. The changes which were proposed, during the crowded days September 12-15, were approved or disapproved with few words and quick votes.

Mason on the 12th "wished the plan had been prefaced with a Bill of Rights, & would second a Motion if made for the purpose." Gerry made the motion. Sherman thought the "State Declarations of Rights" were sufficient. So apparently did the other delegates. On the motion, every vote was cast against it, including Virginia's. A majority of the delegates in every state failed to foresee that the omission of a bill of rights from the Constitution would turn out to be one of the most common arguments against it. On the 14th Madison and Charles Pinckney moved that Congress be given power to establish a university "in which no preferences or distinctions should be allowed on account of religion." Gouverneur Morris thought it was not necessary. The motion was lost. Charles Pinckney and Gerry moved to insert a declaration "that the liberty of the Press should be inviolably preserved." Sherman thought it was unnecessary. The motion was lost. On the 15th Carroll moved that the Convention should prepare an address to the people, to accompany the Constitution. Rutledge said that this would cause delay; and in any case, it would be improper to address the people till Congress had approved. Sherman thought an address was both unnecessary and improper. The motion did not pass.

The question of amendments to the Constitution was left almost to the last. It had been agreed, on September 10, that amendments should be proposed by two-thirds of the members of both Houses of Congress, if they deemed it necessary, or if two-thirds of the state legislatures requested it; and that such amendments should become parts of the Constitution when they had been ratified by three-fourths of the legislatures of the states or by conventions in three-fourths of the states. Rutledge had at once insisted that no amendment might be passed before 1808 affecting importation of slaves or the restriction on direct taxes. This had been agreed to that day. Now on the 15th it was provided that when two-thirds of the state legislatures called for amendments they should be proposed by a general convention called by Congress. At once Sherman insisted that no amendment, at any time, should affect the "internal police" of any state without its consent, or deprive it of its equal suffrage in the Senate. The motion was lost. But on account "of the circulating murmurs of the small states," Gouverneur Morris moved that no state be deprived of an equal vote in the Senate. This was "agreed to without debate, no one opposing it, or on the question, saying no."

Mason was still discontented with the power given Congress to pass navigation acts by a bare majority. This would, he said, "enable a few rich merchants in Philadelphia, New York and Boston, to monopolize the Staples of the Southern States & reduce their value perhaps 50 Per Cent." He moved that no navigation act should be passed before 1808 without the consent of two-thirds of the members of each branch of Congress. This proposal got no such last-minute consideration as had been shown to Rutledge's and Sherman's. All the Northern states and South Carolina voted against it. It had been a hurried day, it was late, and the delegates wished to take the long-desired vote on the Constitution as amended.

But before they could do that, Randolph, Mason, and Gerry announced that they could not vote for it, and gave their reasons.

A RISING SUN

"The warmest friends and the best supporters the
Constitution has, do not contend that it is free from
imperfections; but they found them unavoidable and are
sensible, if evil is likely to arise therefrom, the remedy
must come hereafter; for in the present moment, it is not
to be obtained; and, as there is a Constitutional door open
for it, I think the people (for it is with them to Judge)
can as they will have the advantage of experience on
their Side, decide with as much propriety on the alterations and amendments which are necessary as ourselves. I
do not think we are more inspired, have more wisdom, or
possess more virtue than those who will come after us."
*George Washington to Bushrod Washington, November
10, 1787.*

"I send you enclos'd the propos'd new Federal Constitution for these States. I was engag'd 4 Months of the last
Summer in the Convention that form'd it. It is now sent
by Congress to the several States for their Confirmation.
If it succeeds, I do not see why you might not in Europe
carry the Project of good Henry the 4th into Execution,
by forming a Federal Union and One Grand Republick of
all its different States and Kingdoms, by means of a like
Convention, for we had many Interests to reconcile."
*Benjamin Franklin to Ferdinand Grand (in Paris), October
22, 1787.*

IN THE late, impatient afternoon of Saturday, September 15,
Randolph, with his "most harmonious voice, fine person, and
striking manners," spoke first. He was governor of Virginia, and
it was he who had originally proposed the resolutions of the
Virginia plan. He had come to Philadelphia in the belief that
the Confederation government was not "so eminently defective,
as it had been supposed." During the first days of discussion
with his Virginia colleagues he had been convinced that the
Confederation lacked the energy which the government of the
United States ought to have. In those days he agreed with
Madison. But as time went on, he found himself agreeing with
Mason on various points of dissent from the majority. It was
difficult for Randolph, who was no political philosopher, to

make up his own mind. It became increasingly important for him, as a politician, to think about his constituents in Virginia, and how they would regard the work of the Convention. On August 31 Mason had declared that he "would sooner chop off his right hand than put it to the Constitution" as it then stood. Unless it could be corrected, he thought the whole plan should go over to another "general Convention." Randolph had seized upon this suggestion. Let the state conventions, he added, study the Constitution, propose their amendments, and then let these be submitted to a second general convention which might "reject or incorporate them" as it thought proper. On September 10 Randolph had repeated his proposal.

Now on the 15th he put the proposal in the form of a motion. He felt, he said, "pain at differing from the body of the Convention, on the close of the great & awful subject of their labours." Yet he could not sign the Constitution if his motion were to be disregarded. Whether he should oppose ratification by Virginia he could not now decide, but he must keep himself free to do that if "the course should be prescribed by his final judgment." In other words, which he did not speak, he must wait to see which way his constituents would jump.

Mason seconded the motion. He was as much aroused as so reasonable a man could be. The Convention, he later told Jefferson, had been "precipitate & intemperate not to say indecent" in its conduct for the past week. Day after day, step by step, Mason had opposed the rush of final decisions. Little attention had been paid to his motions or his arguments. Though there is no record to prove it, the majority had no doubt been short with him, as well as resistant and indifferent to his objections. He was still willing, he now said, to sign the Constitution if it were made subject to amendment by the people in state conventions for their amendments, and then confirmed by another general convention with ultimate authority. But without that provision he could neither sign it here nor support it in Virginia.

"This Constitution," he said according to Madison's notes, "had been formed without the knowledge or idea of the people. A second Convention will know more of the sense of the people, and be able to provide a system more consonant to it. It was improper to say to the people, take this or nothing." Whether Mason that afternoon went into the details of his objections does not appear. Everybody present knew that he thought the Constitution should contain a bill of rights; that the Southern states would suffer from commercial regulation by Congress; that it was wrong to permit the importation of slaves for another twenty years. Nobody else seems clearly to have foreseen how important all these matters were to be in the future. And Mason probably did not go into detail when he rose to prophecy, in the words, or nearly the words, he wrote on the blank pages of his printed copy of the report of the Committee of Style: "This government will set out a moderate aristocracy; it is at present impossible to foresee whether it will, in its operation, produce a monarchy, or a corrupt, tyrannical aristocracy; it will most probably vibrate some years between the two, and then terminate in the one or the other."

Charles Pinckney said that these "declarations from members so respectable at the close of this important scene" gave "a peculiar solemnity to the present moment." But he could not believe that anything was to be gained by "calling forth the deliberations & amendments of the different States on the subject of Government at large. Nothing but confusion & contrariety could spring from the experiment." The states would never agree in their plans, and the delegates to a second convention, "coming together under the discordant impressions of their Constituents," would never agree either. He had his own objections to the Constitution, but "apprehending the danger of a general confusion, and an ultimate decision by the Sword, he should give the plan his support."

Gerry went into detail as to his scattering objections. Senators under the Constitution were to hold office for too long a term and might be re-elected. The House of Representatives was given the right not to publish parts of its proceedings that seemed to require secrecy. Congress was free to fix the compensation of its own members. Massachusetts had less than her due share of Representatives. Two-thirds of the slaves were to be represented as if they were free men. Congress, with its power over commerce, might establish monopolies. The Vice-President was to be head of the Senate. All these he could perhaps accept, but not the power of Congress to make any laws "they may please to call necessary and proper," to raise armies and money "without limit," and to establish a Supreme Court without juries, which would be a "Star-Chamber as to civil cases." In the circumstances, Gerry held that a second convention was indispensable. He too seems to have believed the Constitution would not be ratified.

It was now six o'clock. The Convention had sat for seven hours without recess, food, or drink. The two final votes were so simple and overwhelming that Madison could enter them in his notes with irreducible brevity.

"On the question on the proposition of Mr. Randolph. All the States answered no.

"On the question to agree to the Convention, as amended. All the States ay.

"The Constitution was then ordered to be engrossed.

"And the House adjourned."

The late hour of adjournment could not escape public notice. Word got out in Philadelphia that the Convention had agreed on a Constitution. Dickinson of Delaware, in bad health throughout the session, had left during the day for home, asking Read to sign Dickinson's name for him if the document was to be signed by the delegates.

On Sunday, Washington wrote letters all forenoon. Franklin summoned the other Pennsylvania delegates to his house. It was reported that he disapproved of the Constitution on certain points, and could not agree with them. But in fact he desired only "to allay every possible scruple, & make their votes unanimous." He had already written out what he had still to say to the Convention. Possibly at this Sunday meeting Gouverneur Morris drew up an "ambiguous form" of execution for the signatures. Since not all the delegates were willing to sign the Constitution, but a quorum of every represented state was, could it not be made to appear that the states were unanimous in approval, with no indications that individual delegates had refused to sign? The form of execution might read: "Done in Convention by the Unanimous Consent of the States present." This was satisfactory to the Pennsylvania delegation, and was no doubt discussed with delegates from other states before the Convention met on Monday morning.

Also on Sunday the Constitution was engrossed by some unknown penman on four sheets of parchment. Dunlap and Clay-

poole began their work on the printing of five hundred copies
that had been ordered.

II

On Monday morning, as soon as the Convention came to order,
the secretary read the "engrossed Constitution." At once Franklin
rose "with a speech in his hand, which he had reduced to writing
for his own conveniency, and which Mr. Wilson read."

"Mr. President," the speech began, "I confess that there are
several parts of this constitution which I do not at present approve, but I am not sure I shall never approve them: For having
lived long, I have experienced many instances of being obliged
by better information or fuller consideration, to change opinions
even on important subjects, which I once thought right, but
found to be otherwise. It is therefore that the older I grow, the
more apt I am to doubt my own judgment, and to pay more
respect to the judgment of others. Most men indeed as well as
most sects in Religion, think themselves in possession of all truth,
and that wherever others differ from them it is so far error. Steele,
a Protestant in a Dedication tells the Pope, that the only difference between our Churches in their opinions of the certainty of
their doctrines is, that the Church of Rome is infallible and the
Church of England is never in the wrong." At this point in the
speech there must have been smiles among the delegates. "But
though," Wilson read on, "many private persons think almost as
highly of their own infallibility as that of their sect, few express
it so naturally as a certain french lady, who in a dispute with
her sister, said 'I don't know how it happens, Sister, but I meet
with no body but myself, that's always in the right'—*Il n'y a que
moi qui a toujours raison.*" At this point there was sure to be
laughter.

But there was no laughter from Randolph, Mason, and Gerry,
who were grim in their disagreement and could not like to hear
it compared with sectarian orthodoxy or the bright complacency
of one of the French ladies Franklin was supposed to have known
so well during his gay years in France. (He had mentioned her
as "a certain great lady here" in a letter from Paris in March
1784.)

"In these sentiments, Sir," the speech continued, "I agree to this Constitution with all its faults, if they are such; because I think a general Government necessary for us, and there is no form of Government but what may be a blessing to the people if well administered, and believe farther that this is likely to be well administered for a course of years, and can only end in Despotism, as other forms have done before it, when the people shall have become so corrupted as to need despotic Government, being incapable of any other. I doubt too whether any other Convention we can obtain may be able to make a better Constitution. For when you assemble a number of men to have the advantage of their joint wisdom, you inevitably assemble with those men, all their prejudices, their passions, their errors of opinion, their local interests, and their selfish views. From such an Assembly can a perfect production be expected? It therefore astonishes me, Sir, to find this system approaching so near to perfection as it does; and I think it will astonish our enemies, who are waiting with confidence to hear that our councils are confounded like those of the Builders of Babel; and that our States are on the point of separation, only to meet hereafter for the purpose of cutting one another's throats. Thus I consent, Sir, to this Constitution because I expect no better, and because I am not sure, that it is not the best. The opinions I have had of its errors, I sacrifice to the public good— I have never whispered a syllable of them abroad— Within these walls they were born, and here they shall die— If every one of us in returning to our Constituents were to report the objections he has had to it, and endeavor to gain partizans in support of them, we might prevent its being generally received, and thereby lose all the salutary effects & great advantages resulting naturally in our favor among foreign Nations as well as among ourselves, from our real or apparent unanimity. Much of the strength & efficiency of any Government in procuring and securing happiness to the people, depends on opinion, on the general opinion of the goodness of the Government, as well as of the wisdom and integrity of its Governors. I hope therefore that for our own sakes as a part of the people, and for the sake of posterity, we shall act heartily and unanimously in recommending this Constitution (if approved by Congress & confirmed by the Conventions) wherever our influence may extend, and turn our future thoughts & endeavors to the means of having it well administered.

"On the whole, Sir, I cannot help expressing a wish that every member of the Convention who may still have objections to it, would with me, on this occasion, doubt a little of his own infallibility—and to make manifest our unanimity, put his name to this instrument."

Here Wilson ceased reading, and Franklin himself moved that the Constitution be signed by the delegates, with the form devised by Gouverneur Morris.

Before debate on the motion began, Gorham proposed that, if it was not too late, one final change be made in the Constitution. It had been felt by several of the delegates, Mason among them, that 40,000 was a large number of citizens to be represented by one member of the popular House of Congress. Gorham suggested that this number be changed to 30,000. King of Massachusetts and Carroll of Maryland seconded and supported the motion. It is likely that all three of them, and other delegates as well, knew that Washington favored the change.

"When the President rose," as Madison's notes record, "for the purpose of putting the question," he said that "although his situation"—as president—"had hitherto restrained him from offering his sentiments on questions depending in the House, and it might be thought, ought now to impose silence on him, yet he could not forbear expressing his wish that the alteration proposed might take place. It was much to be desired that the objections to the plan recommended might be made as few as possible— The smallness of the proportion of Representatives had been considered by many members of the Convention, an insufficient security for the rights & interests of the people. He acknowledged that it had always appeared to himself among the exceptionable parts of the plan; and late as the present moment was for admitting amendments, he thought this of so much consequence that it would give much satisfaction to see it adopted."

Without a word in opposition the motion was unanimously agreed to. The word "forty" was erased from the engrossed parchment and "thirty" crowded into its place.

But before the vote was taken on Franklin's motion there was further discussion. Randolph had evidently been stung by those philosophical observations on infallibility and unanimity. He now apologized for setting up his own judgment against "the vast majority & venerable names that would give sanction" to the wisdom and worth of the Constitution. His refusing to sign, he repeated, did not mean that he would "oppose the Constitution without doors." He was only keeping himself free to be governed by his duty as he should see it later. He did not believe that nine states would ratify. And if they should not, he made it plain without saying so, he would not have the political disadvantage of having put his name to an unacceptable measure. He was keeping himself free, as it turned out, to change sides later and support the Constitution in the Virginia convention— an apostasy which led Mason for the rest of his life to refer to Randolph as "Young Arnold," meaning a minor Benedict Arnold.

Gouverneur Morris said he too had objections, but "considering the present plan as the best that was to be attained, he should take it with all its faults." The question was, should there be a national government or a general anarchy? The form of signing, he explained, meant only that the states were unanimous, not the delegates.

Hamilton, who had seldom spoken during the past month, and had been absent almost half of that time, "expressed his anxiety that every member should sign." There was now a certain public enthusiasm in favor of the Convention, but it might soon subside if some of its distinguished members refused to sign the Constitution and then opposed it. "No man's ideas were more remote from the plan than his own were known to be," but he would sign (as an individual of course, since he was the only New York delegate present and could not by himself represent his state officially). The choice the country faced, he thought, was between anarchy and convulsion on one side and the chance of good on the other.

Williamson of North Carolina suggested that the delegates sign only the letter to Congress accompanying the Constitution. Some might be willing to sign that, if not the Constitution. Blount of the same state said he had declared he would not sign the Constitution, but in the form proposed he was willing to join with the others in attesting that this was the unanimous act of the states in the Convention.

Franklin insisted that he had not meant, in his remarks, to allude to any individual, for when he wrote them he had not been sure that any of the delegates would finally refuse to sign. "He professed a high sense of obligation to Mr. Randolph for having brought forward the plan in the first instance," and hoped he might yet, "by concurring with his brethren, prevent the great mischief which the refusal of his name might produce." But Randolph said the change of form made no difference to him. He still could not sign. He believed that the refusal of individuals to sign it was not so likely to produce anarchy and civil convulsion as the Convention's insistence on submitting the Constitution as a whole to the states, to be accepted or rejected as a whole.

Gerry could not doubt that Franklin's remarks had been directed at the men who refused to sign. Nevertheless he himself could not change his mind. He knew that in Massachusetts, and he seemed to believe this was true elsewhere in America, there were two fiercely antagonistic parties, one devoted to "Democracy, the worst of all possible evils," and the other "as violent in the opposite extreme." The Constitution as drawn and submitted would, he was sure, only intensify that antagonism. He should have preferred to propose it "in a more mediating shape"—presumably by offering it to the states for their amendments and then considering them all in a second general convention.

Charles Cotesworth Pinckney did not like the equivocal form of execution. He thought it best to have the signers put their names to the Constitution and mean it. He would sign it as evidence of his support, and he wished to pledge himself accordingly. Franklin pointed out that it was too early "to pledge ourselves before Congress and our Constituents shall have approved the plan." Jared Ingersoll of Pennsylvania, who had not spoken during the entire Convention, now said he did not regard signing as a pledge of support, or as a mere attestation, but as a "recommendation of what, all things considered, was the most eligible."

On Franklin's motion that the Constitution be signed as "Done in Convention by the Unanimous Consent of the States present," all the states voted aye except South Carolina, which was divided because General Pinckney and Butler did not like the ambiguous form, although they intended to sign.

Before the signing was begun, King suggested that the "Journals of the Convention should be either destroyed, or deposited in the custody of the President." He thought that if the records were made public, "a bad use would be made of them by those who would wish to prevent the adoption of the Constitution." Wilson thought the second suggestion the better of the two. False accusations might be brought against the delegates, and if the records had been destroyed it would be impossible to answer with proof.

All the states but Maryland were in favor of "depositing the Journals and other papers of the Convention in the hands of the President." Maryland was opposed only because its delegates were required by their instructions to report the "Proceedings" to the Maryland legislature and so could not vote to have them either destroyed or withheld. When Washington, after the vote, asked what he should do with the Convention records, and whether delegates should be furnished with copies on request, it was resolved without dissent that he should "retain the Journal and other papers subject to the order of Congress, if ever formed under the Constitution."

If ever formed under the Constitution. Not one of the delegates about to sign could feel certain that their plan would be accepted by the state conventions or ever go into effect. They might have wasted all their time and effort. They might by their proposals have raised up political enmities which would put an end to their own public careers. They could not foresee that to have signed the Constitution would in the future make them all remembered, however little else they might have done—as the Founding Fathers of their country. They could not imagine how many of them would have an active share in the establishment of the government they had planned. It is easy now to look behind the curtain, so blank to them, and know that Washington and Madison were to be Presidents and Madison also Secretary of State; Hamilton, Secretary of the Treasury; McHenry, Secretary of War; Rutledge (for a short term) Chief Justice of the Supreme Court; Paterson, Wilson, and Blair, Associate Justices; Langdon, Gilman, King, Johnson, Sherman, Dayton, both the Morrises, Read, Bassett, Carroll, Blount, Butler, Few, and Baldwin, all Senators; Clymer, FitzSimons, Spaight, Williamson, Representatives; and Dayton also Speaker of the House; King, Minister to Great Britain, Gouverneur Morris and Charles Cotesworth Pinckney to France, Charles Pinckney to Spain; Brearley, Ingersoll, Bedford, federal judges in district courts. Still less could any of them guess that Gerry, now refusing to sign, would be Representative in the First Congress, vigorous supporter of Hamilton, and Vice-President with Madison; or that Randolph, also refusing, would be Attorney General and Secretary of State under Washington.

Without any of the certainty which a little prophetic knowledge might have given them, the delegates signed with doubt and concern in their minds. McHenry was so insecure that he took pains to write down in his notes that day a short account of his reasons for signing. Franklin, McHenry thought, had by his confession of disapproval of some parts of the Constitution, "guarded the Doctor's fame" no matter what might happen. What Franklin had done, McHenry would do. He said he was opposed to "many parts of the system," yet signed it and meant to support it. He distrusted his own judgment in opposition to "a majority of gentlemen whose abilities and patriotism" were "of the first cast"; and, almost quoting Franklin, "I have had already frequent occasions to be convinced that I have not always judged right. . . . Comparing the inconveniences and the evils which we labor under and may experience from the present confederation, and the little good we can expect from it—with the possible evils and probable benefits and advantages promised us by the new system, I am clear that I ought to give it all the support in my power."

Probably most of the delegates felt as McHenry did while they came forward, in the traditional order of the states from north to south, and signed their names. It was Franklin who spoke the closing words recorded by Madison in his immortal notes.

"Whilst the last members were signing it Doctor Franklin looking towards the President's Chair, at the back of which a rising sun happened to be painted, observed to a few members near him, that Painters had found it difficult to distinguish in their art a rising from a setting sun. I have, said he, often and often in the course of the Session, and the vicissitudes of my hopes and fears as to its issue, looked at that behind the President without being able to tell whether it was rising or setting: But now at length I have the happiness to know that it is a rising and not a setting Sun."

With the Constitution, as engrossed and signed, went the Resolution informing Congress how the Convention thought the Constitution ought to be ratified and the new government put into operation; and the letter to Congress, probably drafted by

Gouverneur Morris but signed by Washington as president of the Convention, with which the Constitution was to be submitted.[1]

That afternoon William Jackson, the secretary, burned all the miscellaneous papers in his charge, and later deposited with Washington the formal Journal of the Convention, the journal of the committee of the whole, and an incomplete, undated table of the details of ayes and noes on various questions. Jackson was to leave the next morning to carry the engrossed Constitution to Congress in New York.

Washington that night summed up the day's transactions in his diary, in grave words which give an unforgettable weight to their plain meaning.

"*Monday, 17th.* Met in Convention, when the Constitution received the unanimous vote of 11 States and Colonel Hamilton's from New York (the only delegate from thence in Convention), and was subscribed to by every member present except Governor Randolph and Colonel Mason from Virginia, and Mr. Gerry from Massachusetts.

"The business being thus closed, the Members adjourned to the City Tavern," in Second Street near Walnut and much favored for large public dinners, "dined together and took a cordial leave of each other; after which I returned to my lodgings, did some business with, and received the papers from the Secretary of the Convention, and retired to meditate on the momentous work which had been executed, after not less than five, for a large part of the time Six, and sometimes 7 hours sitting every day, except Sundays and the ten days adjournment to give a committee opportunity and time to arrange the business, for more than four months."

[1] See Appendix 10, 11.

10

THE WAR OF WORDS
AND IDEAS

"Upon the whole I doubt whether the opposition to the Constitution will not ultimately be productive of more good than evil; it has called forth, in its defence, abilities which would not perhaps have been otherwise exerted that have thrown new light upon the science of Government, they have given the rights of man a full and fair discussion, and explained them in so clear and forcible a manner, as cannot fail to make a lasting impression upon those who read the best publications on the subject, and particularly the pieces under the signature of Publius." *George Washington to John Armstrong, April 25, 1788.*
"So numerous indeed and so powerful are the causes which serve to give a false bias to the judgment, that we, upon many occasions, see wise and good men on the wrong as well as on the right side of questions of the first magnitude to society. This circumstance, if duly attended to, would furnish a lesson of moderation to those who are ever so much persuaded of their being in the right in any controversy. And a further reason for caution, in this respect, might be drawn from the reflection that we are not always sure that those who advocate the truth are influenced by purer principles than their antagonists. Ambition, avarice, personal animosity, party opposition, and many other motives not more laudable than these, are apt to operate as well upon those who support as those who oppose the right side of a question. Were there not even inducements to moderation, nothing could be more ill-judged than that intolerant spirit which has, at all times, characterized political parties. For in politics, as in religion, it is equally absurd to aim at making proselytes by fire and sword. Heresies in either can rarely be cured by persecution." *Alexander Hamilton, The Federalist No. 1, October 27, 1787.*

O N SEPTEMBER 20 the Constitution was laid before Congress, which set the 26th as the day on which the new plan would be considered. Objections were at once raised by various members, among whom Richard Henry Lee of Virginia took the lead. He had received a letter, now missing, from George

Mason in which Mason's objections came as a warning to Lee, if he needed any. Lee agreed with Mason that the proposed Constitution ought to include a bill of rights, provide for a council to advise and assist the President, do away with the office of Vice-President, and make the common law and trial by jury secure throughout the United States. In Lee, Mason found an ally who was to stand with him on the same grounds in the opposition.

Whatever warnings other members of Congress may have had from Philadelphia, they could see that the Constitution was no mere amendment of the Articles of Confederation. Even those who favored a fundamental change in the government of the United States were unprepared not only for the large outlines but also for many of the details which the Federal Convention had worked out in four months of hard thinking and skillful contriving. Congress in September was, as to its opinions on the subject, about where the Convention had been in May. But the members had more than the bare document to guide them in their study of it. Ten of the Convention delegates who were also members of Congress promptly resumed their seats in New York. Langdon and Gilman of New Hampshire, Gorham and King of Massachusetts, Johnson of Connecticut, Madison of Virginia, Blount of North Carolina, Butler of South Carolina, and Few and Pierce of Georgia made up just short of a third of the members who debated the Constitution on the 26th and 27th, and on the 28th resolved to transmit it to the states.

This was not done without a conflict and a bargain. Lee proposed a series of amendments which he thought Congress should make before submitting the Constitution to the states. He was supported in the minority opposition by Melancton Smith of New York. The minority accused the majority of desiring, in Lee's words, "to push the business on with dispatch . . . that it may be adopted before it has stood the test of reflection and due examination." The majority wished to recommend the Constitution to the states. The minority were willing to transmit it, out of respect to the Convention, but wished to point out that, under the Articles, Congress had no power to create "a new confederacy of nine states." In the end the majority agreed to make no recommendation, and the minority to resolve unanimously, though noncommittally, that the Constitution should be transmitted to the legislatures in order "to be submitted to a convention of Delegates chosen in each state by the people thereof in conformity to the resolves of the Convention made and provided in that case."

Copies of the Constitution went out to the states from Congress, by post road and packet boat, to take its chances with the states and their conventions. In the meantime, it reached the people through newspapers, pamphlets, and a quick outburst of discussion. First printed for the public in Dunlap and Claypoole's *Pennsylvania Packet* of September 19, the Constitution was reprinted as fast as printers could get their hands on it. The Convention delegates sent copies to their correspondents everywhere, Franklin particularly to friends in England, France, and Italy. Franklin, Washington, Madison, and probably others, sent copies to Jefferson. The friends of the Constitution unmistakably hoped to make more friends for it as soon as possible.

Its enemies were no less enterprising. Mason on October 4 published his objections in the *Packet* in Philadelphia, and three days later sent a copy to Washington. Randolph on the 10th wrote at length to the Virginia House of Delegates, explaining why he had refused to sign the Constitution, and still insisting that it ought to be referred by the states to a second Convention. On the 18th Gerry furnished the Massachusetts legislature with a statement of his reasons—a new set in this case—for not signing. On the whole the three were temperate in their language, and they did not agree on what were the defects of the Constitution; but they were convinced that unless it could be amended at once it must be a threat to the liberties of America. Their strategy was to delay adoption. If the Constitution "be found good after mature deliberation," Lee wrote in a public letter to Randolph on the 16th, "adopt it: if wrong, amend it at all events: for to say, as many do, that a bad government must be established, for fear of anarchy, is really saying, that we must kill ourselves, for fear of dying."

These were arguments bound to win the approval of cautious men, who needed time in which to readjust their political conceptions. Here was a new government with a President who had powers never exercised by any executive in the United States since they rid themselves of a king. Might not the President become himself a king, as the opposition said he was sure to? The proposed Senate had powers by which, the minority spokesmen declared, it could make itself an aristocracy and the government an oligarchy. The House of Representatives, Mason said, was "not the substance, but the shadow only of representation"; and Lee echoed him by saying that the House was "a mere shred, or rag of representation."

The central government, as the debate went on, was magnified into a monstrous overshadowing force, outside and above any given state, which would be free to dominate, tax, and enslave a helpless people. There was a widespread fear that the federal district ten miles square which was to be the seat of the projected government would develop into something malign and alien. Mason, and with him Patrick Henry, in time took up this cry. A backwoods Baptist elder won election to the ratifying convention in North Carolina by telling his constituents that the federal capital would be a walled or fortified town with an enormous standing army to sally forth and reduce the people to submission. The anonymous author of an extremely rare pamphlet, *The Government of Nature Delineated,* published at Carlisle, Pennsylvania, early in 1788 prophesied that the federal district would draw in treasure "from every corner of the land" and become "a place of refuge for well-born bankrupts, to shelter themselves and property from the rapacity of their persecuting creditors."

Within a few weeks after the Constitution was made public, the people were sharply aligned in two parties for or against it. Those who supported it called themselves Federalists, and denied the charge that they were aiming at a consolidated government with the states abolished. Those who opposed it came naturally to call themselves Antifederalists, since they were united chiefly in their dislike of the Constitution and were otherwise of various opinions on a desirable government for the United States. Some of them thought the Constitution was not strong enough. Some of them thought the country was too large for a single central authority, and talked again of regional confederations. Some of them were jealous for their states and their own rank in them. Some of them were theoretical republicans, who distrusted the novelties in this federal scheme. Most of them were simply conservatives, disturbed by a threat to their peace, suddenly fond of the traditional ways of life in their separate states, afraid of taxation and tyranny from an uncontrolled super-state, and genu-

inely unable to form in their minds a new pattern of the United
States in which the individual states would gain more than they
would lose by a federal union of the kind proposed.

II

The conflict between the two instinctive parties was put
quickly, and too hastily, to the test in Pennsylvania. On the day
after the Constitution was signed, the Pennsylvania delegates,
with Franklin at their head, appeared before the Pennsylvania
Assembly. Mifflin, one of them, was speaker of the house. On the
suggestion of a delegate, Mifflin read the Constitution to the
members, to the applause of citizens who had been admitted to
the chamber. Franklin then presented a letter from the delegates,
recommending that the Assembly immediately cede to Congress
a tract of land in the state to be the seat of government called
for by the Constitution. Since Congress had still to approve the
Constitution, nothing could that day be done by the Assembly,
but a powerful appeal had been made to the interest of Pennsylvania in having the capital of the United States so close at hand.
Congress resolved ten days later to transmit the Constitution
to the states. An express rider, changing horses along the road,
arrived in Philadelphia on the morning of the 29th with the
news. The Federalist majority in the Assembly demanded that a
state convention be called without delay. The Antifederalist minority protested at being hurried. Some members of the opposition had absented themselves so that there would be no quorum
present. The sergeant-at-arms and a clerk were sent to bring in
at least two members to complete the quorum. Two members
refused to come. A crowd of Federalist bystanders highhandedly
dragged them to the State House, and would not let them leave
till the involuntary quorum had appointed the first Tuesday in
November for the election of delegates to the state convention.
Because the Federalists had put themselves clearly in the
wrong, there was an uproar of furious polemics. The proposed
government, the Antifederalists said, would be intolerably expensive. It was not a confederation of states, as it ought to be,
but a rule directly over individuals. The states were to be ob-
literated. Unprotected by their states, the citizens would be at
the mercy of the general government; and there was no bill of

rights in the Constitution. The Constitution, being the "supreme law of the land," might do what it liked to the common law and trial by jury. Congress had almost unlimited power to lay taxes. The President was too strong. The Senate was too aristocratic. The House of Representatives was too small to represent the people. The Supreme Court had a jurisdiction too extensive.

The publication of George Mason's objections in Philadelphia on October 4 was followed the next day by the first appearance in another newspaper of a vigorous, unidentified Antifederalist who called himself Centinel. The "wealthy and ambitious, who in every community think they have the right to lord it over their fellow creatures," he said, were supporting the Constitution. "These characters flatter themselves that they have lulled all distrust and jealousy of their new plan, by gaining the concurrence of the two men"—Washington and Franklin—"in whom America has the highest confidence, and now triumphantly exult in the completion of their long meditated schemes of power and aggrandizement. I would be very far from insinuating that the two illustrious personages alluded to, have not the welfare of their country at heart; but that the unsuspecting goodness and zeal of the one has been imposed upon, in a subject of which he must be necessarily inexperienced, from his other arduous engagements; and that the weakness and indecision attendant on old age, has been practiced on in the other." Having more than hinted that Washington was incompetent and Franklin senile, Centinel then went on to a detailed study of the Constitution to prove that it must lead to the creation of "a *permanent* ARISTOCRACY." The Federalists, he charged, were trying to stampede the people by saying there was "no alternative between adoption and absolute ruin." This, he declared, was "the argument of tyrants." Let his fellow citizens remember that "of all *possible* evils, that of *despotism* is the *worst* and the most to be dreaded."

On October 6 James Wilson appeared at a public meeting in the State House Yard and there addressed a large crowd in answer to the Antifederalist objections. He painstakingly explained that the states reserved to themselves every power not granted to the federal government. As they had not granted the power to make rules about a bill of rights or trial by jury, these matters still stood in the states exactly where they had stood

before, and were not required in the federal Constitution. The
states were not destroyed. The President was to be chosen by
electors in the states. The Senators were to be elected by the
state legislatures. The Representatives were to be elected by the
voters who elected the popular legislative houses in the states.
To the accusation that the friends of the Constitution were the
wealthy and ambitious, he retorted that its enemies were most
of them state officials who were afraid of losing comfortable posts
which, under the Constitution, might cease to exist or be transferred to the federal government.

For a month the controversy went on, with abuse and counter-
abuse. Wilson came to be considered "the principal fabricator"
of the Constitution in the "Dark Conclave" which had made it.
There were so many attacks on the Pennsylvania delegates to the
Federal Convention that only Wilson was nominated for the
state convention, though the Antifederalists used Franklin's name
as a ruse to draw votes. He got more than any Antifederalist
candidate in the election on November 6, but they were obviously for him rather than for the party. The Federalist candidates
were overwhelmingly elected in Philadelphia. A mob of rioters
threw stones through the windows of the boarding house where
several Antifederalist members of the Assembly lodged.

The state convention met in the State House on the 21st. Two-
thirds of the sixty-nine members were Federalists. As soon as the
body was organized, Thomas McKean, chief justice of Pennsylvania, moved that they adopt and ratify the Constitution: not
that he expected this to be done at once but that he desired to
bring the matter to debate. Wilson opened the discussion with
a careful survey of what the Federal Convention had under-
taken to do and what the Constitution really intended. "America,"
he said, "has it in her power to adopt either of the following
modes of government: She may dissolve the individual sovereignty of the States, and become one consolidated empire: she
may be divided into thirteen separate, independent and uncon-
nected commonwealths; she may be erected into two or more
confederacies; or, lastly, she may become one comprehensive
Federal Republic." The Federal Convention had considered all
these, and had chosen the last as the one most suited to the situation and character of the United States. Wilson went patiently
through the chief reasons for this choice, summing up the es-

sence of many profound debates and conflicts in which he had taken part.

John Smilie of Fayette County, a leading Antifederalist, accused McKean of trying to hurry the adoption. Robert Whitehill of Cumberland County, another Antifederalist, proposed that the convention go into a committee of the whole, to discuss the Constitution article by article. The convention voted against going into committee, but agreed that in convention every member might speak as often as he wished. It was voted also, however, that the speeches should not be printed, because of the unnecessary expense. The minority objected, but the majority was strong. Consequently the records of the convention are to be found chiefly in contemporary newspapers. Thomas Lloyd, an expert shorthand writer, took down the deliberations and announced that he would publish them all after the close of the convention. He appears to have been bought off by the Federalists, and published only one volume, containing speeches by the Federalists Wilson and McKean.

The debate continued till December 12. So far as the imperfect records show, Smilie, Whitehill, and William Findley of Westmoreland County, the three leaders of the Antifederalists, opposed ratification principally on three points: that the Federal Convention had exceeded its authority in creating a new government instead of revising the old one; that there was no bill of rights; and that the proposed Constitution destroyed the sovereignty of the states. Wilson, aided by McKean, had to go again and again over the familiar arguments. The Federal Convention had thought rather of the spirit than of the letter of its instructions; a federal bill of rights was superfluous, since the states had their own; the states gave up their sovereignty only in matters which no one of them had a right to decide upon.

On December 1 Findley attacked the Constitution for setting up a "consolidated government, and not a confederation of the states." The Preamble said "*We the people,* and not *We the States,*" which implied "a compact between individuals entering into society, and not between separate states enjoying independent power, and delegating a portion of that power for their common benefit." In a true confederation, "from the very nature of the things, a state can have only one voice"; but under the Constitution each member of Congress would have a vote. Both the United States and the separate states would have power to tax. But, Findley said, "there cannot exist two independent sovereign taxing powers in the same community, and the strongest will of course annihilate the weaker." Under the Constitution, Congress would regulate and judge elections. The judicial power was to be "co-extensive with the legislative." And in other respects, not clearly reported, Findley declared that the new government must destroy the states.

"The secret is now disclosed," Wilson answered, "and it is discovered to be a dread that the boasted state sovereignties will, under this system, be disrobed of part of their power. . . . Upon what principle is it contended that the sovereign power resides in the state governments? . . . My position is, that the sovereignty resides in the people. They have not parted with it; they have only dispensed such portions of it as were conceived primarily for the public welfare. This constitution stands upon this broad principle. I know very well, Sir, that the people have hitherto been shut out of the federal [Confederation] government, but it is not meant that they should any longer be dispossessed of their rights. In order to recognize this leading principle, the proposed system sets out with a declaration that its existence depends upon the supreme authority of the people alone. . . . When the principle is once settled that the people are the source of authority, the consequence is that they may take from the subordinate governments powers with which they have hitherto entrusted them, and place those powers in the general government, if it is thought that there they will be productive of more good. . . . *States* now exist and others will come into existence; it was thought proper that they should be represented in the general government. But gentlemen will please to remember, this constitution was not framed merely for the States; it was framed for the PEOPLE also."

It was on this day that Benjamin Rush, most ardent of all the Federalists in the Pennsylvania convention, said a "passion for separate sovereignty had destroyed the Grecian Union." And he went further to say that "this plurality in politics is what plurality of gods is in religion—it is the idolatry, the heathenism of government." Rush would be happy to see Pennsylvania surrender sovereignty to the United States. "I have now a vote for Members of Congress. I am a Citizen of every State." Smilie

thought this more ridiculous than anything he had ever heard
except some earlier observation of the same speaker. No matter
what changes might be made in the Confederation, the rights
of mankind must not be forgotten.

The minority would not forget them or stop talking about them.
On December 11 Wilson admitted that they were contending for
those rights; but "what then are the majority contending for? If
the minority are contending for the rights of mankind, the majority must be contending for the doctrines of tyranny and slavery.
Is it probable that this is the case? Who are the majority in this
assembly? Are they not the people? Are they not the representatives of the people, as well as the minority? Were they not elected
by the people as well as the minority? Were they not elected by
the greater part of the people? Have we a single right separate
from the rights of the people? Can we forge fetters for others, that
will not be clasped round our own limbs? . . . On what fancied
distinction shall the minority assume to themselves the merit of
contending for the rights of mankind?"

But no argument convinced the Antifederalist minority, and
the votes varied no more than three or four on a side in the entire
session. The minority objected to the laughter or applause of
citizens in the "gallery"—that is, behind the rail inside the door.
Things would be different, Smilie said on December 10, if the
convention were meeting elsewhere in the state. "No, Sir, this
is not the voice of the people of Pennsylvania." He, like Findley
and Whitehill, was from an inland county, where the opposition
to the Constitution was generally stronger than in and near
Philadelphia. The "cold and sour temper of the back counties,"
as Gouverneur Morris described it in a letter to Washington on
October 30, was already hostile to Philadelphia, resentful of its
dominance in Pennsylvania politics, and convinced that the interests of the interior could never be the same as the interests
of the seaboard. The Constitution had been made in Philadelphia. It appeared to have its strongest support in the larger cities.
It looked to the western Pennsylvanians like another threat to
their independence and their individualism. When news reached
the convention that Delaware, on December 7, had been the first
state to ratify the Constitution, Smilie said that Delaware had
"reaped the honor of having first surrendered the liberties of the
people."

On December 12 the Pennsylvania convention voted, 46 to 23, "to assent to and ratify" the Constitution. The next day the members, with "the President [Franklin] and Vice-President of the State, members of Congress, the faculty of the University, the magistrates and militia officers of the city," went in procession to the old Court House at Market and Second Streets, where the ratification was read from the balcony "to a great gathering." At three that afternoon the members of the convention, with numerous officials and citizens, dined at Epple's Tavern in Race Street. The first of their thirteen toasts was "The *People* of the United States." The last was "Peace and free governments to all the nations in the world."

The convention sat for two more days, concerning itself with the seat of the new federal government. In spite of opposition from the minority, the majority resolved that when the new government should have been organized, Pennsylvania would cede to Congress full jurisdiction over any district within the state except the city of Philadelphia, Southwark, and a part of the Northern Liberties; and that until Congress should have chosen the "place of their permanent residence," in Pennsylvania or elsewhere, they would be free to use the needed public buildings in Philadelphia or anywhere else in the state.

The Antifederalists in the convention, still unconvinced and still angry at the rough tactics of the majority, published on December 18 their "Reasons for Dissent" in an address to their constituents. It was a thoroughgoing attack on the secrecy of the Federal Convention, the bullying haste with which the Pennsylvania Federalists had pressed for ratification by their state, and the lack of consideration shown the Antifederalist minority in the state convention. The minority's objections argued that (1) the United States was too large to be governed "on the principles of freedom" except as a confederation of republics; (2) that the Constitution as proposed must "necessarily annihilate and absorb the legislative, executive, and judicial powers of the several States, and produce from their ruins one consolidated government, which from the nature of things will be *an iron handed despotism*"; (3) even if it were practicable to form a consolidated government over so large a territory, this Constitution was "not calculated to attain the object." The "Reasons for Dissent" assumed that the "consolidated government" would speedily overpower the people, who were given no adequate representation and no bill of rights. Trial by jury in civil cases would be lost. Taxation by Congress would be unlimited, with a standing army to enforce collection. The state militias, under the control of Congress, could be used to suppress all public liberty. "The militia of Pennsylvania may be marched to New England or Virginia to quell an insurrection occasioned by the most galling oppression." Pennsylvania, with its popular constitution, would suffer particularly from the creation of a central government so unlike that of Pennsylvania. And yet, the Antifederalist dissenters declared, they were not thinking of Pennsylvania alone, but rather of "the cause of the present and future ages—the cause of liberty and mankind."

The minority dissenters were supported by many of their constituents, and Pennsylvania had a vigorous Antifederalist opposition which did not give up till months after the Constitution had been ratified by the necessary nine states. The "Reasons for Dissent" reached other states and strengthened the hands of Antifederalists there. Some of the responsibility for the persistence of the Pennsylvania opposition must be laid to the Federalist leaders who used their advantage of numbers in a ruthless drive to make Pennsylvania the first to ratify and therefore perhaps most likely to win the seat of government. Their actions amounted to a kind of majority *coup d'état*. There was bound to be resistance from men of spirit, especially from those who, having all their lives been inhabitants of Pennsylvania, could not quickly think of themselves as citizens of the United States. But it may be pointed out that the Antifederalist leaders, Findley, Smilie, and Whitehill, all later served willingly and effectively in Congress.

A picturesque incident, overlooked by historians of the making and ratifying of the Constitution, throws a hard light on the conflict between Federalists and Antifederalists in Philadelphia. Some time in the fall of 1787 a Philadelphia painter, Matthew Pratt, painted a signboard, now long lost, which was hung in front of an unidentified tavern at Fourth and Chestnut Streets. The picture on it was called "The Representation of the Constitution," and it contained portraits, said to be lifelike, of thirty-eight of the thirty-nine delegates who had signed the document. They were shown inside the room where they had sat, with Washington in the Chair, Wilson at his right, "the venerable head and spectacles of Dr. Franklin in conspicuous relief," and the other delegates ranged in some no doubt heroic composition. Crowds are said to have gathered before the tavern and eagerly occupied themselves with identifying the likenesses. Beneath it were two lines of Pratt's own verse:

"These 38 great men have signed a powerful deed
That better times to us, should very soon succeed."

This was in the first weeks after the signing of the Constitution, when the Federal Convention was generally approved. But in the following spring, after a winter of controversy, the Antifederalist *Independent Gazette* on April 24 published a ribald piece called "A New Federal Song" which told, or purported to tell, of different treatment of the "federal sign." Some "mischievous Anti's seeing it cut such a dash" spattered the sign with filth from the street, particularly the figures of the Pennsylvania delegates: FitzSimons, the Scottish James Wilson, General Thomas Mifflin, Benjamin Franklin, the rich Robert Morris, and one-legged Gouverneur Morris. Or as the stumbling verses put it:

"As for 'Simons and the Caledonian, their eyes were turned green,
And General Tommy, Benny and Bobby, were also unclean.
Bob seemed to hold guineas and Jamie to beg,
But old Harry had hold of the man with one leg."

Nor did the rollicking Antifederalists confine themselves to the Pennsylvania delegates.

"In short, the shape of most of the figures were altered,
And instead of masqued patriots, rose up rogues ready haltered.
All that was wanted to complete the black scene
Was a gallows that would hold at least ten or fifteen."

III

No single writer, with pamphlets like trumpets, celebrated the Constitution as Thomas Paine had celebrated the Declaration of Independence. The Declaration had been ringing first principles about liberty and the rights of man. The Constitution was second thoughts about how that liberty and those rights, once obtained, might be perpetuated in an orderly government. Instead of the language of poets and prophets it used the language of lawyers and administrators. It was addressed to minds not to emotions. Its worst enemies, however violent in their abuse of it, did not achieve a contagious unity of eloquence. Nor did its best friends. Benjamin Rush in the Pennsylvania convention, on the day the Constitution was ratified, said he "as much believed the hand of God was employed in this work"—the Constitution—"as that God had divided the Red Sea to give a passage to the children of Israel, or had fulminated the ten commandments from Mount Sinai." But Gouverneur Morris, the next month, observed in a letter that "while some have boasted it as a work from Heaven, others have given it a less righteous origin. I have many reasons to believe that it is the work of plain honest men, and such, I think, it will appear."

Since the Federal Convention on its last day had given up the rule of secrecy, several of the delegates took part, actively or passively, in the public discussions of the Constitution. Franklin gave copies of his final remarks about infallibility and unanimity to Carroll of Maryland and Gorham of Massachusetts for use in their states; and probably other copies to other delegates for similar purposes. On November 29 Carroll read the speech to the Maryland legislature. It was printed in the *Virginia Independent Chronicle* of Richmond for December 5, the same month in Boston and Philadelphia, and soon in newspapers throughout the country. On December 14 Washington, in a letter to a friend, said he thought there was no alternative between the adoption of the Constitution and anarchy; and that a second Convention would be "more discordent or less Conciliatory than the last." The paragraph got into the papers and was printed everywhere. Washington was distressed and vexed that his private remarks had been made public: but only because they were casually phrased in his letter, not because they misrepresented his sentiments in general. From Mount Vernon he watched the war of words and ideas with intense concern. His letters are an instructive commentary on the campaign.

Ellsworth of Connecticut, himself absent when the Constitution was signed, corrosively impugned the motives of the delegates who had refused to sign it. Mason, Ellsworth wrote on December 10, had objected to the Constitution's permitting slaves to be imported for twenty years. But "Mr. Mason has himself about three hundred slaves, and lives in Virginia, where it is found by prudent management they can breed and raise slaves faster than they want for their own use, and could supply the deficiency in Georgia and South Carolina; and perhaps Col. Mason may suppose it more humane to breed than import slaves." And so on through all Mason's objections.

Gerry, Ellsworth charged on December 24, had moved in the Convention that the old continental paper money ought to be redeemed by the new government. "As Mr. Gerry was supposed to be possessed of large quantities of this species of paper, his motion appeared to be founded in such barefaced selfishness and injustice, that it at once accounted for all his former plausibility and concession, while the rejection of it by the Convention inspired the author with an utter rage and intemperate opposition to the whole system he had formerly praised." Gerry replied on January 5 that he had never made any such motion (the records bear him out in this) and that he had not during the Convention owned, and did not now own, "the value of ten pounds in continental money." But Ellsworth had put the story into circulation.

Ellsworth made no attack on Randolph, but he trained all his guns on Martin of Maryland, whom Ellsworth accused of being an insufferable bore in the Convention, and a blustering obstructionist, and a collaborator with Gerry, and now of falsifying what had happened. Martin replied to Ellsworth, in the same temper but of course more volubly. Between them, Ellsworth writing as The Landholder in the *Connecticut Courant* of Hartford and Martin under his own name in the *Maryland Journal* of Baltimore, they carried on a long-range debate that the whole country read. As to Richard Henry Lee, whose *Letters of a Federal Farmer*, published in October, were a popular textbook of the Antifederalists, Ellsworth on December 10 said: "The factious spirit of R. H. L., his implacable hatred to General Washington, his well-known intrigues against him in the late war, his attempts to displace him and give the command to General [Charles] Lee, is so recent in your minds it is not necessary to repeat them."

Roger Sherman, writing as A Countryman in the *New Haven Gazette* from November 14 to December 20, was as terse and homely as Poor Richard. "You do not hate," he said in the last of these papers, "to read Newspaper Essays on the new constitution more than I hate to write them. Then *we will be short*—which I have often found the *best* expression in a dull sermon, except the *last*."

In the first paper, Sherman, who in the Federal Convention had urged the advantage of small states, now said that if any "corner of this State of ten miles square, was now, and long had been independent," the people living there "would consider a proposal to unite them to the other parts of the State, as a violent attempt to wrest from them the only security for their persons or property. They would lament how little security they should derive from sending one or two members to the legislature at Hartford & New Haven," where the Connecticut legislature met alternately, "and all the evils that the Scots predicted from the proposed union with England, in the beginning of the present century, would be thundered with all the vehemence of American politics, from the little ten miles district." But the Scots, "instead of becoming a poor, despicable, dependent people, have become much more secure, happy, and respectable."

As to the bill of rights, over which so much clamor had been raised by the Antifederalists: "No bill of rights ever yet bound the supreme power longer than the *honeymoon* of a new married couple, unless the *rulers were interested* in preserving the rights." In this respect, the interest of Congress was the same as the interest of the states. The people of Connecticut had already granted the powers of government to their legislature. Under the Constitution they would simply, for reasons of general security, transfer some of those powers to Congress.

Martin of Maryland, who had spoken at great length before the Maryland legislature on November 29, expanded his speech in *The Genuine Information* which ran through the *Maryland Gazette* from the end of December into the beginning of February and appeared also as a separate pamphlet. It gave, besides its voluminous arguments against the Constitution, a great deal of information, some of it highly colored, about the inside workings of the Convention which is to be found nowhere else.

So, through fall and winter, and the following spring and summer, the vast debate went on, covering the United States with a net of arguments which reached even to the backwoods, though here less closely and in some remote places little comprehended or felt. But the supreme contribution was made by Hamilton and Madison, with some help from John Jay, in the series of essays all signed Publius, and called *The Federalist,* which began on October 27 and continued in New York newspapers till after the eighty-five numbers were brought together in two volumes in March and May respectively. *The Federalist* at once took its place as almost a part of the Constitution itself, and the masterpiece of all thinking and writing about federal government.

Gouverneur Morris was asked to join the others in the undertaking, but for some reason declined. Jay, who had assisted in making the treaty of peace with England and was now Congress's secretary of foreign affairs, contributed five essays concerned with the Constitution and international relations. Madison, in New York as member of Congress from Virginia, did not take a hand till after nine essays had been printed, and left for home after writing No. 63. From then on the whole burden, except for No. 64 by Jay, fell on Hamilton, who had originated the series in order to counteract the powerful New York opposition led by Governor Clinton.

The Federalist could not be a systematic exposition, because it was written under the fire of miscellaneous objections which had to be answered. Jay had not been a delegate to the Federal Convention, and came in as a well-disposed outsider. Hamilton did not even like the federal government which had been chosen instead of the consolidated national government he preferred. Madison, who could regard the Constitution as at so many points his own achievement, might be expected to be partial. All three of the writers might have been irritable under Antifederalist abuse. But they avoided personalities and picayune contentions, raised the whole argument to the highest level of political theory and practice, and followed an order that gave their discussions a cumulative effect. Most of the points they made had come up in the Convention, and had there been stormily debated. Now they were brought to public scrutiny, clarified, enlarged, put into permanent language. To read and understand them was the next thing to having had a hand in making the Constitution. They were widely reprinted. Their immediate influence is hard to trace, for they were without the passion and prejudice which rouse quick responses. But there can be no doubt that these papers, so rigorously anonymous at the time, made their way through the most reflective minds of the time and then on into posterity.

In the midst of so much controversy, Delaware on December 7, New Jersey on December 18, and Georgia on January 2 unanimously ratified the Constitution. Delaware and New Jersey, at first so resistant in the Convention, were now convinced that small states had every reason to enter the federal system. Washington on January 18, more than two weeks after Georgia had ratified but days before the news was able to reach him, summed up Georgia's situation in words any Georgia Federalist might have used: "if a weak State with the Indians on its back and the Spaniards on its flank does not see the necessity of a General Government there must I think be wickedness or insanity in the way."

11

NINE NECESSARY STATES

"To get the bad Customs of a Country chang'd, and new ones, though better, introduc'd, it is necessary first to remove the Prejudices of the People, enlighten their Ignorance, and convince them that their Interest will be promoted by the propos'd Changes; and this is not the Work of a Day." *Benjamin Franklin to Alexander Small, September 28, 1787.*

"I pant for the time when the establishment of the new government, and the safety to individuals which shall arise from it, shall excuse men who like myself wish only to be passengers from performing the duty of sailors on board the political ship in which our all is embarked. I have yielded to a deep sense of the extreme danger of my country, in quitting the cabin for a station at the pump. As soon as the storm is over, and our bark safely moored, the first wish of my heart will be to devote the whole of my time to the peaceable pursuits of science, and to the pleasures of social and domestic life." *Benjamin Rush to Jeremy Belknap, February 28, 1788.*

FROM Hartford, where the Connecticut convention met on January 1 in the State House (later in a church warmed with stoves for the comfort of the members), Jonathan Trumbull, one of Washington's aides during the Revolution, wrote to Washington on the 9th. "With great satisfaction," he said, "I have the honor to inform you that, last evening, the Convention of this State, by a great majority, voted to ratify and adopt the new proposed Constitution for the United States; yeas one hundred and twenty-seven [actually 128], nays forty. With additional pleasure I can inform you, that the debates on this subject have been conducted with a spirit of great candor, liberality, and fairness, and the decision approved with the universal applause of a numerous body of the people of the State, who attended the public deliberations of their Convention, and expressed their cordial assent, on the moment of decision, with a general clap."

Yet there had been opposition from nearly a third of the delegates. William Williams, senior member of the Council, wished

to see the Preamble assert "a firm belief of the being and per-
fections of the one living and true god," though he gave up his
demand for what the majority regarded as a form of religious test.
General Jeremiah Wadsworth, with other former officers of the
Continental Army, objected to giving Congress "both the sword
and purse"—that is, control over both the army and the treasury;
but Wadsworth voted for ratification. Some of those who opposed a stronger central government sympathized with Shays'
followers in Massachusetts, and were at odds with the ministers
and magistrates who dominated Connecticut. Most of the dissenters were simply rural Yankees who were satisfied with their
tight communities and did not wish to be drawn into a government that would reach from New Hampshire to Georgia and
from the Atlantic to the Mississippi. But Connecticut was an
orderly state, and the minority accepted the majority vote without resentments or recriminations.

All the state's delegates to the Federal Convention were present
at Hartford, and all spoke. The *Connecticut Journal* of New
Haven praised Oliver Ellsworth's "Demosthenian energy," William Samuel Johnson's "learning and eloquence," and the "genuine good sense and discernment" of Roger Sherman; but only
Ellsworth's speeches seem to have been recorded.

"Our being tributaries to our sister states," Ellsworth said, "is
in consequence of the want of a federal system. The state of
New York raises 60 or £80,000 a year by impost. Connecticut
consumes about one third of the goods upon which this impost
is laid; and consequently pays one third of this sum to New York.
If we import by the medium of Massachusetts, she has an impost,
and to her we pay a tribute. If this is done when we have the
shadow of a national government, what shall we not suffer, when
even that shadow is gone?"—that is, when the states should have
fallen even further apart by refusing to accept the Constitution.
Connecticut had paid her share of expenses during the war and
since, Ellsworth said, but some other states had not. There must
be power to raise the needed money from all the states, if the
burden on the willing states was not to be intolerable. The right
to lay imposts must be granted to Congress, otherwise the separate states would oppress the others "and destroy all harmony
between them." Some of the delegates had thought that Congress
could not be trusted with the sword and the purse. But Congress

must have both. "Else how could the country be defended? For the sword without the purse is of no effect: it is a sword in the scabbard."

There was no reason why Congress and the state legislatures should not both make laws, if they were restrained from making laws in conflict with each other. "The road is broad enough; but if two men will justle each other, the fault is not in the road." There might be conflicts between individual states or between the states and the central government. But such conflicts existed already, with nothing to settle them. Under the Constitution, there was "every reasonable check against it." In republics it was "a fundamental principle that the majority govern, and that the minority comply with the general voice." Under the Confederation a single state could "put a veto upon the most important public measures." This had happened: "a minority, a very small minority has governed us. So far is this from being consistent with republican principles, that it is in effect the worst species of monarchy. Hence we see how necessary for the union is the coercive principle. No man pretends the contrary: we all see and feel this necessity. The only question is, shall it be a coercion of law, or a coercion of arms? . . . I am for coercion by law—that coercion which acts only upon delinquent individuals. This constitution does not attempt to coerce sovereign bodies, states, in their political capacity. . . . But this legal coercion singles out the guilty individual, and punishes him for breaking the laws of the union. All men will see the reasonableness of this; they will acquiesce, and say, let the guilty suffer."

The speeches of the opposition have been lost, and can only be guessed from the replies to them. Little appears to have been said about a bill of rights. To the objection that the new government would annihilate the state governments, Richard Law, chief judge of Connecticut's superior court and mayor of New London, said: "this general government rests upon the state governments for its support. It is like a vast and magnificent bridge, built upon 13 strong and stately pillars; now the rulers who occupy the bridge, cannot be so beside themselves as to knock away the pillars which support the whole fabric." Some of the delegates had said that "a free government, like this," could not have enough energy "to pervade a country of such vast extent." Law replied: "We are not satisfied with this assertion. We want to try the experiment." The delegates no doubt included many holders of public securities which would be safer if the new government should strengthen public credit; and these no doubt voted for ratification in their own interest. But the scanty records of the convention do not show that any of them spoke of this as a reason for adopting the Constitution.

II

Massachusetts was the first of the states to print anything like a full record of its ratifying convention: the speeches not only of its eminent citizens but also of plain men who now sound like characters in a living drama, not like politicians in a dead convention.

There was Abraham White of Norton who said: "we ought to be jealous of rulers. All the godly men we read of failed—nay, he would not trust a flock of Moseses." Samuel Thompson, of Topsham in the District of Maine, began: "Sir, gentlemen have said a great deal about the history of old times—I confess, I am not acquainted with such history—but I am, sir, acquainted with the history of my own country." Again he said: "I suspect my own heart, and I shall suspect our rulers." And again: "There are some parts of this constitution which I cannot digest: and, sir, shall we swallow a large bone for the sake of a little meat? Some say swallow the whole now, and pick out the bone afterwards. But I say, let us pick off the meat, and throw the bone away." William Widgery, of New Gloucester in Maine, insisted that everybody was subject to passions and prejudices. "In the late general court, of which I was a member, I would willingly have deprived the three western counties"—where the Shays uprising had been strongest—"from sending delegates to this house; as I *then* thought it was necessary." Now he knew he would have been wrong.

Amos Singletary of Sutton wished the Federalists "would not play round the subject with their fine stories, like a fox round a trap, but come to it." He said: "These lawyers, and men of learning, and monied men, that talk so finely and gloss over matters so smoothly, to make us poor illiterate people, swallow down the pill, expect to get into Congress themselves; they expect to be the managers of this constitution, and get all the power and all the money into their own hands, and then they will swallow up all us little folks, like the great *Leviathan,* Mr. President: yes, just as the whale swallowed up *Jonah.*"

These remarks on January 25 brought on the most dramatic speech of the Convention, made by Jonathan Smith of Lanesboro in Berkshire County. "Mr. President, I am a plain man, and get my living by the plough. I am not used to speak in public, but I beg your leave to say a few words to my brother ploughjoggers in this house. I have lived in a part of the country where I have known the worth of good government, by the want of it. There was a black cloud that rose in the east last winter, and spread over the west."

At this Widgery of Maine interrupted to ask "what the gentleman means by the east?" Widgery knew that Smith was referring to the uprising of 1786 against oppressive taxes, and wanted it understood that this had not begun in Maine. It had in fact been general through much of the state, but the first county to protest had been Bristol, in the southeast.

"I mean, sir, the county of Bristol," Smith replied, and went on: "The cloud rose there and burst upon us, and produced a dreadful effect. It brought on a state of anarchy and that led to tyranny. I say, it brought anarchy. People that used to live peaceably, and were before good neighbors, got distracted, and took up arms against government."

Here Major Martin Kinsley of Hardwick in Worcester County "called to order and asked what had the history of last winter to do with the constitution? Several gentlemen, and among the rest the hon. Mr. [Samuel] Adams, said the gentleman was in order—let him go on in his own way."

Smith went on in his own way, which was the only way he knew. "I am going, Mr. President, to shew you, my brother farmers, what were the effects of anarchy, that you may see the reasons why I wish for good government. People, I say, took up arms, and then, if you went to speak to them, you had the musket of death presented to your breast. They would rob you of your property, threaten to burn your houses; oblige you to be on your guard night and day; alarms spread from town to town; families were broke up; the tender mother would cry, O, my son is among them! What shall I do for my child! Some were taken captive, children taken out of their schools, and carried away. Then we should hear of an action, and the poor prisoners were set in the front, to be killed by their own friends. How dreadful, how distressing was this! Our distress was so great that we should have been glad to snatch at anything that looked like a government. Had any person, that was able to protect us, come and set up his standard, we should all have flocked to it, even if it had been a monarch, and that monarch might have proved a tyrant; so that you see that anarchy leads to tyranny, and better have one tyrant than so many at once.

"Now, Mr. President, when I saw this constitution, I found that it was a cure for these disorders. It was just such a thing as we wanted. I got a copy of it and read it over and over. I had been a member of the convention to form our own state constitution, and had learnt something of the checks and balances of power, and I found them all here. I did not go to any lawyer, to ask his opinion—we have no lawyer in our town, and we do well enough without. I formed my own opinion, and was pleased with this constitution. My honorable old daddy there (pointing to Mr. Singletary) wont think that I expect to be a congress-man and swallow up the liberties of the people. I never had any post, nor do I want one. But I dont think the worse of the constitution because lawyers and men of learning, and monied men are fond of it. I dont suspect that they want to get into congress and abuse their power. I am not of such a jealous make. They that are honest men themselves are not apt to suspect other people. I dont know why our constituents have not as good a right to be jealous of us, as we seem to be of the congress; and I think those gentlemen who are so very suspicious that as soon as a man gets into power he turns rogue, had better look at home.

"We are by this constitution allowed to send ten [actually eight] members to congress. Have we not more than that number fit to go? I dare say, if we pick out ten, we shall have another ten left, and I hope ten times ten; and will not these be a check upon those that go? Will they go to congress and abuse their power and do mischief, when they know they must return and look the other ten in the face, and be called to account for their conduct? Some gentlemen think that our liberty is not safe in the hands of monied men, and men of learning. I am not of that mind.

"Brother farmers, let us suppose a case, now: Suppose you

had a farm of fifty acres, and your title was disputed, and there was a farm of 5000 acres joined to you that belonged to a man of learning, and his title was involved in the same difficulty; would you not be glad to have him for your friend, rather than to stand alone in the dispute? Well, the case is the same—these lawyers, these monied men, these men of learning, are all embarked in the same cause with us, and we must all swim or sink together; and shall we throw the constitution overboard, because it does not please us alike? Suppose two or three of you had been at the pains to break up a piece of rough land, and sow it with wheat— would you let it lay waste, because you could not agree what sort of a fence to make? Would it not be better to put up a fence that did not please every one's fancy, rather than not to fence it at all, or keep disputing about it, until the wild beast came and devoured it? Some gentlemen say, dont be in a hurry, take time to consider, and dont take a leap in the dark. I say, take things in time—gather fruit when it is ripe. There is a time to sow and a time to reap; we sowed our seed when we sent men to the federal convention, now is the harvest, now is the time to reap the fruit of our labor, and if we wont do it now, I am afraid we never shall have another opportunity."

Some of the art of this speech may perhaps be credited to George Richards Minot, the historian of Shays' Rebellion, who was secretary of the Massachusetts convention. But there was no disguising the blunt eloquence of the solid farmer who could see beyond his township in the Berkshire hills.

The management of the convention by the Federalist leaders seems to have had more to do with the outcome than the debates had. The delegates were much divided when they appeared in Boston, probably a majority against the Constitution. The Atlantic cities and counties, with their commercial and shipping interests, were generally Federalist. So was the southwestern part of the state, which resented its dependence on New York. But between these Federalist sections were many farmers and villagers who instinctively resisted change, distrusted the motives of the prosperous and educated spokesmen for the Constitution, and believed that a federal government would be intrusive and oppressive. The counties in Maine were strongly Antifederalist, in part because of a conviction that if they joined with Massachusetts in ratifying the Constitution they might find it difficult to become a separate state, as they desired.

On the whole there were more wordless prejudices than articulate principles among the Antifederalists. In debate they were no match for their opponents, who included Governor John Hancock, the former governor James Bowdoin, and, as Gorham wrote to Madison, "three judges of the supreme court, fifteen members of the Senate, twenty from among the most respectable of the clergy, ten or twelve of the first characters at the bar, judges of probate, high sheriffs of counties," besides three generals of the Continental Army and the three delegates from Massachusetts—Gorham, King, and Strong—who had signed the Constitution. Gerry was invited by the convention to be present to answer questions, but he was not a member.

Aware of the strength of the Antifederalists when the convention met in the State House on January 9, the Federalists after several days spent in preliminaries managed on the 14th to get a vote, moved by Strong, that the convention would take up the Constitution paragraph by paragraph before trying to come to any decision on the whole. This meant that the Federalist leaders would have every opportunity to explain the provisions in detail and so win a gradual assent which would not be given to the whole at the outset. They managed also to get the sessions transferred from the State House to the church in Long Lane, which had room in the gallery for "a vast many people" who were as a rule Federalist in sympathy.

Most important of all, the Federalists managed to win John Hancock to active support of a cause to which he at first cautiously refused to commit himself. A popular figure in the state, on account of his attitude toward the Shays rebels, he was elected president of the convention on the opening day. But, alleging an attack of the gout which had more than once saved him from taking part in controverted affairs, he did not put in an appearance till January 30; and then only after he had been told by King and the others that, if Virginia did not ratify the Constitution, which he was told was *problematical,* then Hancock would be the *only fair candidate for President.* This was enough to win him over. He had been bitterly disappointed in June 1775 when he aspired to be commander in chief and had to see Washington chosen instead. Now, on the chance of becoming President of the United States, Hancock was willing to support the Constitution.

He supported it by offering a series of amendments, drawn up by Federalist leaders but presented by Hancock as his own, which Massachusetts would recommend along with the ratification of the Constitution. The ratification was not to be conditional on the acceptance of the amendments, but the convention made it clear that certain alterations in the Constitution "would remove the fears and quiet the apprehensions of many of the good people of the commonwealth [of Massachusetts], and more effectually guard against an undue administration of the federal government."

These suggested amendments removed enough fears and quieted enough apprehensions among the members of the convention to bring a vote in favor of ratification on February 6, but only by the narrow majority of 187 over 168. Afterwards, however, the minority acquiesced in a spirit very different from that of the minority in Pennsylvania, where the Federalist leaders had been less mannerly in their management. The Pennsylvania tactics would have alienated a man like Hancock—or a man like Samuel Adams, who also did not support the Constitution till he saw how many supporters it had among the mechanics of the town, headed by Paul Revere.

Nobody in Pennsylvania spoke, after defeat, as Widgery did when the vote had been counted. He said "that he should return to his constituents, and inform them, that he had been overruled, and that it had been carried by a majority of wise and understanding men; that he should endeavour to sow the seeds of union and peace among the people he represented; and that he hoped, and believed, that no person would wish for, or suggest, the measure of a *Protest:* for, said he, we must consider that this body is as full a representation for the people, as can be convened. . . . He concluded by saying, that he should support, as much as in him lay, the constitution, and that he believed, as this state had adopted it, that not only nine, but the whole thirteen would come into the measure." Two days later, in a letter to a friend, Widgery expressed, in his own frontier spelling, his approval of Federalist Boston: "One thing I mus menchen, the Gallerys was very much Crowded, yet on the Desition of so emportant a Question as the present you might have heard a Copper fall on the Gallery floor, their was Sush a profound Silence. . . . Notwithstanding my opposition to the Constitution, and the anxiety of Boston for its adoption I most Tel you I was never Treated with So much politeness in my Life as I was afterwards by the Treadesmen of Boston Merchants & every other Gentleman."

During the course of the convention a rumor spread in Boston, and was printed in the *Boston Gazette,* that large sums of money had been brought from a neighboring state—by which New York was meant—to bribe and corrupt the Antifederalist members. The convention on January 21 took note of the rumor, and assigned a committee to investigate it. No confirmation was found, and there is no reason to believe there was any truth in it. But this was another sign of the suspicions with which the Antifederalists were filled.

The debates in the convention covered most of the general grounds of opposition, with some special to Massachusetts. There was a long contest over the two-year term for representatives in Congress. Massachusetts preferred one year, as for its own legislature. Charles Turner of Scituate seemed to argue that annual elections were as much a law of nature as the annual renewal of the seasons. Major Thomas Lusk of West Stockbridge, noting that there was no religious qualification for Federal officers, "shuddered at the idea, that Roman Catholics, Papists, and Pagans might be introduced into office; and that Popery and the Inquisition may be established in America."

And there was much dislike of the Constitution for taking slavery for granted and permitting the importation of slaves for at least another twenty years.

The South, with its many slaves, seemed to some of the members very far away from Massachusetts, with none. If Massachusetts should be joined with the slave states under the Constitution, would this not mean that Massachusetts must become responsible for the evil of slavery and its people be "partakers of other men's sins"? Benjamin Randall of Antifederalist Sharon felt that there could be no safe union of the South and New England. "Our manners," he said, "are widely different from the southern states—their elections were not so *free and unbiassed;* therefore, if the states were consolidated, he thought it would introduce manners among us which would set us at continual variance." General William Heath of Federalist Roxbury argued that, much as Massachusetts might detest slavery, it had no right to interfere with slavery in the slave states. "Each state," he said, "is sovereign and independent to a certain degree, and they have a right, and they will regulate their own internal affairs, as to themselves appear proper; and shall we refuse to eat, or to drink, or to be united, with those who do not think, or act, just as we do?" Thomas Dawes Jr. of Boston said that the Southern states, "like ourselves, have *their* prejudices. It would not do to abolish slavery, by an act of congress, in a moment, and so destroy what our southern brethren consider as property." But, and here Dawes said what was said more than once in the convention, slavery would not last long in the United States. Or as he put it: "Although slavery is not smitten with an apoplexy, yet it has received a mortal wound and will die of a consumption."

III

Almost no words survive from all those spoken at the New Hampshire convention. General John Sullivan of the Continental Army, now president of the state and convention chairman, made a speech on the jurisdiction of the Federal courts which was reported in the *Freeman's Oracle* (at Exeter) for March 7, 1788. Joshua Atherton, of Amherst, in an attack on slavery which may have been revised at a later date before it was ever printed, uncompromisingly said: "We do not think ourselves under any obligations to perform works of supererogation in the reformation of mankind; we do not esteem ourselves under any necessity to go to Spain or Italy to suppress the inquisition of those countries; or of making a journey to the Carolinas to abolish the detestable custom of enslaving the Africans; but, sir, we will not lend the aid of our ratification to this cruel and inhuman merchandise, not even for a day."

Except for these two speeches or parts of speeches the New Hampshire convention is hardly more than an official act on the record. The state, like Massachusetts, was divided, and its people were less well informed. The seaboard was generally Federalist; so was the section along the Connecticut River, which resented the domination of its trade by New York and wished to be protected by Federal regulations. But the farmers and villagers of the interior, like those in Massachusetts, preferred their traditional hardy isolation. When the state convention met in the courthouse at Exeter on February 13 (to adjourn at once to the First Congregational meetinghouse), it was found, as John Langdon wrote to Washington, that "a small majority of (say, four) persons appeared against the system." A good many of the delegates came from remote communities which at the time of the elections had been told "by a few designing men, who wished for confusion," according to Langdon, that the Massachusetts convention would certainly refuse to ratify; "that the liberties of the people were in danger, and the great men, as they call them, were forming a plan for themselves; together with a thousand other absurdities, which frightened the people almost out of what little senses they had. This induced them to choose not only such men as were against the plan, but to instruct them positively against receiving it."

For ten days the unrecorded debate went on, with the Antifederalists bound by their instructions and the Federalists unable to make headway. But finally some of the instructed delegates were convinced, and wished to go back to their constituents and lay the matter again before them. This seemed to the Federalists the most they could get from the convention. Against a strong minority, the convention voted to adjourn to June 3, later changed to the 17th.

On June 2 Tobias Lear, Washington's private secretary at Mount Vernon but now on a visit to his native state of New Hampshire, wrote to Washington about the prospects for ratification. The enemies of the Constitution, he said, had been imprudent in their strategy. "Instead of alarming the fears of the people, by telling them that their immediate and individual interest would be affected by the adoption of the Constitution, they acknowledged that this State would be more benefited thereby than any other in the Union; but declared that, if the Constitution obtained, the rights and liberties of all American citizens would be destroyed, and that the people of this State, as a part of the community, would suffer in the general wreck." This had produced the Antifederalist majority in the first session of the convention. But on further reflection, aided by Federalist arguments between February and June, the public came to feel that the inhabitants of other states were competent to judge what was injurious to their liberties, and that, if the New Hampshire people "had more to hope and less to fear from its obtaining than almost any other State, it would be doing injustice to themselves not to accept it."

In that spirit the convention reassembled at Concord on June 17, after Maryland and South Carolina had ratified in the interval. This would make New Hampshire the ninth and deciding state, but the convention could not know that. The Virginia convention had already met, and might ratify before New Hampshire. Some sense of the crucial decision may have encouraged promptness in Concord, but the chief motive was the simple interest New Hampshire had in the event. After four days the convention on the 21st voted in favor of the Constitution by a majority of 57 to 46. Amendments were recommended, as in Massachusetts. These, as Lear wrote to Washington, "were drawn up more with the view of softening and conciliating the adoption to some who were moderate in their opposition, than from an expectation that they would ever be ingrafted into the Constitution." Again as in Massachusetts, the defeated minority, "except a few," yielded without anger or complaining.

Lear, reporting to Washington on the 22nd, added a postscript. "The Constitution was ratified on Saturday, at one o'clock, P.M. I am thus particular, as Virginia might have adopted it the same day, and, in that case, the hour must be known, to determine which was the ninth State."

IV

In Maryland the delegates to the Federal Convention were called before the legislature in Annapolis on November 29 "to explain the Principles, upon which the proposed Constitution for the United States of America were formed." McHenry supported the Constitution clearly and sensibly; Martin attacked it with vigor and at length on the grounds that it would create a consolidated, not a federal, government in which the rights of Maryland were not protected and indeed none of the states would be safe from encroachment by the central authority. He accused Washington and Franklin of neglecting the rights of the states and the liberties of the people. Mercer also was energetic in opposing the Constitution, Carroll and Jenifer in supporting it. The legislature voted by a majority of seven to call a state convention to debate ratification.

The real contest in Maryland came during the campaign for the election of the delegates to the convention. Martin in his "tavern harangues," according to Carroll, told members of the legislature that more than twenty members of the Federal Convention had been in favor of a "Kingly Government." Mercer made assertions which grew into rumors that the French Minister had had a hand in the Convention; and that Langdon of New Hampshire had said he would be willing, on certain terms, to have Washington made "despot of America." These and other stories reached the public "When they attended the Polls," again according to Carroll, "a wildness appeared in many which show'd they were really frightened." And yet the Federalists must have been in the majority, no matter how skillful the Federalist leaders were, for at the election for members of the state convention more than half the counties instructed their delegates to ratify without considering any amendments. Only a few of the delegates were opposed to the Constitution, and nearly two-thirds were opposed to any amendments. The Constitution was particularly popular with the shipbuilders, merchants, mechanics, and sailors of Baltimore, who believed the new general government would bring them quick prosperity by its encouragement to commerce.

The convention, which met in the noble State House at Annapolis on April 21, was firmly under Federalist control. The members spent two days in organizing and making rules for the transaction of business. On the 23rd the Constitution was first read to them. By a large majority it was voted that there would be no debate on "any particular part of the proposed plan of federal government for the United States: but that the whole thereof shall be read through a second time, after which, the subject may be fully debated and considered; and then the president shall put the question, 'That this convention do assent to and ratify the same constitution.'"

Nothing was done on the 24th, but on the 25th William Paca, who had signed the Declaration of Independence, produced a series of amendments, "not to prevent, but to accompany the ratification," which he asked leave to read. Whereupon a delegate from each of eleven counties and from the city of Annapolis rose and announced that they had been elected "to ratify the proposed constitution, and that as speedily as possible, and to do no other act. After this, Mr. Paca was not permitted even to read his amendments. The opponents continued to make their objections to the constitution," until noon of the 26th. "The advocates of the government, although repeatedly called on, and earnestly requested to answer the objections, if not just, remained inflexibly silent, and called for the question." On the vote 63 were for ratification, 11 against it.

The majority, having settled the matter, was now willing to appoint a committee of fifteen to consider Paca's amendments and to report on Monday the 28th to the convention. With Paca on the committee were Samuel Chase, who had signed the Declaration but was opposed to the Constitution, Mercer, McHenry, and other distinguished citizens. They agreed on thirteen amendments, most of them concerned with the rights of individual citizens under the new government, and rejected fifteen. But the majority decided against making any formal report, or recommendation, to the convention. Paca read the thirteen amendments agreed on, but the convention refused to approve them or even to enter the vote on the record. On the motion to adjourn, 27 were opposed, presumably because they were in favor of at least some of the amendments. The motion was carried. Four members of the amendments committee and eight of the convention afterward published an account of the transactions, with the text of all the amendments, in an *Address to the People of Maryland,* but nothing came of it. Paca later served as district federal judge, Chase as an associate justice of the Supreme Court. Martin, chiefly out of his hatred for Jefferson, later became one of the most ardent and stormy of Federalists, the "bull-dog of federalism."

v

In South Carolina the debate in the legislature was more interesting than that in the ratifying convention. The legislature had among its members a strong opposition from the up country not only to the proposed new central government but also to the low country which supported it. The delegates to the Federal

Convention, Rutledge, the Pinckneys, and Butler, spoke in favor of the Constitution. Few of the up-country members spoke, so far as the record shows, but their cause was represented with unrelenting pertinacity by Rawlins Lowndes. Lowndes, born in the West Indies, had been long a conspicuous figure in South Carolina, for one term president of the state, and was now taking his last stand in public affairs. The debate in the legislature was largely between him on one side and the Convention delegates on the other.

"The security of a republic is jealousy," Lowndes declared on January 16, the first day of the debate; "for its ruin may be expected from unsuspecting security; let us not, therefore, receive this proffered system with implicit confidence, as carrying with it the stamp of perfection; rather let us compare what we already possess, with what we are offered for it." He called the Articles of Confederation "a most excellent constitution, one that had stood the test of time." The new Constitution was an experiment. "What, risk the loss of political existence, on experiment!" If this experiment were tried, he "sincerely believed . . . that the sun of the southern states would set, never to rise again." The Northern states would have a majority in Congress, and in the nature of things would not consider Southern interests. Those Northern states had already, in the Constitution, limited the importation of slaves to twenty years. "For his part he thought this trade could be justified on the principles of religion, humanity, and justice; for certainly to translate a set of human beings from a bad country to a better, was fulfilling every part of these principles. But they"—the Northern states—"don't like our slaves, because they have none themselves; and therefore want to exclude us from this great advantage."

Lowndes said he had been very much against the Declaration of Independence, but after it was approved by the people he had accepted it. He was very much against the Constitution, "but if it was sanctioned by the people, it would have his hearty concurrence and support."

Rutledge in his reply that day wondered that Lowndes could "pass such eulogium on the old confederation," which Rutledge represented in very different terms. And how could Lowndes, "so strenuous an advocate for the powers of the people . . . distrust the people the moment that power is given to them," and feel sure that under this Constitution the representatives of the people would be corrupt and the people themselves become negligent? Rutledge insisted that the South had gained more than it had given up in agreeing to the Constitution, and that its advantage would grow with the certain increase of population in the Southern states while the Northern states stood still in that respect.

Charles Cotesworth Pinckney the next day doubted that Lowndes could be serious in his "warm panegyric on the old confederation," in spite of its known inability "to secure us tranquillity at home, or respect abroad." As to slaves, General Pinckney was as convinced as Lowndes could be that without them "South Carolina would soon be a desert waste." The Middle states, including Virginia, in the Convention at Philadelphia had been in favor of immediate and total prohibition of the importation of slaves. The Northern states had given up some of their "religious and political prejudices" and had joined with the Southern in making a compromise.

Lowndes said that even against such "a phalanx of able antagonists" he must continue to oppose the Constitution because "a number of respectable members, men of good sense, though not in the habit of speaking in public, had requested that he would state his sentiments, for the purpose of gaining information on such points as seemed to require it." He insisted that representation in Congress would be "merely virtual, similar to what we were allowed in England, whilst under the British rule; we were then told that we were represented in Parliament." There would be difficulties in electing representatives. And this was as nothing compared with the difficulty of electing a President. "For the first president there was one man to whom all America looked up, (General Washington) and for whom he most heartily would vote; but after that gentleman's administration ceased, where could they point out another so highly respected" as to win a majority of the Presidential electors? If that could not be done, "then the government must stand still." Lowndes advanced through a series of detailed objections and closed, for the moment, with wishing that another Federal Convention might be called to make another Constitution.

Robert Barnwell, of the Parish of St. Helena, who was in favor of the Constitution, said he had expected from "a gentle-

man of such acknowledged abilities, and such great experience"
as Lowndes "a train of reasoning, and a power of argument, that
would have made the federal fabric totter to its foundation; but
to him they rather appeared like those storms which shake the
edifice to fix it more strongly on its basis." Barnwell did not
believe that the North was prejudiced against the South. In
the Revolution, when the North was most heavily attacked, it
had not demanded assistance from the South. Yet when war had
shifted to the South, then the North had sent forces to Virginia
and Yorktown. Barnwell thought the Constitution was "like the
laws of Solon, not the best possible to be formed, but the best
that our situation will admit of: he considered it as the panacea
of America, whose healing power will pervade the continent."

Arthur Simkins, of the up-country District of Ninety-Six, "asked
for information, whether congress had a right to interfere in
religion." General Pinckney answered, "they had no power at
all, and explained this point to Mr. Simkins' satisfaction."

On the 18th General Pinckney reminded Lowndes that the
Declaration of Independence had not even mentioned the states
by name; and went in detail over Lowndes's familiar objections,
replying to them with the familiar answers. Lowndes knew he
had been accused of obstinacy, but he insisted he was as open
to conviction as any man. Once more he spoke of the glories of
the Confederation, "and ridiculed the depraved inconsistency
of those who pant for the change." He did not believe that
population would shift from the North to the South, because of
its "excessive heats." He did not believe the United States was
in the least danger from any foreign foe. "Was it to be supposed
that the policy of France would ever suffer America to become
an appendage of the crown of Great Britain; or that Great
Britain, equally jealous of France, would permit her to reduce
us to subjection?" If the new government was so wonderful, why
delay at all. "Let us go plump into the adoration of it; let us at
once surrender every right which we at present possess." He
ascribed fantastic powers to the President, and then pointed
out the danger in them. "This was the best preparatory plan for
a monarchical government he had read. . . . How easy the
transition, no difficulty occurred in finding a king; the president
was the man proper for this appointment."

Concluding his last speech, Lowndes thanked the members

for their "very great indulgence" in listening to him, and the speakers on the other side for their "candid, fair" answers. "Popularity was what he never courted; but on this point he spoke merely to point out those dangers to which his fellow citizens were exposed; dangers that were so evident, that when he ceased to exist, he wished for no other epitaph, than to have inscribed on his tomb, 'Here lies the man that opposed the constitution, because it was ruinous to the liberty of America.' "

Lowndes spoke like an advocate for a client, with something unconvincing in his rhetoric. James Lincoln of Ninety-Six, one of the up-country men whom Lowndes represented, was blunter and closer to the position of the Antifederalist minority. He agreed that something should be done to remedy the defects of the Confederation. But this proposed Constitution "totally changes the form of your present government; from a well digested, well formed democratic, you are at once rushing into an aristocratic government.—What have you been contending for these ten years past? Liberty. What is liberty? The power of governing yourselves. If you adopt this constitution, have you this power? No: you give it into the hands of a set of men, who live one thousand miles distant from you." A "haughty, imperious aristocracy" would follow, and be followed by a "tyrannical monarchy." Americans were the freest people in the world, yet here they were deliberating whether they should throw away the blessings of freedom. The President was to be elected for four years, but might be re-elected indefinitely. The Constitution said not a word about the liberty of the press. "Was it forgot? impossible! Then it must have been purposely omitted." The Constitution said that the government of the United States would guarantee to each state a republican form of government. "But pray who are the United States—a president and four or five senators." And why was there no bill of rights? "Perhaps this same president and four or five senators would by and by, declare them." Lincoln "much feared they would."

General Pinckney, replying, said the Convention had omitted a bill of rights because these rights already belonged to the people and the power over them had not been granted to the central government. "Another reason weighed particularly with the members from this state, against the insertion of a bill of rights; such bills generally began with declaring, that all men are by nature born free; now we should make that declaration with a very bad grace, when a large part of our property consists in men who are actually born slaves."

At the close of the debate Colonel James Mason of Little River District, "by the desire of several gentlemen, members of that house," thanked Lowndes for his opposition, which had drawn from the other side "most valuable information." He thanked the Federalists for giving the information "with so much good nature; those gentlemen who lived in the country were now enabled to satisfy their constituents." The legislature then voted unanimously to call a convention "for the purpose of ratifying, or rejecting," the proposed Constitution.

The convention met in the Hall of the Exchange at Charleston on May 12, on the 13th chose Governor Thomas Pinckney (brother of Charles Cotesworth Pinckney) for president, and on the 14th began the debate. Again, as in the legislature, Charles Pinckney ably presented and argued the merits of the Constitution for Americans. It was particularly suited, he said, to agricultural states, like South Carolina. He quoted Franklin, unnamed but called "a very celebrated author," on the three ways by which nations could acquire wealth: the Roman way of conquest, which was "robbery"; the way of commerce, which was "generally cheating"; and the way of agriculture, "the only honest way, wherein a man receives a real increase of the seed thrown into the ground, in a kind of continual miracle wrought by the hand of God in his favor." Pinckney spoke of the diversity of the individual states, "differing in extent of territory, manners, population and products." New England was very different from the Middle states. The greater part of the "interior country" of New York was still Dutch and spoke the Dutch language. Pennsylvania and Delaware were Quaker states, Maryland had many Roman Catholics. There were great differences between North and South. "The southern citizen beholds, with a kind of surprise, the simple manners of the east [New England], and is too often induced to entertain undeserved opinions of the apparent purity of the Quakers, while they, in turn, seem concerned at what they term the extravagance and dissipation of their southern friends, and reprobate, as unpardonable, moral and political

evil, the dominion they hold over a part of the human race."
There was much variety in the state governments. The United
States was very large. "All the republics we read of, either in
the ancient or modern world, have been extremely limited in
territory; we know of none a tenth part so large as the United
States." And yet the delegates to the Federal Convention from
such varied commonwealths and so extensive a territory had by
harmony and concession been able to plan a "superintending
government" which would bind the people of the United States
together in a union without which they must perish as a nation.

The records of the debates in the convention are scanty for
the remaining days, and tell little about the nature and quality
of the opposition. Patrick Dollard of Prince Frederick's said all
his constituents were opposed to the Constitution and would not
accept it unless they were compelled by force of arms—"and then,
they say, your standing army, like Turkish Janissaries enforcing
despotic laws, must ram it down their throats with the points
of bayonets." (But four of the seven members from Dollard's
parish voted for ratification.) On the 21st General Thomas
Sumter of the District eastward of Wateree moved to adjourn to
October for *"further consideration"*—which meant word had come
that Virginia might not ratify, and some of the South Carolinians
wished to follow Virginia. The motion was lost by a majority of
46. On May 23 the convention voted for ratification by 149 to 73.

According to the historian David Ramsay, a member of the
convention, "when the result of the vote was announced, an
event unexampled in the annals of Carolina took place. Strong
and involuntary expressions of applause and joy burst forth
from the numerous transported spectators. The minority com-
plained of disrespect—unpleasant consequences were expected.
The majority joined with the complaining members in clearing
the house, and in the most delicate manner soothed their feelings.
In the true style of republicanism the minority not only acquiesced, but heartily joined in supporting the determination of
the majority."

South Carolina was the eighth state to ratify, and did not know
which would be the ninth, or whether there would be a ninth.
New Hampshire, completing the nine necessary states on June
21, had heard of the ratification in South Carolina. In a Federal
Procession at Portsmouth on the 26th to celebrate the happy

outcome the spectacular feature was "The Ship Union, completely rigged, armed and manned under an easy sail with colours flying, elevated on a carriage, drawn by nine horses, a tenth (emblematical of Virginia) completely harnessed, led and ready to join the rest." Nobody in Portsmouth could know that Virginia had become the tenth the day before.

12

THE REMAINING STATES

"The plot thickens fast. A few short weeks will determine the political fate of America for the present generation and probably produce no small influence on the happiness of society through a long succession of ages to come. Should every thing proceed with harmony and consent according to our actual wishes and expectations; I will confess to you sincerely, my dear Marquis; it will be so much beyond any thing we had a right to imagine or expect eighteen months ago, that it will demonstrate as visibly the finger of Providence, as any possible event in the course of human affairs can ever designate it." *George Washington to the Marquis de Lafayette, May 28, 1788.*
"You will permit me to say, that a greater Drama is now acting on this Theatre than has heretofore been brought on the American stage, or any other in the World. We exhibit at present the Novel and astonishing Spectacle of a whole People deliberating calmly on what form of government will be most conducive to their happiness; and deciding with an unexpected degree of unanimity in favour of a System which they conceive calculated to answer the purpose." *George Washington to Sir Edward Newenham, August 29, 1788.*

THE nine states which had ratified by June 21, 1788 were, in principle, enough to put the new United States into operation. In practice they faced a serious difficulty in their geographical arrangement. New England, with Connecticut, Massachusetts (including Maine), and New Hampshire assenting, could be counted on as a homogeneous and substantial element in the union. Intractable Rhode Island was too small to be more than a nuisance; Vermont, once its independence should be recognized by Congress, would probably come in. The Middle states, Delaware, Pennsylvania, New Jersey, and Maryland had committed themselves, two unanimously, and the others by good majorities. The most Southern states, Georgia and South Carolina, had joined, the one unanimously, the other without dangerous hesitation. But between New England and the Middle

216

states, ambitious New York held out in organized resistance; and between Maryland and South Carolina lay Virginia (still including Kentucky) and North Carolina (still claiming Tennessee), both of them reaching from the Atlantic to the Mississippi, and both of them with such strong oppositions that nobody could be sure whether they would ratify or not.

The geographical situation of Virginia and New York gave their Antifederalists a strategic advantage. So long as those two barrier states refused to enter the proposed general government they could make it almost impossible for the other states to inaugurate it with any prospect of success. In New York there was a stubborn party opposed to any fundamental change in the Confederation government. The leaders of the opposition in Virginia favored a stronger union, but thought their state should propose amendments to the Constitution and insist that they be acted on by another Federal Convention. Jefferson in Paris was at first—though not later—of this opinion. He wished to see nine states ratify, so that the new government would be assured, and the remaining four hold out for what he considered indispensable amendments: a bill of rights included and the President limited to a single term of office. The Virginia Antifederalists believed that Virginia could not do without the union, but also that the union could not do without Virginia, which was then the largest of the states and had at least a fifth of the total population of the United States.

Before the Virginia convention met at Richmond on June 2, 1788, the leaders of the opposition were very active. Mason was joined by Patrick Henry, who fought the Constitution as he had formerly fought the British rule. He assured Virginians that under the Constitution an established religion would be set up. He wrote to Kentuckians that under the Constitution they would lose the right to navigate the Mississippi. Mason was intemperate. He told his constituents, it was reported, that they must not think the Constitution had been made by an assemblage of great men. The delegates from New England were "Knaves and Fools"; those from the lower South "a parcel of Coxcombs"; those from the Middle states "Office Hunters not a few." Randolph was first active, then gradually quieter.

The Federalist leaders in the convention were the venerated, crippled Edmund Pendleton, who was chosen president, George

Wythe, chairman of the committee of the whole, James Madison, Henry ("Light Horse Harry") Lee, and John Marshall. Probably no one of them was so influential as Washington, who did not attend the convention but who was known by the delegates to be powerfully in favor of the constitution and the ratification of it by Virginia.

Of all the state conventions Virginia's was the most dramatic and most fully reported, the most philosophical and wide-reaching in its debates. Its delegates ranged from the planter-statesmen of the Northern Neck to the frontiersmen who had come from Kentucky, armed with pistol and hanger against prowling Indians. Without much doubt the majority was at the outset, if only from inertia, opposed to ratification. Skillful management by the Antifederalists, aided by Henry's enormous eloquence, might have given them victory. They were less skillful than the Federalists, who had made concerted plans in advance and kept to them throughout the session.

As soon as the convention, meeting in the New Academy on Shockoe Hill, had on its third day agreed to a set of rules and resolved itself into a committee of the whole, Mason warned the delegates that "the curse denounced by the divine vengeance will be small, compared with what will justly fall upon us, if from any sinister views we obstruct the fullest inquiry"; and he urged that the whole Constitution be taken up, clause by clause, before any question should be put. Madison at once concurred. This was precisely what the Federalists had hoped for, but had not expected. It would be easier for the Antifederalists to win votes by attacking the proposed new government at large than by finding fault with parts of it which the Federalists could justify with expert reasons. Patrick Henry asked that the instructions given by the Virginia legislature to the Virginia delegates to the Federal Convention be read. President Pendleton said it was not for this house to consider whether the Convention delegates had exceeded their instructions. The Convention had reported the Constitution to Congress, Congress had transmitted it to the Virginia legislature, the Virginia legislature had called the state convention; and "the people have sent us hither to determine whether this government be a proper one or not." Henry withdrew his motion. The clerk began the reading of the Constitution, and read the Preamble and the first two sections of

Article I. George Nicholas, one of the Federalists, seized the initiative and spoke ably in defense of the system of representation in Congress which was provided.

Then Henry took the floor, "as the servant of the people of this commonwealth," he said, "as a sentinel over their rights, liberty, and happiness. . . . A year ago," he said, "the minds of our citizens were at perfect repose." Now all were "uneasy and disquieted." The republic was in extreme danger. Why? Because of this "proposal of establishing nine states into a confederacy, to the eventual exclusion of four states." He had the "highest veneration" for the men who had drafted the Constitution: "but, sir, give me leave to demand, what right had they to say, *We the people?* My political curiosity, exclusive of my anxious solicitude for the public welfare, leads me to ask, who authorized them to speak the language of *We the people,* instead of, *We the states?* States are the characteristics and the soul of a confederation. If the states be not the agents of this compact, it must be one great consolidated national government, of the people of all the states. . . . The people gave them no power to use their name. . . . You must, therefore, forgive the solicitation of one unworthy member, to know what danger could have arisen under the present confederation, and what are the causes of this proposal to change our government."

When Randolph stood up everybody expected him to give further reasons for refusing to sign the Constitution and insisting that it be returned with amendments to a second Convention. Instead he announced that he had come to believe it was too late to ask for amendments before ratification and adoption. The union would be endangered by delay. "And I will assent to the lopping of this limb (meaning his arm) before I assent to the dissolution of the union." Eight states, by ratifying the Constitution, had testified that it was suited to the genius of the American people.

Mason must have been stunned at finding himself, without notice, deserted by Randolph, the governor of the state, popular with citizens of all kinds, and certain to affect a good many votes in this convention. But without a word of reference to Randolph, Mason began with the right to lay direct taxes which was included in the clause on representation. That right, he declared, changed the confederation of states into a government "calculated to annihilate totally the state governments. . . . Is it to be supposed that one national government will suit so extensive a country, embracing so many climates, and containing inhabitants, so very different in manners, habits, and customs?" Where in history was there any record of so large a country governed without the loss of the people's liberties? No man, Mason said, was a "greater friend to a firm union of the American states" than he, but he thought the union could be secured without "hazarding the rights of the people." Taxation was fundamental. The states ought to be asked to contribute the amount required of each of them for the Federal government, and only if they refused should Congress lay a direct tax on the people.

On June 5 Pendleton replied to Henry's and Mason's arguments that the new government was a threat with the profound observation: "There is no quarrel between government and liberty; the former is the shield and protector of the latter. The war is between government and licentiousness, faction, turbulence, and other violations of the rules of society, to preserve liberty." Under the Confederation the states had been living without order or peace. The Constitution promised to bring both. If not, it had been made by the people and could be corrected by them.

Henry swung into one of his tremendous speeches, taking up most of the day. As read now, he seems often shrill, prolix, and theatrical; but as heard then he must have seemed like fire and music. He warmed every prejudice in his hearers, and chanted words that comforted them in their oldest prepossessions.

The Constitution, he said, was as "radical" as the resolution "which separated us from Great Britain. . . . The rights of conscience, trial by jury, liberty of the press, all your communities and franchises, all pretentions to human rights and privileges, are rendered insecure, if not lost, by this change. . . . Is this tame relinquishment of rights worthy of freemen? . . . It is said eight states have adopted this plan. I declare that if twelve states and a half had adopted it, I would with manly firmness, and in spite of an erring world, reject it. . . . Liberty, greatest of all earthly blessings—give us that precious jewel, and you may take every thing else! But I am fearful I have lived long enough to become an old fashioned fellow."

Well, he had years ago been thought a traitor for supporting the rights of his country, and he was willing to be thought so again in so good a cause as this. Congress, under this Constitution, would have more than a tyrant's powers. It could lay what taxes it chose. With a standing army it could keep the people in submission. The President, if he should be ruthless and able, could make himself absolute. "I would rather infinitely, and I am sure most of this convention are of the same opinion, have a king, lords, and commons, than a government so replete with such insupportable evils." The thought of the President sent Henry off into a torrent with which the reporter could not keep up, and he reduced it to a note: "Here Mr HENRY strongly and pathetically expatiated on the probability of the president's enslaving America, and the horrid consequences that must result." And so on for pages in the record, with the threatening conclusion: "I have, I fear, fatigued the committee, yet I have not said the one hundred thousandth part of what I have on my mind, and wish to impart."

On the 6th Madison made his first extended speech in the convention. After the stately, elegant Randolph and the orchestra-voiced Henry who looked like an eagle in an ill-fitting wig, Madison was so small he could hardly be seen by the spectators, and his voice so low he could hardly be heard. He stood there with his hat in his hand and his notes in his hat, beginning with words which the reporter could not catch. When Madison became audible he was saying: "I shall not attempt to make impressions by any ardent professions of zeal for the public welfare; we know the principles of every man will, and ought to be judged, not by his professions and declarations, but by his conduct." So "we ought to examine the constitution on its merits solely: we are to inquire whether it will promote the public happiness."

Henry had said the Constitution endangered the public liberty in many instances, but he had not pointed out clearly what these were. Madison called attention to the inconsistencies in Henry's arguments, to the inaccuracies in his historical examples, to the looseness in his political reasoning. Some of the objections to the form of government now proposed had arisen because it was misunderstood. "It is of a mixed nature; it is in a manner unprecedented; we cannot find one express example in the ex-

perience of the world." Let the delegates therefore consider the
Constitution with open minds and not measure it by outmoded
standards. With perfect clarity Madison disposed of most of the
objections which Henry had raised, so far as they could be
disposed of "by a calm and rational investigation."

On Saturday the 7th Francis Corbin, who was only twenty-
eight, brilliantly answered some of Henry's objections. Randolph
and Madison continued at the request of Henry, who did not want
to follow the attractive and effective young man, but gave as
his reason that he wished further information. Then, with un-
changed opinions and untired rhetoric, Henry resumed his attack
in a speech which kept up to the end of the session in order
that he might have the floor when the session opened on Monday, when he spoke more than half the day.

This was the pattern of the convention. Of the six hundred
printed pages of the record, Henry's speeches make up nearly a
fifth. His principal allies were Mason and William Grayson, recently member of Congress from Virginia, with some help from
James Monroe, who also had served in Congress. Henry's most
effective antagonists were Madison, Randolph, George Nicholas,
Henry Lee, and (later in the session) John Marshall, the young
Richmond lawyer who was to be Chief Justice of the Supreme
Court and next to Madison, of all those present in the convention, was to have the largest influence on the subsequent fortunes
of the Constitution. Many of the speakers were much of the time
out of order. The Antifederalists would not confine themselves to
a particular clause under consideration, but ran over into general arguments against the Constitution. Their opponents were
obliged to answer them at the time or else lose the chance to
reply while the objections were before the house.

Now and then, though infrequently, the debaters came to personalities. Henry on June 7 bore hard on Randolph for his
apostasy. "That honorable member will not accuse me of want
of candor," Henry said, "when I cast in my mind what he has
given to the public"—in Randolph's letter to the Virginia legislature explaining why he had not signed the Constitution—"and
compare it to what has happened since. It seems to me very
strange and unaccountable, that that which was the object of
his execration, should now receive his encomiums. Something
extraordinary must have operated so great a change in his

opinions." Randolph controlled his anger at this insinuation till the 9th, when he blazed up. "I disdain his aspersions, and his insinuations," Randolph told the convention. "His asperity is warranted by no principle of parliamentary decency, nor compatible with the least shadow of friendship: and if our friendship must fall—*let it fall, like Lucifer, never to rise again.*" Henry declared that he had no "personal intention of offending any one —that he did his duty." There was a passage of sharp words between them, after which Randolph read part of another letter, to his constituents, threw the letter on the clerk's table, and announced that it might lie there "for the *inspection of the curious and malicious.*"

Henry had hinted that Randolph was an apostate for some hidden (and therefore perhaps discreditable) reason. Randolph had replied that Henry was discourteous and malicious. According to the sensitive code of the day, here were words that must be answered with deeds. Henry's second called on Randolph that night, and there was tension in Richmond over the possibility of a duel between the present governor and a former governor of the proud state. But matters were somehow adjusted, and the two remained merely debaters.

The Antifederalists, in the midst of their discussions of relevant constitutional issues, often repeated the most commonplace sensational arguments against the Constitution. There was for instance that bogey, the district which was to be the seat of the federal government. "This ten miles square," Mason said on June 14, "may set at defiance the laws of the surrounding states, and may, like the custom of the superstitious days of our ancestors, become the sanctuary of the blackest crimes. . . . Now, sir, if an attempt should be made to establish tyranny over the people, here are ten miles square where the greatest offender may meet protection. If any of their officers, or creatures, should attempt to oppress the people, or should actually perpetrate the blackest deed, he has nothing to do, but get into the ten miles square." Grayson, agreeing with Mason as to the danger of sanctuary, added that the citizens of the federal district would have every interest to "aggrandize themselves by every possible means in their power, to the great injury of the other states. If we travel all over the world, we will find that people have aggrandized their own capitals. Look at Russia and Prussia."

Henry was even more alarming. "Will not this clause give them"—Congress and the President—"a right to keep a powerful army continually on foot, if they think it necessary to aid in the execution of their laws? Is there any act, however atrocious, which they cannot do by virtue of this clause? Look at the use which has been made in all parts of the world of that human thing called power. Look at the predominant thirst of dominion which has invariably and uniformly prompted rulers to abuse their power." And then Henry was off on the subject of power in general. "I conjure you once more to remember the admonition of that sage man who told you that when you give power, you know not what you give. . . . I have reason to suspect ambitious grasps at power. The experience of the world teaches me the jeopardy of giving enormous power."

Henry seemed regularly to regard the projected general government as something foreign to Virginia, and indeed to all the states. It did no good for Madison and Marshall to point out that Congress and the President and the Supreme Court would be Americans elected by Americans. Still Henry declaimed against a new, inhuman force which would destroy the liberties of the people. Congress, under the influence of the Northern states, would in effect conspire with Spain to give up the navigation of the Mississippi, and so damage the Southern states and the future states to the west of them. On June 13 Madison admitted that under the Confederation seven states, for the sake of an advantageous treaty with Spain, had consented to Spanish control of navigation on the Mississippi for a term of twenty-five years; but this had not yet gone into effect, and he argued that it was much less likely under a strong new government than under the weak old one. Henry, in one of the most magnificent of his speeches, aimed at the Kentucky delegates, spoke of the mighty West that might be "the strength, the pride, the flower of the Confederacy," if the Mississippi were kept open for American trade; then of the wilderness the West must become if the Mississippi under the Constitution should be "controlled by those who had no interest in its welfare." Nothing could offset his eloquence, and in the end ten of the fourteen Kentuckians voted against ratification.

On the 20th Henry, following Mason on the same subject, dealt with the threat to Virginia and the individual states from the proposed Federal judiciary. "The purse is gone; the sword is gone," he said, as so many had said in so many conventions. And now the scales of justice were in danger. The state courts were to be at the mercy of the federal courts. Citizens of the states were to be at the mercy of an alien jurisdiction. John Marshall replied with a masterful exposition of the proposed judiciary, which he insisted was no more likely to be unjust in its operations than that of Virginia, which it much resembled. But Henry on the 21st, while paying compliments to Marshall, whom he admired, was sure that the Constitution, still only on paper, could not be trusted. "It will be an empire of men and not of laws. Your rights and liberties rest upon men. Their wisdom and integrity may preserve you—but on the contrary, should they prove ambitious, and designing, may they not flourish and triumph upon the ruins of their country?" Henry implied they might and would. And again he was eloquent about the threat of the Constitution to the immemorial right of trial by jury.

No doubt many of the members of the convention followed the constitutional arguments with difficulty. It is as hard for an untrained person to read a printed constitution and visualize its workings as to read a musical score and hear the complex sounds indicated by the notes on the page. No wonder Henry was, of all the debaters, the most popular with the members, and with the spectators who crowded the New Academy whenever he spoke. His arguments were as exciting as a play. And, like a play, they moved the emotions of the hearers. Virginia, the mother of the states and of American liberties, must not be lost in a general government with its head elsewhere. The agricultural South must not be put at a disadvantage with the commercial North. The West must not be sacrificed to interests of the East. And there was the matter of the heavy debts still owed by Virginia planters to British creditors. A general government might demand that these be paid, and might make treaties which Virginia, and any state, would have to accept and act upon. Should Virginia impoverish herself to benefit the union? Or, as Grayson put it on the 24th: "Is it right for a rich nation to consolidate with a poor one? . . . In all nations where a rich state is joined with a poor one, it will be found that the rich one will pay in that disproportion. . . . I can see what she [Virginia] gives up, which is immense. The little states gain in proportion as we lose."

As to slavery, Mason stood in Richmond where he had stood in Philadelphia. "The augmentation of slaves," he said on the 18th, "weakens the states; and such a trade is diabolical in itself, and disgraceful to mankind. Yet, by this constitution, it is continued for twenty years. As much as I value an union of all the states, I would not admit the Southern states"—South Carolina and Georgia—"into the union, unless they agree to the discontinuance of this disgraceful trade. . . . And though this infamous traffic be continued, we have no security for the property of this kind which we have already." The Constitution, that is, now tolerated slavery and yet might abolish it later to the ruin of slaveholders. Madison replied that South Carolina and Georgia would not have entered the union without the "temporary permission of that trade," and that it had seemed better to win them by the concession than to do without them. If the importation of slaves had been prohibited, those states would have had to buy slaves in Virginia, at a higher price. "I need not expatiate on this subject."

Henry on the 24th thundered on both sides of the issue. Congress under the Constitution might decree *"That every black man must fight"* in its standing army. Or Congress might free all the slaves. "In this situation, I see a great deal of the property of the people of Virginia, in jeopardy, and their peace and tranquillity gone.—I repeat it again, that it would rejoice my very soul that everyone of my fellow beings was emancipated. As we ought with gratitude to admire that decree of heaven which has numbered us among the free, we ought to lament and deplore the necessity of holding our fellow men in bondage. But is it practicable by any human means to liberate them, without producing the most dreadful and ruinous consequences? We ought to possess them, in the manner we inherited them from our ancestors, as their manumission is incompatible with the felicity of our country. But we ought to soften, as much as possible, the rigor of their unhappy fate. . . . This is a local matter and I can see no propriety in subjecting it to congress."

The convention was more than the debates on the floor. Before and after the sessions there was continuous lobbying. Both sides courted the Kentuckians, who might have the balance of power. Every night the managers of both sides tried to tabulate the prospective votes. Robert and Gouverneur Morris from Philadelphia were in Richmond, on business of their own but busy also with the Virginia Federalists. Eleazer Oswald, printer of the intensely Antifederalist *Independent Gazetteer* of Philadelphia, came to Richmond and secretly conferred with Henry, Mason, and others of their party. Madison was in close correspondence with Hamilton in New York, as rapidly as express riders could carry their letters back and forth. There were other communications between the Antifederalists of New York and Virginia.

Most important of all was a letter from George Clinton, governor of New York, to Governor Randolph of Virginia. In that letter Clinton informed his fellow governor, supposed by Clinton to be opposed to ratification, that the New York convention, called for June 17, would cordially "hold a communication with any sister State on the important subject" of a second Federal Convention, and especially with any state "so respectable in point of importance, ability, and patriotism as Virginia." Clinton went as far as he could go, in diplomatic language, toward saying that if Virginia would hold out against ratifying the Constitution without previous amendments, so would New York. If the Virginia Antifederalists had known of this offer, they might have been able to win enough votes to ratify only on condition that their amendments be incorporated in the Constitution. But Randolph deliberately suppressed the letter till the 25th. Then he delivered it to the Virginia legislature, where it was not read because all the members had gone to the convention to hear the final debate on ratification, voted that day.

On June 23 the convention completed the reading of the Constitution clause by clause. Mason's closing words were bitter prophecy. "He dreaded popular resistance" to the proposed government, so "vague, indefinite, and ambiguous" in its assurances of liberty, and otherwise so defective. "He expressed, in emphatic terms, the *dreadful effects* which must ensue, should the people resist"; and warned the convention against voting hastily at the risk of rousing the people to rebellion. Henry Lee had never believed that he could live to hear from "the honorable gentleman . . . opinions so injurious to our country, and so opposite to the dignity of this assembly. If the dreadful picture which he has drawn, be so abhorrent to his mind as he has declared, let me ask the honorable gentleman if he has not pursued the very means to bring into action the horrors which he deprecates? Such speeches within these walls, from a character so venerable and estimable, easily progress into overt acts, among the less thinking and the vicious. Then, Sir, I pray you to remember, and the gentlemen in opposition not to forget, that should these impious scenes commence, which my honorable friend might abhor, and which I execrate, whence and how they began."

In this temper the convention on the 24th moved toward its decision. The Federalists held that Virginia should ratify the Constitution but should propose amendments to be considered afterwards in the manner which the Constitution provided. The Antifederalists demanded that Virginia propose amendments to be agreed on by the states before its ratification could go into effect. If the Constitution was defective, why should it be ratified and then patched up later, if at all? "Do you enter into a compact first," Henry asked, "and afterwards settle the terms of the government?" The opposition, who could not yet know that New Hampshire had ratified three days before, believed that Virginia was the ninth state. This put Virginia in the strongest possible position. It was to their interest to insist on making the Constitution more satisfactory, and it was their duty to support the other states which were unsatisfied.

Madison set forth with shining cogency the argument against delay. The American states had stirred the admiration of the world, he said, by setting up their free governments under the pressure of war. How much more would they win admiration, and astonishment, if they should be able, "peaceably, freely, and satisfactorily, to establish one general government, when there is such a diversity of opinions, and interests, when not cemented or stimulated by any common danger?" But it was still uncertain that they were able to do that. Suppose nine states ratified it, without Virginia, and then Virginia asked them all to acknowledge that they had been wrong. Suppose only eight states should ratify, and Virginia refused to make the ninth except on her own terms. Then, even if the others agreed to her terms, which was doubtful, every state must call new conventions to consider the amendments. Here there would be endless disagreements; and there would be still more when the states came together again in a general convention. Every state would be encouraged to offer its own amendments. The difficulty of agreement would be greater than it had been in Philadelphia. If Virginia held out, the United States might never have a government. If Virginia consented, it might bring about "one of the most fortunate events that ever happened for human nature."

Henry was a tempest all that day. He introduced a long series of amendments which if put into effect would have deprived Congress of important powers and would have reduced the Supreme Court to the narrowest jurisdiction. And these must be "previous" not "subsequent" amendments. "I conceive it my duty," he said, "if this government is adopted before it is amended, to go home." Later, in reply to Randolph, Henry said he had not meant he would leave the convention without voting: only that, if the convention voted for subsequent amendments, then he would have no further hand in them. But he spoke at greater length in reply to Madison.

"He tells you," Henry said, "of important blessings which he imagines will result to us and mankind in general, from the adoption of this system. I see the awful immensity of the dangers with which it is pregnant. I see it. I feel it. I see beings of a higher order anxious concerning our decision. When I see beyond the horizon that binds human eyes, and look at the final consummation of all human things, and see those intelligent beings which inhabit the ætherial mansions, reviewing the political decisions and revolutions which in the progress of time will happen in America, and the consequent happiness or misery of mankind, I am led to believe that much of the account of one side or the other will depend on what we now decide. Our own happiness alone is not affected by the event. All nations are interested in the determination. We have it in our power to secure the happiness of one half of the human race. Its adoption may involve the misery of the other hemispheres."

While Henry spoke, a storm had been gathering over Richmond. And now suddenly, as if those beings in their ætherial mansions were perturbed by the doings in the New Academy, darkness closed in, with fierce lightning and roaring thunder. These things, according to the record, "put the house in such disorder, that Mr. Henry was obliged to conclude." Nature itself seemed to confirm and assist the orator.

On the 25th the Federalists pushed for the vote. The speeches in favor of ratification were better planned and better than those opposed to it. Although nobody could be sure what the vote would be, Henry may have believed it would be against him. "If I shall be in the minority," he said, "I shall have those painful sensations, which arise from a conviction of *being overpowered in a good cause*. Yet I will be a peaceful citizen! My head, my hand, and my heart shall be at liberty to retrieve the loss of liberty, and remove the defects of that system, in a constitutional way. I wish not to go to violence, but will wait with hopes that the spirit which predominated in the revolution, is not yet gone, nor the cause of those who are attached to the revolution yet lost. I shall therefore patiently wait in expectation of seeing that government changed, so as to be compatible with the safety, liberty, and happiness of the people."

By 88 to 80 the convention voted against referring previous amendments to the other states for their consideration. By a vote of 89 to 79 it voted to ratify the Constitution; but, "in order to relieve the apprehensions of those who may be solicitous for amendments," also to recommend amendments to Congress to be acted upon "according to the mode prescribed" in the Constitution. On the 26th an engrossed form of the ratification was read and signed by Pendleton, as president, in behalf of the convention. On the 27th another engrossed copy was signed for the archives of the Virginia legislature, and the twenty formidable amendments and the bill of rights reported by a committee were accepted by the convention in an affirmative vote which was not counted. Not till the next day, at the earliest, did Richmond learn that New Hampshire and not Virginia had been the ninth state to ratify.

The news of the Virginia ratification reached Alexandria the evening of the 27th, and before morning came the news from New Hampshire. The citizens of Alexandria, Washington wrote to General Pinckney, "constituted the first public company in America, which had the pleasure of pouring a libation to the prosperity of the ten States that had actually adopted the general government." He attended the celebration on the 28th, and recollected that it was the anniversary of the battles of Sullivan's island in South Carolina and of Monmouth in New Jersey.

II

The opposition was better organized in New York than in any other state. George Clinton, who had been governor for eleven years, and who had his state almost in his pocket, had the strongest personal interest in keeping New York as distinct as possible within the Confederation. He had the support of the "peculiar aristocracy," the lords of the manors lying northward along the Hudson, who naturally liked to see the public expenses paid rather out of import duties, collected by New York, than out of taxes on land. The British occupation of New York City and the adjacent islands during the Revolution had forced the state to carry on its government at various towns inland, and the counties above Westchester had had much political experience. Clinton himself lived in Ulster County. John Lansing and Robert Yates, delegates from New York to the Federal Convention, both lived in Albany. As soon as they left Philadelphia, in July 1787, they disregarded the rule of secrecy and informed Clinton that the Convention was exceeding its instructions; and they gave it as their own opinion that "a general government, however guarded by declarations of rights, or cautionary provisions, must unavoidably, in a short time, be productive of the destruction of the civil liberty of such citizens as could be effectually coerced by it." Clinton, already wary, became more emphatic. He began what was called "a campaign of education" against the Convention and the Constitution which went on with accumulating vigor until the state convention met the next year on June 17 at the court house in Poughkeepsie. Two-thirds of the members were Antifederalists, from all the up-state counties north of Westchester, and some members from the lower counties on the New York islands.

The contest in the campaign of education was managed on one side by Clinton, on the other by Alexander Hamilton. Hamilton and John Jay (with the help of Madison) produced *The Federalist,* but it was too learned and reasonable to catch votes in the hustings. Interested local politicians did that better. But though the Antifederalists had a majority in the convention, they could not simply reject the Constitution. As Hamilton wrote to Madison on June 8, the Antifederalist leaders were afraid that outright rejection would "bring matters to a crisis" between New York and the states which had ratified. Moreover, the Federalist southern counties might try to break away from the northern and join the union. Consequently the New York Anti-federalists, Hamilton said, preferred "a long adjournment as the safest and most artful course to effect their final purpose." Once the new government got under way, there were bound to be complaints from particular states. "If any considerable discontent should show itself, they will stand ready to head the opposition. If, on the contrary, the thing should go on smoothly, and the sentiments of our own people should change, they can elect to come into the Union. They at all events take the chances of time and the chapter of accidents."

The chance of time and accidents, it turned out, was against them. When Clinton took the chair of the convention on June 17 he and his followers knew that the New Hampshire and Virginia convention were debating the Constitution, but there was no knowing what they would do, or how soon they would do it. New Hampshire had adjourned once before. The opposition in Virginia, Poughkeepsie kept hearing, was energetic and resolute. Either state might reject the Constitution, or accept it on conditional terms that would amount to a demand for amendments. In that case, New York could be the ninth state or not as it chose. But if one or two of the others should ratify, then New York would be the tenth or the eleventh: in a weak strategic position no matter what it chose to do.

On June 24 the news of New Hampshire's ratification came; on July 2, the news of Virginia's. The first of these communications had little effect, but the second had so much that the later procrastinating days were a scramble of debates of which there is almost no record.

Only a few of the debaters distinguished themselves. Robert R. Livingston, chancellor of the State Supreme Court, was witty and intelligent. In his opening speech, on the 19th, he said plainly what everybody knew: that if New York did not join the union, it would be hard put to defend itself. Its ports were on islands, close to New Jersey and Connecticut, which, "in case of a disunion, must be considered as independent, and perhaps unfriendly powers." To the northeast was Vermont, inhabited by "a brave and hardy body of men" with whom New York had been at war before and might be again. To the northwest were the British posts, still held by strong forces, and hostile Indians. "He shewed, that in case of domestic war, Hudson river, that great source of our wealth, would also be that of our weakness; by the intersection of the state, and the difficulty we should find in bringing one part to support the other." The Confederation was said to be "thirteen distinct governments, and yet they are not thirteen governments, but one government," he remarked on July 1. "It requires the ingenuity of St. Athanasius to understand this political mystery." What was needed was a federal government such as the Constitution offered, in which the central government should be supreme over central affairs, and the local governments supreme over local. This was no mystery, but good sense.

Neither Clinton for the Antifederalists nor Jay for the Federalists spoke often. The convention was largely a debate, now and then interrupted by various speakers, between Hamilton from New York County and Melancton Smith, a self-taught and well-taught merchant and lawyer who had lately lived in New York City but had been elected from Dutchess County, where he had large estates. Smith thought a confederated government better than a consolidated. While he was in favor of a union of the states, and agreed that the central government ought to operate upon individuals rather than upon states, still he thought it ought to operate upon individuals only "to a certain degree." The state legislatures had been placed by the Articles of Confederation between Congress and the people to protect the people. "We were then, it is true, too cautious," Smith admitted on June 21; "and too much restricted the powers of the central government. But now it is proposed to go into the contrary, and a more dangerous extreme; to remove all barriers to give the new government free access to our pockets, and ample command of our persons, and that without providing for a genuine and fair representation of the people." Once started on this course, there was no telling how far the process might go.

If the people were properly represented in Congress, as Smith thought they were in the state legislatures, the central government would be too expensive and the officials probably become corrupt. He thought it fantastic to talk about providing so costly a thing as a navy. That must come later, if ever. "It was our duty to calculate for the present period," he said on July 1, "and not attempt to provide for the contingencies of two or three centuries to come. . . . In three or four hundred years" the population of America "might amount to a hundred million"; but by that time "two or three great empires might be established, totally different from our own."

James Kent, of the famous *Commentaries*, was then a young lawyer in Poughkeepsie, and he attended all the debates in the convention. Smith, Kent later said, was "the most prominent and responsible speaker on the part of the anti-federalist majority. There was no person on that side to be compared to him in acute and logical discussion. He was Hamilton's most persevering and formidable antagonist. But even Smith was routed in every contest." Hamilton's experience in the Federal Convention and in the writing of *The Federalist* had filled his mind with "the principles and history of federal governments, and with every topic of debate. He was prompt, ardent, energetic, and overflowing with an exhaustless store of argument and illustration." In the end, after the news of Virginia's ratification, Smith was won over to Hamilton's side.

Hamilton kept as a rule close to strict constitutional arguments. On June 28, which was Saturday, Lansing accused Hamilton of having urged, in the Federal Convention, that the states ought to be "subverted" in the interest of the general government. Hamilton denied this. "This produced a warm personal altercation between those gentlemen, which engrossed the remainder of the day." On Monday the "personal dispute" was again brought forward, and took up a "considerable part of this day." But Hamilton made no replies to the usual trifling objections raised by timid men who saw in the Constitution a monster threat to their peace and liberty. With brilliant precision he analyzed the defects of the Confederation, explained the advantages of the proposed new government, defended the powers of Congress and particularly the Senate, and insisted that the states still had all the rights they could need in the union. The New York convention was a triumph for Hamilton as no other state convention was for any other man.

The last two weeks of wrangling, barely recorded debate was about the form of ratification. Finally on Smith's motion, modified by others, the Convention on July 26 voted to ratify, "in full confidence" that until a second Federal Convention should be called for "proposing amendments" certain specified state rights claimed by New York should not be interfered with. The vote was 30 to 27. It would not have been carried at all but for the "in full confidence" which in the minds of the Antifederalists was virtually the equivalent of "upon condition." The convention voted unanimously to issue a circular letter, to be sent by Governor Clinton to the governors of all the other states, recommending that a second Federal Convention be called to consider the amendments that had been proposed by the various state conventions.

To punish Hamilton for his share in this narrow Federalist victory, the New York legislature refused to elect him to Congress that winter to serve while the new government was put in operation. But he became Secretary of the Treasury in Washington's first administration. John Jay was the first Chief Justice of the Supreme Court. Clinton, sturdily Antifederalist, served as Vice-President under both Jefferson and Madison, now called Republicans. In the long run New York has without much doubt profited more than any other state from the adoption of the Constitution.

III

Washington and many Virginians believed that the action of their state on the Constitution would be followed by North Carolina. It was not. The North Carolina convention, which met in a church at Hillsboro on July 21, 1788, was from the first irresistibly Antifederalist. On August 2 it voted 184 to 84 neither to ratify nor to reject till a second Federal Convention should have considered the declaration of rights and amendments proposed by North Carolina. This was of course a rejection, and meant that for the time being the state would rather be out of the union than in it.

The Constitution was supported in the convention by Governor Samuel Johnston, two of the delegates—William Richardson Davie and Richard Dobbs Spaight—to the Federal Convention, and James Iredell, an Edenton lawyer, later Associate Justice of the United States Supreme Court, who was the ablest leader of the state's Federalists. The chief spokesman for the Antifederalists was Willie Jones, born in North Carolina but educated in England at Eton. He had refused to serve as delegate to the Federal Convention and now took his stand with the people, who thought their rights were in danger from the new government.

The debates on constitutional points tell less about the spirit of the convention than some of the speeches of the unlearned members of the opposition. William Goudy on July 23 wondered that "these gentlemen learned in the law should quibble upon words. I care not whether it [the Constitution] be called a compact, agreement, covenant, bargain or what. Its intent is a concession of power on the part of the people to their rulers. We know that private interest governs mankind generally. Power belongs originally to the people, but if rulers be not well guarded, that power may be usurped from them. People ought to be cautious about giving away power. . . . If we give away more power than we ought, we put ourselves in the situation of a man who puts on an iron glove, which he can never take off till he breaks his arm. Let us beware of the iron glove of tyranny." And again on the 26th: "I am not able to follow these learned gentlemen through all the labyrinths of their oratory.—Some represent us as rich and not honest; and others again represent us as honest and not rich. We have no gold or silver, no substantial money to pay taxes with." To give Congress the power to lay and collect taxes would, Goudy thought, "totally destroy our liberties." The Constitution asked the people to give up their power over both purse and sword. "There is no danger we are told. It may be so, but I am jealous and suspicious of the liberties of mankind. . . . Suspicions in small communities, are a pest to mankind; but in a matter of this magnitude, which concerns the interest of millions yet unborn, suspicion is a very noble virtue. . . . It is said that those who formed this constitution were great and good men. We do not dispute it. We also admit that great and learned people have adopted it. But I have a judgment of my own, and though not so well informed always as others, yet I will exert it when manifest danger presents itself."

The words of Goudy expressed the opinions of the majority. North Carolina, including the counties in Tennessee, was a large state with a population widely dispersed, often in isolated communities. Most of its people were farmers or frontiersmen who had to depend on their own resources to live, and who consequently lived as individuals, self-sufficiently. They suspected their state government, which was for the most part in the hands of men living close to the Atlantic. All the more they suspected the proposed federal government, which seemed vast, remote, and not likely to be attentive to the people's interests. The arguments against the Constitution which had run through the state before the convention were often fantastic, mere political folklore. The federal district which was to be the seat of the government would be an armed stronghold. The Pope of Rome might be elected President of the United States. The absence of any religious test would encourage the immigration to America of Jews, Pagans, Mahometans, any one of whom might hold office. Many of the delegates to the state convention were Presbyterians from the north of Ireland (or from Ireland by way of Virginia) and fiercely Protestant. The Baptists in North Carolina, as in Virginia, were generally Antifederalist. At least one of the members of the convention at Hillsboro could not write his name, and there may have been others. All these circumstances combined to make the North Carolina majority, in the state and in the convention, instinctively averse to any general government, and certainly to this one offered for a quicker decision than they could give without more knowledge and reflection.

Willie Jones thought North Carolina should remain out of the union for several years, till it could enter more nearly on its own terms. But after the new government of the United States was set up, with North Carolina regarded—though not altogether treated —as a foreign state like any other, there was a prompt change in North Carolina opinion. A second convention met at Fayetteville on November 19, 1789, and on the 21st ratified the Constitution by a vote of 194 to 77.

Rhode Island, where the conflict between the townspeople and the "country party," particularly over paper money, had been so intense that the state could not agree to send delegates to the Federal Convention, held out in resentful isolation. But in 1790, after the Senate had passed a bill severing commercial relations between the United States and Rhode Island, a state convention voted on May 29, by a stubborn vote of 34 to 32, to ratify the Constitution and enter the United States. Washington, in a letter to Governor Arthur Fenner of Rhode Island on June 4, handsomely closed the long account. "Since the bond of union is now complete, and we once more consider ourselves as one family, it is much to be hoped that reproaches will cease and prejudice be done away; for we should all remember that we are members of that community upon whose general success depends our particular and individual welfare; and, therefore, if we mean to support the Liberty and Independence which it has cost us so much blood and treasure to establish, we must drive far away the dæmon of party spirit and local reproach."

While North Carolina and Rhode Island had delayed, the other states had not. As soon as news of the ratifications by New Hampshire and Virginia reached Congress, it proceeded to make arrangements for putting the Constitution into effect. On August 6, 1788, Congress agreed that the first Wednesday of the following January should be the day for choosing the electors in several states, the first Wednesday in February for the electors to assemble and vote for the President, and the first Wednesday in March for the first proceedings of the new government. Washington was inaugurated President on April 30. In the first session of the new Congress the first ten amendments to the Constitution,[1] known as the Bill of Rights, were proposed by Congress to the states. After ratification in the manner provided for they became effective on December 15, 1791. Since among them they protect virtually all the rights which had been urged by the various state conventions, they may be regarded as the contribution of the people through those conventions to the Constitution.

---

[1] See Appendix 12, 13.

13

THE FEDERAL PROCESSION

"It is a flattering and consolatory reflection, that our rising Republics have the good wishes of all the Philosophers, Patriots, and virtuous men in all nations: and that they look upon them as a kind of Asylum for mankind. God grant that we may not disappoint their honest expectations, by our folly or perverseness." *George Washington to the Marquis de Chastellux, April 25-May 1, 1788.*

"God grant, that not only the Love of Liberty, but a thorough Knowledge of the Rights of Man, may pervade all the Nations of the Earth, so that a Philosopher may set his Foot anywhere on its Surface, and say, 'This is my Country.'" *Benjamin Franklin to David Hartley, December 4, 1789.*

AS THE number of ratifications, from December 1787 to July 1788, increased, so did the size and variety of the Federal Processions which celebrated the progress of the Constitution. On the afternoon of December 12, the day Pennsylvania ratified, a party of sailors and ship carpenters mounted a boat on a wagon drawn by five horses and conducted it through the Philadelphia streets, pretending to take soundings as they went. They would throw out a line, and shout: "Three and twenty fathom—foul bottom"; or "Six and forty fathom—sound bottom, safe anchorage." All the spectators knew that the minority against ratification had been 23, the majority 46. The *Gazetteer* reported that "many thousand" of Philadelphians were amused. An Antifederalist writing to the *Packet* declared that though the sailors did all they could to attract attention—"huzzaed at the corners, had the sweet music of a fiddle, etc."—they interested nobody but the children who tagged after them.

Boston, whether taking a hint from Philadelphia or hitting on the same idea independently, had a ship called the *Federal Constitution*, mounted on runners and drawn through the snow-covered streets by thirteen horses on February 8, after Massachusetts had ratified. In Boston besides sailors and ship carpenters

239

there were men of many other trades marching—four or five thousand, the *Massachusetts Centinel* estimated, praising the "perfect order and urbanity, the dignity and solemnity" of the occasion. Some Philadelphia Antifederalist sneered in a quatrain, later reprinted by the *Centinel,* about the "GRAND procession" of the "Boston folks."

> "There they went up, up, up
> And there they went down, down, downy,
> There they went backwards and forwards
> And poop for Boston towny!"

In Charleston, on May 27, the allegorical ship of state was the *Federalist,* drawn by eight white horses, each bearing on his forehead the name of a state that had ratified. The *Union* in Philadelphia on July 4 was a barge which had been captured with the *Serapis* by John Paul Jones in the *Bon Homme Richard.* Decked and built up to look like a fighting ship of twenty guns, the *Union* had a crew of twenty-five, including officers and four small midshipmen in uniform. One of these was John Rush, Benjamin Rush's eleven-year-old son, who could proudly show his commission gravely signed by William Jackson, secretary of the Federal Convention and now secretary of the Federal Procession. "Sir," the commission read, "This is to request you to repair on board the federal Ship the Union commanded by John Green Esquire in the character of Midshipman, the duties of which station you are faithfully and diligently to perform. For which This shall be your sufficient warrant."[1]

But the unmistakable masterpiece of all these Procession ships was the *Hamilton* in New York City on July 23, three days before the state ratified the Constitution. The *Hamilton* was a "Frigate of thirty-two guns, twenty-seven feet keel, and ten feet beam, with galleries and every thing complete and in proportion, both in hull and rigging; manned with upwards of thirty seamen and marines, in their different uniforms; Commanded by Commodore [James] Nicholson, and drawn by ten horses."

Shipshape in the Fields (now City Hall Park) at ten o'clock the *Hamilton* fired thirteen guns "as a signal for marching," the *New York Packet* told the story. "She then got under way, with her top-sails a-trip, and courses in the brails, proceeding in the

---

[1] Rush Papers, Library Company of Philadelphia.

centre of the procession. When abreast of Beaver-street, she made the proper signal for a pilot, by hoisting a jack at the fore top mast head, and firing a gun. The pilot-boat appearing upon her weather quarter, the frigate threw her main top-sail to the mast; the boat hailed, and asked the necessary questions; the hail was, From whence came ye? Answered by Capt. [Luke] Matthewman, From the old Constitution. Where bound? To the new Constitution. Will you have a pilot? Ay. I'll board you at the starboard bow. The pilot was received aboard, and the boat dismissed. The frigate then filled and moved abreast of the fort [the old Fort George at Bowling Green], where the crew discovered the President and Members of Congress. She immediately brought to, and fired a salute of 13 guns, which was followed by 3 cheers, and politely answered by the gentlemen of Congress.

"The procession then moved; when the ship came opposite to Mr. Constable's, the crew discovered at the window Mrs. Edgar, who had generously honored the ship with the present of a suit of silk colors; immediately they manned ship and gave three cheers. When she arrived abreast of the old Slip, she was saluted by 13 guns from his Most Catholic Majesty's Packet, then in the harbour, which was politely returned. She then made sail and proceeded through Queen-street [now a part of Pearl Street] to the Fields, when squalls came on, and the wind ahead, she beat to windward by short tacks, in which the pilot displayed his skill in navigation, heaving the lead, getting ready for stays, putting the helm a-lee, by bracing and counter-bracing the yards, &c.

"In the Fields, she had to descend several hills, in rising which she afforded a delightful prospect to the spectators, her top-sails appearing first, and then her hull, in imitation of a ship at sea; exhibiting an appearance beyond description splendid and majestic. When she arrived at her station abreast of the dining tables, she clued up her top-sails and came to, in close order with the rest of the procession, the officers going ashore to dine.

"At four o'clock she gave the signal for marching, by a discharge of 13 guns, when the procession moved by the lower road. The manner in which the ship made her passage through the narrow parts of the road, was highly interesting and satisfactory, being obliged to run under her fore-top-sail, in a squall, and keep in the line of procession; this was accomplished with great hazard, by the good conduct of the commander and the assiduity of the seamen and pilot; she arrived at her moorings abreast of the Bowling-green at half after five, amidst the acclamations of thousands; and the different orders in procession, as soon as they were dismissed, honored her with three cheers, as a mark of appreciation for the good conduct of the Commodore and his crew."

The New York Federal Procession had a touch of Paris in it, as well as of New York, for the whole spectacle had been designed by Major Pierre-Charles L'Enfant, the dashing young French engineer who had served as a volunteer at his own expense in the Continental Army and was later to design the Federal City of Washington. No Boston or Philadelphia designer on that day would have encouraged the Tailors to march, as the New York Tailors did, under a "flag, 10 by 11 feet, field sky blue, a fine landscape—Adam and Eve represented naked, excepting fig leaves for aprons, nearly in full stature, in a sitting posture—motto, 'And they sewed fig leaves together.'" There was the Chair of State sitting on the four-wheeled carriage manned by the Upholsterers. The Chair was "seven feet high and four wide, exclusive of decorations, covered with rich light blue satin; down the back on each side hung a piece of drapery, drawn in festoons, a valance at the bottom, in festoons; a rich white fringe with Circassian tassels decorated the drapery." And the Brewers had a cask containing three hundred gallons of ale loaded on a dray, and on top of the cask a tun of wine, and standing on the tun a "living Bacchus—a very handsome boy, of 8 years old, dressed in flesh colored silk, sewed tight round from his chin to his toes—a cap ornamented with hop vines and barley—a silver goblet in his hand, drinking and huzzaing the whole day with the greatest cheerfulness."

II

New York, while gayer than Philadelphia in its Federal Procession, was not less patriotic; and Philadelphia, without the benefit of Major L'Enfant's flair for public spectacles, combined its Federal Procession with a Fourth of July celebration in a spectacle never equaled in the United States before, and seldom since.

Sunrise was greeted that morning with a full peal of bells from the Christ Church steeple and the discharge of cannon from the armed ship *Rising Sun* anchored in the Delaware off Market Street. Ten peaceful vessels lay in the harbor with broad white flags at the masthead, and on the flags in gold letters the names of the ratifying states from New Hampshire to Georgia, arranged in order from north to south. The *Rising Sun* was decorated with the flags of various nations. The other ten, and the vessels tied up at the wharves, were dressed with flags and pennants which fluttered in a brisk, cool south wind all day long.

The Procession formed at the corner of South and Third Streets, where by eight o'clock nine marshals, with General Mifflin at their head, on horseback, with white plumes on their hats and speaking trumpets in their hands, were in charge. The "different companies of Military, Trades, and Professions" had met still earlier at appointed places in the city. As they arrived at the "general rendezvous" they were assigned by the marshals to the neighboring streets from which they might fall into their prearranged order when the Procession moved.

The line of march had been announced. Crowds filled the "footways," windows, and rooftops from the starting point along Third Street to Callowhill; up Callowhill to Fourth; on Fourth to Market; and thence to Union Green in front of Bush Hill, the residence of William Hamilton, who had offered the use of his grounds for the oration and feast which were to crown the day. The pavements had been swept, by order of the committee of arrangements, overhanging branches cut off the trees, and all other obstacles removed.

The Procession got under way about half past nine. It was a mile and a half long. It took three hours to travel the three miles of its route. There were estimated to be five thousand persons in the Procession, and about seventeen thousand—at least half the city's population—finally assembled on Union Green.

First in the Procession went "Twelve Axemen, dressed in white frocks, with black girdles round their waists." Then came the First Troop of City Cavalry, gentlemen on fine horses, in smart uniforms of brown and white, with black hats with buck tails for crests. Then *Independence*, represented by "*John Nixon*, Esq; on horseback, bearing the staff and cap of Liberty, under the cap a silk flag, with the words, '4th of July, 1776,' in large gold letters." Then four pieces of artillery, with a detachment from the artillery train. Then *French Alliance*, represented by Thomas

FitzSimons on a horse that had formerly belonged to the Comte de Rochambeau. FitzSimons carried a flag of white silk, with "three fleurs-de-lys and thirteen stars in union, over the words, '6th of February, 1778,' in gold letters." Then a corps of light infantry with the standard of the First Regiment. Then *Definitive Treaty of Peace* represented by George Clymer, "carrying a staff adorned with olive and laurel," with a flag which had "3d of September, 1783" in gold letters. Then Colonel John Shee on horseback, "carrying a flag, blue field, with a laurel and an olive wreath over the words, 'washington, the Friend of his Country,' in silver letters." Another troop of City Cavalry, commanded by Major William Jackson.

So far it had been all history, the Revolution, the French alliance, the treaty of peace with England. But now came a Herald on horseback, "attended by a trumpet, proclaiming a New Æra—the words, 'New Æra,' in gold letters, pendant from the Herald's staff, and the following lines:

> Peace o'er our land her olive wand extends,
> And white robed Innocence from Heaven descends;
> The crimes and frauds of Anarchy shall fail,
> Returning Justice lifts again her scale."

The Herald was Richard Bache, Franklin's son-in-law. "His Excellency the President," the official account of the Procession said, "was too much indisposed to attend." Franklin may have seen the Procession saluted by Captain David Ziegler's company of Continental infantry at the corner of Fourth and Market Streets near Franklin's house; but he could not have endured a long ride in his sedan chair.

After the Herald of the New Æra came Peter Muhlenberg, representing the *Convention of the States,* with the words "17th of September, 1787" in silver letters on a blue flag. Then "a Band of Music performing a grand March, composed by Mr. *Alexander Reinagle* for the occasion." And only then *The Constitution:* "The Honorable Chief Justice M'Kean, the Hon. Judge Atlee, the Hon. Judge Rush (in their Robes of Office), in a lofty, ornamented Car, in the form of a large eagle, drawn by six horses, bearing the constitution, framed and fixed on a staff, crowned with the cap of Liberty, the words 'the people' in gold letters, on the staff, immediately under the Constitution."

The Constitution was No. 13 in the Procession, which ran to eighty-eight numbered parts. No doubt the spectators lost count, and after a time paid little attention to the less dramatic features of the parade. Ten gentlemen representing the ten states which had ratified the Constitution walked arm in arm "emblematical of the Union." They were all natives or naturalized inhabitants of their states, but lived or were visiting in the capital city of Philadelphia. The consuls or representatives of the foreign states in alliance with the United States—France, the United Netherlands, Sweden, Prussia, and Morocco—rode together in an "ornamented Car" drawn by four horses. Peter Baynton, as a citizen, and Colonel Isaac Melcher, as an Indian chief, sat in a carriage "smoking the Calumet of Peace together,—the Sachem magnificently dressed according to the Indian custom."

Preceded by thirty dragoons of the Berks County troop came the "New Roof, or grand Fœderal Edifice," which was a symbol popular in Philadelphia ever since it had been thought of by Francis Hopkinson, poet, musician, signer of the Declaration of Independence, judge of admiralty, and now director of the Federal Procession. In December 1787 he had written a satirical story allegorizing the Constitution as a New Roof, and had ridiculed the Antifederalists who preferred the old one and were afraid the new one would be bad for the house. His cheerful fable was realized in "an elegant building . . . begun and finished in the short space of four days." It stood on a carriage drawn by ten white horses: "the dome supported by thirteen corinthian pillars, raised on pedestals proper to that order; the frieze decorated with thirteen stars; ten of the columns complete, and three left unfinished; on the pedestals of the columns were inscribed, in ornamented cyphers, the initials of the Thirteen American States; on the top of the dome a handsome *cupola,* surmounted by a figure of Plenty, bearing her cornucopias, and other emblems of her character." Round the pedestal of the edifice were the words: "In Union the Fabric stands firm."

Seated in chairs on the floor of the Federal Edifice were ten gentlemen "as Representatives of the Citizens at large, to whom the Constitution was submitted previous to the ratification. When the Grand Edifice arrived safe at *Union Green,* these Gentlemen gave up their seats to the representatives of the States"—those ten gentlemen already mentioned who had come on foot. The walking representatives of the ratifying states "entered the temple, and hung their flags on the corinthian columns to which they respectively belonged." At the end of the ceremonies the New Roof, with the ten representatives, was brought back "in great triumph and with loud Huzzas to the State House," where it stood for days to the admiration of the public.

With the New Roof marched the Architects and House Carpenters, four hundred and fifty of them, and the Saw Makers and File Cutters, the first body of tradesmen to appear in the Procession. The Federal Edifice was an exhibit of their art and craft.

The Manufacturing Society, No. 29, was another industrial exhibit with a motto: *"May the Union Government protect the manufactures of America."* On a carriage thirty feet long and thirteen wide were a carding machine worked by two persons; a spinning machine of eighty spindles worked by a woman, "a native of and instructed in this city"; a lace loom on which a man was weaving "a rich scarlet and white livery lace"; and a loom on which a man was weaving jean with a fly-shuttle. "Behind the looms was fixed the apparatus of Mr. Hewson, printing muslins of an elegant chintz pattern, and Mr. Lang designing and cutting prints for shauls; on the right was Mrs. Hewson and her 4 daughters pencilling a piece of very neat sprigged chintz of Mr. Hewson's printing, all dressed in cottons of their own manufacture." Behind the carriage walked about a hundred Weavers, and the Cotton Card Makers.

This display probably attracted more attention than the Pennsylvania Society of the Cincinnati, and the detachments of light infantry that came at intervals, and the Marine Society: eighty-nine shipmasters with quadrants, trumpets, spyglasses, charts, and other implements of their profession. But there was no overlooking the Federal Ship *Union*, "perfectly proportioned and complete throughout, decorated with emblematical carving, and finished even to a stroke of the painter's brush. And what is truly astonishing, she was begun and compleated in less than four days, viz, begun at 11 o'clock on Monday morning, the 30th of June, and on the field of rendezvous on Thursday morning, fully prepared to join in the Grand Procession. The workmanship and appearance of this beautiful object commanded universal admiration and applause, and did high honor to the artists of Philadelphia, who were concerned in her construction."

She was followed by the Pilots of the Port, forty Boat Builders, Sail Makers, three hundred and fifty Ship Carpenters, about thirty Ship Joiners, the Rope Makers and Ship Chandlers, and Merchants and Traders, with their clerks and apprentices. The Merchants and Traders had for standard the flag of a merchant ship of the United States. On one side was painted a ship, the *Pennsylvania,* and on the other a globe with the motto *"Par tout le Mond."*

Nos. 33 to 77 in the line of march were all Trades and Professions in an order determined by lot. The mere names of their callings make up a panorama of the life of Philadelphia. Philadelphia was marching under the banner of the Constitution.

Cordwainers (6 men actually making shoes and 300 marching). Coach Painters (10 with palettes and pencils in their hands). Cabinet and Chair Makers (a moving workshop with a master, journeymen, and apprentices at work). Brick Makers (over 100, with a motto "It was found hard in Egypt, but this prospect"— the new government—"makes it easy"). House, Ship, and Sign Painters (68, with equipment for grinding paint). Porters (that is, draymen, with five barrels of "Fœderal flour" which were afterwards delivered to the overseers for the use of the poor). Clock and Watch Makers (24). Fringe and Ribband Weavers. Bricklayers (masters and workmen with aprons and trowels, and a flag with a picture of "The Fœderal city rising out of a forest: workmen building it, and the sun illuminating it—Motto— *Both Buildings and Rulers are the Works of our hands'"*). Tailors (250). Instrument Makers, Turners, Windsor Chair and Spinning Wheel Makers (60 in green aprons). Carvers and Gilders (with an elaborate car in which a number of artists were at work). Coopers (150 in white leather aprons). Plane Makers. Whip and Cane Manufacturers. Blacksmiths, Whitesmiths, and Nailers (over 200, several of them at work in a moving forge. "Mr. *John Mingler,* and his assistant, *Christian Keyser,* blacksmiths, completed a set of plough irons out of old swords, worked a sword into a sickle, turned several horse shoes, and performed several jobs on demand").

Coach Makers (150, with the motto: *"No tax on American carriages"*). Potters (a potter's wheel and men at work turning out cups, mugs, bowls). Hatters (125). Wheelwrights (22). Tinplate Workers. Skinners, Breeches Makers, and Glovers (58 in buckskin breeches and gloves). Tallow Chandlers (a flag with the picture of a chandelier with thirteen branches). Victuallers (86 masters, a band of music, and two oxen weighing 3000 pounds. "The oxen to be killed, the hides and tallow to be sold for bread and given, with the meat, to the poor").

Printers, Booksellers, and Stationers. There were fifty of these. On a stage drawn by four horses was a complete small printing house. The printers composed and struck off many copies of an Ode written by Francis Hopkinson. "This Ode, together with one in the German language, fitted to the purpose, and printed by Mr. Steiner, were thrown amongst the people as the procession moved along." The motto: *"We protect and are supported by Liberty."*

Saddlers (a shop in which a workman, "having the different parts at readiness, compleated a neat saddle"). Stone Cutters. Bread and Biscuit Bakers (130). Gunsmiths. Coppersmiths. Goldsmiths, Silversmiths, and Jewellers. Distillers (12). Tobacconists (70). Brass Founders. Stocking Manufacturers (30). Tanners and Curriers (25 tanners, 35 curriers). Upholsterers (nothing like the splendor of the upholsterers in New York). Sugar Refiners (36 with white aprons, "on which were painted sugar loaves"). Brewers (with two hogsheads and a butt marked "Beer, Ale, Porter" with the motto *"Home brew'd is best"*—meaning brewed in America, not imported). Peruke-Makers and Barber Surgeons (72 of them, with the arms of their professions). Plaisterers. Brush Makers. And at the end Stay Makers ("represented by Mr. *Francis Serre,* with his first journeyman carrying an elegant pair of lady's stays in the procession").

After that, another corps of light infantry, and public officials. The civil and military officers of Congress in the city. The Supreme Executive Council of Pennsylvania (without President Franklin who was ill, and Vice President Muhlenberg who was representing the Pennsylvania convention nearer the head of the Procession). Various city officials. The gentlemen of the bar, and students of law. "The clergy of the different christian denominations, and the Rabbi of the Jews, walking arm in arm." The College of Physicians, and students of medicine. Students of the University, and of the Episcopal Academy, and most of the schools of the city, preceded by their principals, masters, and tutors. The county troop of light horse "brought up the rear of the whole."

At Bush Hill the Grand Edifice was placed in the center of a great circle and the ship *Union* moored beside it, with the flags of the consuls and other standards planted round them. The boundary of the circle was a range of tables, covered with canvas awnings and "plentifully spread with a cold collation." As soon as the rear of the Procession arrived, James Wilson delivered his oration from the Federal Edifice. The companies of light infantry were drawn up on an "eminence nearly opposite," where they fired a *feu de joie,* three rounds by battalion, and gave three cheers, "to testify their satisfaction." At dinner no spirits or wines were served, only American porter, beer, and cider.

Instead of the usual thirteen toasts there were ten, for the ten states which had ratified: (1) The People of the United States; (2) Honor and Immortality to the Members of the late Fœderal Convention; (3) General Washington; (4) The King of France; (5) The United Netherlands; (6) The foreign Powers in Alliance with the United States; (7) The Agriculture, Manufactures, and Commerce of the United States; (8) The Heroes who have fallen in Defence of our Liberties; (9) May Reason, and not the Sword, hereafter decide all national Disputes; (10) The whole Family of Mankind. Each toast was announced by the trumpet; each was answered by a discharge of ten guns from the artillery, repeated by the *Rising Sun* at her moorings in the river.

By six o'clock Union Green was cleared. The people went home in good order and happy, almost none of them drunk. That evening the *Rising Sun* was handsomely illuminated in honor of the great festival. And the whole sky was filled that night with a beautiful Aurora Borealis.

III

It was easy for the enemies of the Constitution to think, and say, that most of the marchers in this Federal Procession had their minds set on prosperity rather than liberty. The merchants and traders believed that under the new government the ships of Pennsylvania could voyage to the ports of all the world, carrying American exports from any state and bringing back imported goods for American consumers. The manufacturers, long forbidden to operate under British rule and prevented by interstate jealousy from extensive trade under the Confederation, believed they would be protected and supported by the proposed general regulation of commerce. The bricklayers saw themselves as possible builders of the new Federal City, perhaps not far from Philadelphia, and rejoiced in the prospect of work and profits. Hundreds of workers in the various trades were convinced that after the depression which had followed the war there would be good times again; that the new Constitution would help to bring more employment and better wages. They displayed their skills in the Federal Procession.

They understood that the Procession was federal. The symbols of the new order were the Federal Edifice, the New Roof, for all the states that cared to enter it, and the Federal Ship *Union*. Nor was there any evidence that these thronging Philadelphians looked upon the proposed government as an alien rule. All the states that day were neighbors to Pennsylvania. Their names were everywhere: on the flags at the mastheads of the ships in the river; on the pedestals of the Federal Edifice; on the flags the representatives of the ten states carried in the Procession; on the floats of the tradesmen. The union would bring peace among the states. It had been made by the people themselves, in their own right, for their own purposes. "May Reason," said one of the toasts at Union Green, "and not the Sword, hereafter decide all national Disputes." And the people ardently went further and drank to "The whole Family of Mankind."

It was easy for the enemies of the Constitution to think, and say, that many of the people had believed what their leaders or employers told them, without making up their own minds. But in those days almost every American, in Pennsylvania or out of it, was a politician. Americans had gone through a Revolution, with years of argument about independence and liberty and the rights of man. Now for the past year they had talked and heard of nothing, in politics, so much as the defects of the old Confederation and the need of a new Federal order. In the war of ideas there had of course been much irrelevance, much prejudice, much nonsense. But in all American history there had never been a year in which such profound and elevated political thinking had been so clearly stated or so widely published and discussed. To live in that year was to get a political education.

The masters of the Federal Convention had put their faith in the people, and the people had justified it. Some later enemies, or censurers, of the Constitution, have liked to argue that it was almost a conspiracy against the people, in which crafty men built a new government in their own interest, then tricked or cajoled the people into accepting it. The record does not bear this argument out. Of course the friends of the Constitution believed in it and worked for its adoption. Of course they made use of political arts, as their opponents did. Of course the majority was small in some of the ratifying conventions. But eleven states did ratify within a year, by majorities no smaller than had carried much of their own domestic legislation. There was no violent resistance. The minorities accepted the decision. And the bricklayers of Philadelphia could march in their Federal Procession under the brave motto: *"Both Buildings and Rulers are the Works of our hands."*

That Fourth of July in Philadelphia was a day of generous enthusiasm and innocent faith. To many of the people the Constitution seemed a new roof, a new remedy, a new assurance, perhaps a miracle. It was not any of these. What they had was like a child just born, a marriage just solemnized. The Constitution had still to be lived, by the people and their children and children's children after them. It would be worshiped and hated, fought over in a civil war, altered as the changing years brought unforeseeable political circumstances into being. It would become the rule of life for a country larger than any of the founders imagined, and would last longer than most of them dared to hope. Philadelphia celebrated not the end of the struggle for the Constitution, but the beginning. The Philadelphia Federal Procession, like every other Federal Procession of the year, was a dramatic epitome of the life and work of a separate state, a symbolic act of faith in the future of the United States. Those who believed were more right than those who doubted.

APPENDIX

[The documents here printed show the growth of the Constitution from the Randolph resolutions to the final form. They do not include the two Hamilton plans, one read to the Convention and one given to Madison, because they were never discussed by the delegates. They may be found in Farrand's *Records of the Federal Convention*, I, 291-93, and III, 619-30. The Pinckney plan was never discussed, and the text is missing. The one often printed as the original is apparently a later draft and based upon the Constitution as reported by the Committee of Detail. A reconstruction of the original may be found in Farrand's *Records*, III, 604-09. The Constitution as reported by the Committee of Style is not here included, for the reason that it differs from the final Constitution in only a few changes made in the final days of the Convention. It is printed in Farrand, II, 590-603.]

ARTICLES OF CONFEDERATION
AND PERPETUAL UNION

To ALL to whom these Presents shall come, we the undersigned Delegates of the States affixed to our Names send greeting. Whereas the Delegates of the United States of America in Congress assembled did on the fifteenth day of November in the Year of our Lord One Thousand Seven Hundred and Seventy seven, and in the Second Year of the Independence of America agree to certain articles of Confederation and perpetual Union between the States of New-hampshire, Massachusetts-bay, Rhode-island and Providence Plantations, Connecticut, New York, New Jersey, Pennsylvania, Delaware, Maryland, Virginia, North-Carolina, South-Carolina and Georgia in the Words following, viz. "Articles of Confederation and perpetual Union between the states of Newhampshire, Massachusetts-bay, Rhodeisland and Providence Plantations, Connecticut, New-York, New-Jersey, Pennsylvania, Delaware, Maryland, Virginia, North-Carolina, South-Carolina, and Georgia."

Art. I. The Stile of this confederacy shall be "The United States of America."

Art. II. Each state retains its sovereignty, freedom and independence, and every Power, Jurisdiction and right, which is not by this confederation expressly delegated to the United States, in Congress assembled.

Art. III. The said states hereby severally enter into a firm league of friendship with each other, for their common defence, the security of their Liberties, and their mutual and general welfare, binding themselves to assist each other, against all force offered to, or attacks made upon them, or any of them, on account of religion, sovereignty, trade, or any other pretence whatever.

Art. IV. The better to secure and perpetuate mutual friendship and intercourse among the people of the different states in this union, the free inhabitants of each of these states, paupers, vagabonds and fugitives from Justice excepted, shall be entitled to all privileges and immunities of free citizens in the several states; and the people of each state shall have free ingress and regress to and from any other state, and shall enjoy therein all the privileges of trade and commerce, subject to the same duties, impositions and restrictions as the inhabitants thereof respectively, provided that such restriction shall not extend so far as to prevent the removal of property imported into any state, to any other state of which the Owner is an inhabitant; provided also that no imposition, duties or restriction shall be laid by any state, on the property of the united states, or either of them.

If any Person guilty of, or charged with treason, felony, or other high misdemeanor in any state, shall flee from Justice, and be found in any of the united states, he shall upon demand of the Governor or executive power, of the state from which he fled, be delivered up and removed to the state having jurisdiction of his offence.

Full faith and credit shall be given in each of these states to the records, acts and judicial proceedings of the courts and magistrates of every other state.

Art. V. For the more convenient management of the general interests of the united states, delegates shall be annually appointed in such manner as the legislature of each state shall direct, to meet in Congress on the first Monday in November, in every year, with a power reserved to each state, to recal its delegates, or any of them, at any time within the year, and to send others in their stead, for the remainder of the Year.

No state shall be represented in Congress by less than two, nor by more than seven Members; and no person shall be capable of being a delegate for more than three years in any term of six years; nor shall any person, being a delegate, be capable of holding any office under the united states, for which he, or another for his benefit receives any salary, fees or emolument of any kind.

Each state shall maintain its own delegates in a meeting of the states, and while they act as members of the committee of the states.

In determining questions in the united states, in Congress assembled, each state shall have one vote.

Freedom of speech and debate in Congress shall not be impeached or questioned in any Court, or place out of Congress, and the members of congress shall be protected in their persons from arrests and imprisonments, during the time of their going to and from, and attendance on congress, except for treason, felony, or breach of the peace.

Art. VI. No state without the Consent of the united states in congress assembled, shall send any embassy to, or receive any embassy from, or enter into any conference, agreement, or alliance or treaty with any King, prince or state; nor shall any person holding any office of profit or trust under the united states, or any of them, accept of any present, emolument, office or title of any kind whatever from any king, prince or foreign state; nor shall the united states in congress assembled, or any of them, grant any title of nobility.

No two or more states shall enter into any treaty, confederation or alliance whatever between them, without the consent of the united states in congress assembled, specifying accurately the purposes for which the same is to be entered into, and how long it shall continue.

No state shall lay any imposts or duties, which may interfere with any stipulations in treaties, entered into by the united states in congress assembled, with any king, prince or state, in pursuance of any treaties already proposed by congress, to the courts of France and Spain.

No vessels of war shall be kept up in time of peace by any state, except such number only, as shall be deemed necessary by the united states in congress assembled, for the defence of such state, or its trade; nor shall any body of forces be kept up by any state, in time of peace, except such number only, as in the judgment of the united states, in congress assembled, shall be deemed requisite to garrison the forts necessary for the defence of such state; but every state shall always keep up a well regulated and disciplined militia, sufficiently armed and accoutred, and shall provide and constantly have ready for use, in public stores, a due number of field pieces and tents, and a proper quantity of arms, ammunition and camp equipage.

No state shall engage in any war without the consent of the united states in congress assembled, unless such state be actually invaded by enemies, or shall have received certain advice of a resolution being formed by some nation of Indians to invade such state, and the danger is so imminent as not to admit of a delay, till the united states in congress assembled can be consulted: nor shall any state grant commissions to any ships or vessels of war, nor letters of marque or reprisal, except it be after a declaration of war by the united states in congress assembled, and then only against the kingdom or state and the subjects thereof, against which war has been so declared, and under such regulations as shall be established by the united states in congress assembled, unless such state be infested by pirates, in which case vessels of war may be fitted out for that occasion, and kept so long as the danger shall continue, or until the united states in congress assembled shall determine otherwise.

Art. VII. When land-forces are raised by any state for the common defence, all officers of or under the rank of colonel, shall be appointed by the legislature of each state respectively by whom such forces shall be raised, or in such manner as such state shall direct, and all vacancies shall be filled up by the state which first made the appointment.

Art. VIII. All charges of war, and all other expences that shall be incurred for the common defence or general welfare, and allowed by the united states in congress assembled, shall be defrayed out of a common treasury, which shall be supplied by the several states, in proportion to the value of all land within each state, granted to or surveyed for any Person, as such land and the buildings and improvements thereon shall be estimated according to such mode as the united states in congress assembled, shall from time to time direct and appoint. The taxes for paying that proportion shall be laid and levied by the authority and direction of the legislatures of the several states within the time agreed upon by the united states in congress assembled.

Art. IX. The united states in congress assembled, shall have the sole and exclusive right and power of determining on peace and war, except in the cases mentioned in the sixth article—of sending and receiving ambassadors—entering into treaties and alliances, provided that no treaty of commerce shall be made whereby the legislative power of the respective states shall be restrained from imposing such imposts and duties on foreigners, as their own people are subjected to, or from prohibiting the exportation or importation of any species of goods or commodities whatsoever—of establishing rules for deciding in all cases, what captures on land or water shall be legal, and in what manner prizes taken by land or naval forces in the service of the united states shall be divided or appropriated—of granting letters of marque and reprisal in times of peace—appointing courts for the trial of piracies and felonies committed on the high seas and establishing courts for receiving and determining finally appeals in all cases of captures, provided that no member of congress shall be appointed a judge of any of the said courts.

The united states in congress assembled shall also be the last resort on appeal in all disputes and differences now subsisting or that hereafter may arise between two or more states concerning boundary, jurisdiction or any other cause whatever; which authority shall always be exercised in the manner following. Whenever the legislative or executive authority or lawful agent of any state in controversy with another shall present a petition to congress, stating the matter in question and praying for a hearing, notice thereof shall be given by order of congress to the legislative or executive authority of the other state in controversy, and a day assigned for the appearance of the parties by their lawful agents, who shall then be directed to appoint by joint consent, commissioners or judges to constitute a court for hearing and determining the matter in question: but if they cannot agree, congress shall name three persons out of each of the united states, and from the list of such persons each party shall alternately strike out one, the petitioners beginning, until the number shall be reduced to thirteen; and from that number not less than seven, nor more than nine names as congress shall direct, shall in the presence of congress be drawn out by lot, and the persons whose names shall be so drawn or any five of them, shall be commissioners or judges, to hear and finally determine the controversy, so always as a major part of the judges who shall hear the cause shall agree in the determination: and if either party shall neglect to attend at the day appointed, without shewing reasons, which congress shall judge sufficient, or being present shall refuse to strike, the congress shall proceed to nominate three persons out of each state, and the secretary of congress shall strike in behalf of such party absent or refusing; and the judgment and sentence of the court to be appointed, in the manner before prescribed, shall be final and conclusive; and if any of the parties shall refuse to submit to the authority of such court, or to appear to defend their claim, or cause, the court shall nevertheless proceed to pronounce sentence, or judgment, which shall in like manner be final and decisive, the judgment or sentence and other proceedings being in either case transmitted to congress, and lodged among the acts of congress for the security of the parties concerned: provided that every commissioner, before he sits in judgment, shall take an oath to be administered by one of the judges of the supreme or superior court of the state, where the cause shall be tried, "well and truly to hear and determine the matter in question, according to the best of his judgment, without favour, affection or hope of reward:" provided also that no state shall be deprived of territory for the benefit of the united states.

All controversies concerning the private right of soil claimed under different grants of two or more states, whose jurisdictions as they may respect such lands, and the states which passed such grants are adjusted, the said grants or either of them being at the same time claimed to have originated antecedent to such settlement of jurisdiction, shall on the petition of either party to the congress of the united states, be finally determined as near as may be in the same manner as is before prescribed for deciding disputes respecting territorial jurisdiction between different states.

The united states in congress assembled shall also have the sole and exclusive right and power of regulating the alloy and value of coin struck by their own authority, or by that of the respective states—fixing the standard of weights and measures throughout the united states—regulating the trade and managing all affairs with the Indians, not members of any of the states, provided that the legislative right of any state within its own limits be not infringed or violated—establishing and regulating post-offices from one state to another, throughout all the united states, and exacting such postage on the papers passing thro' the same as may be requisite to defray the expences of the said office—appointing all officers of the land forces, in the service of the united states, excepting regimental officers—appointing all the officers of the naval forces, and commissioning all officers whatever in the service of the united states—making rules for the government and regulation of the said land and naval forces, and directing their operations.

The united states in congress assembled shall have authority to appoint a committee, to sit in the recess of congress, to be denominated "A Committee of the States," and to consist of one delegate from each state; and to appoint such other committees and civil officers as may be necessary for managing the general affairs of the united states under their direction—to appoint one of their number to preside, provided that no person be allowed to serve in the office of president more than one year in any term of three years; to ascertain the necessary sums of Money to be raised for the service of the united states, and to appropriate and apply the same for defraying the public expences—to borrow money, or emit bills on the credit of the united states, transmitting every half year to the respective states an account of the sums of money so borrowed or emitted—to build and equip a navy—to agree upon the number of land forces, and to make requisitions from each state for its quota, in proportion to the number of white inhabitants in such state; which requisition shall be binding, and thereupon the legislature of each state shall appoint the regimental officers, raise the men and cloath, arm and equip them in a soldier like manner, at the expence of the united states, and the officers and men so cloathed, armed and equipped shall march to the place appointed, and within the time agreed on by the united states in congress assembled: But if the united states in congress assembled shall, on consideration of circumstances judge proper that any state should not raise men, or should raise a smaller number than its quota, and that any other state should raise a greater number of men than the quota thereof, such extra number shall be raised, officered, cloathed, armed and equipped in the same manner as the quota of such state, unless the legislature of such state shall judge that such extra number cannot be safely spared out of the same, in which case they shall raise, officer, cloath, arm and equip as many of such extra number as they judge can be safely spared. And the officers and men so cloathed, armed and equipped, shall march to the place appointed, and within the time agreed on by the united states in congress assembled.

The united states in congress assembled shall never engage in a war, nor grant letters of marque and reprisal in time of peace, nor enter into any treaties or alliances, nor coin money, nor regulate the value thereof, nor ascertain the sums and expences necessary for the defence and welfare of the united states, or any of them, nor emit bills, nor borrow money on the credit of the united states, nor appropriate money, nor agree upon the number of vessels of war, to be built or purchased, or the number of land or sea forces to be raised, nor appoint a commander in chief of the army or navy, unless nine states assent to the same: nor shall a question on any other point, except for adjourning from day to day be determined, unless by the votes of a majority of the united states in congress assembled.

The congress of the united states shall have power to adjourn to any time within the year, and to any place within the united states, so that no period of adjournment be for a longer duration than the space of six Months, and shall publish the Journal of their proceedings monthly, except such parts thereof relating to treaties, alliances or military operations as in their judgment require secresy; and the yeas and nays of the delegates of each state on any question shall be entered on the Journal, when it is desired by any delegate; and the delegates of a state, or any of them, at his or their request shall be furnished with a transcript of the said Journal, except such parts as are above excepted, to lay before the legislatures of the several states.

Art. X. The committee of the states, or any nine of them, shall be authorised to execute, in the recess of congress, such of the powers of congress as the united states in congress assembled, by the consent of nine states, shall from time to time think expedient to vest them with; provided that no power be delegated to the said committee, for the exercise of which by the articles of confederation, the voice of nine states in the congress of the united states assembled is requisite.

Art. XI. Canada acceding to this confederation, and joining in the measures of the united states, shall be admitted into, and entitled to all the advantages of this union: but no other colony shall be admitted into the same, unless such admission be agreed to by nine states.

Art. XII. All bills of credit emitted, monies borrowed and debts contracted by, or under the authority of congress, before the assembling of the united states, in pursuance of the present confederation, shall be deemed and considered as a charge against the united states, for payment and satisfaction whereof the said united states, and the public faith are hereby solemnly pledged.

Art. XIII. Every state shall abide by the determinations of the united states in congress assembled, on all questions which by this confederation are submitted to them. And the Articles of this confederation shall be inviolably observed by every state, and the union shall be perpetual; nor shall any alteration at any time hereafter be made in any of them; unless such alteration be agreed to in a congress of the united states, and be afterwards confirmed by the legislatures of every state.

AND WHEREAS it hath pleased the Great Governor of the World to incline the hearts of the legislatures we respectively represent in congress, to approve of, and to authorize us to ratify the said articles of confederation and perpetual union. KNOW YE that we the undersigned delegates, by virtue of the power and authority to us given for that purpose, do by these presents, in the name and in behalf of our respective constituents, fully and entirely ratify and confirm each and every of the said articles of confederation and perpetual union, and all and singular the matters and things therein contained: And we do further solemnly plight and engage the faith of our respective constituents, that they shall abide by the determinations of the united states in congress assembled, on all questions, which by the said confederation are submitted to them. And that the articles thereof shall be inviolably observed by the states we respectively represent, and that the union shall be perpetual. In Witness thereof we have hereunto set our hands in Congress. Done at Philadelphia in the state of Pennsylvania the ninth Day of July in the Year of our Lord one Thousand seven Hundred and Seventy-eight, and in the third year of the independence of America.

JOSIAH BARTLETT JOHN WENTWORTH Junr August 8th 1778	On the part & behalf of the State of New Hampshire
JOHN HANCOCK SAMUEL ADAMS ELBRIDGE GERRY FRANCIS DANA JAMES LOVELL SAMUEL HOLTEN	On the part and behalf of The State of Massachusetts Bay
WILLIAM ELLERY HENRY MARCHANT JOHN COLLINS	On the part and behalf of the State of Rhode-Island and Providence Plantations
ROGER SHERMAN SAMUEL HUNTINGTON OLIVER WOLCOTT TITUS HOSMER ANDREW ADAMS	On the part and behalf of the State of Connecticut

JA^S DUANE
FRA^S LEWIS
W^M DUER
GOUV MORRIS
— On the Part and Behalf of the State of New York

JNO WITHERSPOON
NATH^L SCUDDER
— On the Part and in Behalf of the State of New Jersey. Novr 26, 1778.—

ROB^T MORRIS
DANIEL ROBERDEAU
JON^A BAYARD SMITH
WILLIAM CLINGAN
JOSEPH REED   22^d July 1778
— On the part and behalf of the State of Pennsylvania

THO M:KEAN   Feby 12 1779
JOHN DICKINSON   May 5th 1779
NICHOLAS VAN DYKE
— On the part & behalf of the State of Delaware

JOHN HANSON   March 1 1781
DANIEL CARROLL d^o
— On the part and behalf of the State of Maryland

RICHARD HENRY LEE
JOHN BANISTER
THOMAS ADAMS
JN^O HARVIE
FRANCIS LIGHTFOOT LEE
— On the Part and Behalf of the State of Virginia

JOHN PENN   July 21st 1778
CORN^S HARNETT
JN^O WILLIAMS
— On the part and Behalf of the State of N^o Carolina

HENRY LAURENS
WILLIAM HENRY DRAYTON
JN^O MATHEWS
RICH^D HUTSON
THO^S HEYWARD   Junr
— On the part & behalf of the State of South-Carolina

JN^O WALTON   24th July 1778
EDW^D TELFAIR
EDW^D LANGWORTHY
— On the part & behalf of the State of Georgia

2

RESOLUTION OF CONGRESS
February 21, 1787

WHEREAS there is provision in the Articles of Confederation & perpetual Union for making alterations therein by the Assent of a Congress of the United States and of the legislatures of the several States; And whereas experience hath evinced that there are defects in the present Confederation, as a means to remedy which several of the States and particularly the State of New York by express instruction to their delegates in Congress have suggested a convention for the purposes expressed in the following resolution and such Convention appearing to be the most probable means of establishing in these states a firm national government

Resolved that in the opinion of Congress it is expedient that on the second Monday in May next a Convention of delegates who shall have been appointed by the several states be held at Philadelphia for the sole and express purpose of revising the Articles of Confederation and reporting to Congress and the several legislatures such alterations and provisions therein as shall when agreed to in Congress and confirmed by the states render the federal constitution adequate to the exigencies of Government & the preservation of the Union.

3

THE VIRGINIA PLAN AS OFFERED
BY RANDOLPH
May 29, 1787

1. RESOLVED, That the articles of Confederation ought to be so corrected and enlarged as to accomplish the objects proposed by their institution; namely, common defence, security of liberty and general welfare.

2. Resolved, therefore, That the rights of suffrage, in the National Legislature ought to be proportioned to the Quotas of contribution, or to the number of free inhabitants, as the one or the other rule may seem best in different cases.

3. Resolved, That the National Legislature ought to consist of two branches.

4. Resolved, That the members of the first branch of the National Legislature ought to be elected by the people of the several States every   for the term of   ; to be of the age of   years at least; to receive liberal stipends by which they may be compensated for the devotion of their time to public service; to be ineligible to any office established by a particular State, or under the authority of the United States, except those peculiarly belonging to the functions of the first branch, during the term of service, and for the space of after its expiration; to be incapable of re-election for the space of after the expiration of their term of service; and to be subject to recall.

5. Resolved, That the members of the second branch of the National Legislature ought to be elected by those of the first, out of a proper number of persons nominated by the individual Legislatures; to be of the age of   years, at least; to hold their offices for a term sufficient to ensure their independency; to receive liberal stipends, by which they may be compensated for the devotion of their time to public service; and to be ineligible to any office established by a particular State, or under the authority of the United States, except those peculiarly belonging to the functions of the second branch, during the term of service, and for the space of   after the expiration thereof.

6. Resolved, That each branch ought to possess the right of originating Acts; that the National Legislature ought to be impowered to enjoy the Legislative Rights vested in Congress by the Confederation, and moreover to legislate in all cases to which the separate States are

incompetent, or in which the harmony of the United States may be interrupted by the exercise of individual Legislation; to negative all laws passed by the several States, contravening in the opinion of the National Legislature the articles of Union; and to call forth the force of the Union against any member of the Union failing to fulfil its duty under the articles thereof.

7. Resolved, That a national executive be instituted; to be chosen by the National Legislature for the term of   years; to receive punctually at stated times, a fixed compensation for the services rendered, in which no increase or diminution shall be made so as to affect the Magistracy existing at the time of increase or diminution; and to be ineligible a second time; and that besides a general authority to execute the National laws, it ought to enjoy the Executive rights vested in Congress by the Confederation.

8. Resolved, That the executive and a convenient number of the National Judiciary, ought to compose a council of revision with authority to examine every act of the National Legislature before it shall operate, and every act of a particular Legislature before a Negative thereon shall be final; and that the dissent of the said Council shall amount to a rejection, unless the act of the National Legislature be again passed, or that of a particular Legislature be again negatived by   of the members of each branch.

9. Resolved, That a national judiciary be established to consist of one or more supreme tribunals, and of inferior tribunals to be chosen by the National Legislature, to hold their offices during good behaviour; and to receive punctually at stated times fixed compensations for their services, in which no increase or diminution shall be made so as to affect the person actually in office at the time of such increase or diminution. That the jurisdiction of the inferior tribunals shall be to hear and determine in the first instance, and of the supreme tribunal to hear and determine, in the dernier resort, all piracies and felonies on the high seas; captures from an enemy; cases in which foreigners or citizens of other States applying to such jurisdictions may be interested, or which respect the collection of the National revenue; impeachments of any National officer; and questions which involve the national peace or harmony.

10. Resolved, That provision ought to be made for the admission of States lawfully arising within the limits of the United States, whether from a voluntary junction of Government and Territory, or otherwise, with the consent of a number of voices in the National Legislature less than the whole.

11. Resolved, That a Republican Government and the territory of each State, except in the instance of a voluntary junction of Govern-

ment and territory, ought to be guaranteed by the United States to each State.

12. Resolved, That provision ought to be made for the continuance of Congress and their authorities and privileges, until a given day after the reform of the articles of Union shall be adopted, and for the completion of all their engagements.

13. Resolved, That provision ought to be made for the amendment of the articles of Union whensoever it shall seem necessary; and that the assent of the National Legislature ought not to be required thereto.

14. Resolved, That the legislative, executive, and judiciary powers within the several States, ought to be bound by oath to support the articles of union.

15. Resolved, That the amendments which shall be offered to the Confederation, by the Convention ought at a proper time, or times, after the approbation of Congress, to be submitted to an assembly or assemblies of Representatives, recommended by the several Legislatures to be expressly chosen by the people, to consider and decide thereon.

4

THE VIRGINIA PLAN AS REPORTED BY THE COMMITTEE OF THE WHOLE

June 13, 1787

(The text follows, with some rearrangements, that of Farrand's *Records of the Federal Convention,* I, 228-32)

1. RESOLVED, That it is the opinion of this Committee, that a national government ought to be established, consisting of a Supreme Legislative, Judiciary, and Executive.

2. Resolved, That the National Legislature ought to consist of Two Branches.

3. Resolved, That the members of the first branch of the national Legislature ought to be elected by the People of the several States, for the term of Three years; to receive fixed stipends, by which they may be compensated for the devotion of their time to public service, to be paid out of the National Treasury; to be ineligible to any Office established by a particular State, or under the authority of the United States (except those peculiarly belonging to the functions of the first branch) during the term of service, and under the national government for the space of one year after its expiration.

4. Resolved, That the Members of the second Branch of the national Legislature ought to be chosen by the individual Legislatures; to be of the age of thirty years at least; to hold their offices for a term sufficient to ensure their independency, namely, seven years; to receive fixed stipends, by which they may be compensated for the devotion of their time to public service, to be paid out of the National Treasury; to be ineligible to any Office established by a particular State, or under the authority of the United States (except those peculiarly belonging to the functions of the second branch) during the term of service, and under the national government, for the space of one Year after its expiration.

5. Resolved, That each branch ought to possess the right of originating acts.

6. Resolved, That the national Legislature ought to be empowered to enjoy the legislative rights vested in Congress by the confederation; and moreover to legislate in all cases to which the separate

States are incompetent, or in which the harmony of the United States may be interrupted by the exercise of individual legislation; to negative all laws passed by the several States contravening, in the opinion of the national legislature, the articles of union, or any treaties subsisting under the authority of the union.

7. Resolved, That the right of suffrage in the first branch of the national Legislature ought not to be according to the rule established in the articles of confederation, but according to some equitable ratio of representation; namely, in proportion to the whole number of white and other free citizens and inhabitants, of every age, sex, and condition, including those bound to servitude for a term of years, and three fifths of all other persons not comprehended in the foregoing description, except Indians not paying taxes in each State.

8. Resolved, That the right of suffrage in the second branch of the national Legislature ought to be according to the rule established for the first.

9. Resolved, That a national Executive be instituted to consist of a Single Person; to be chosen by the National Legislature, for the term of Seven years; with power to carry into execution the National Laws; to appoint to Offices in cases not otherwise provided for; to be ineligible the second time; and to be removable on impeachment and conviction of malpractice, or neglect of duty; to receive a fixed stipend, by which he may be compensated for the devotion of his time to public service, to be paid out of the national Treasury.

10. Resolved, That the national executive shall have a right to negative any legislative act, which shall not be afterwards passed unless by two third parts of each branch of the national Legislature.

11. Resolved, That a national Judiciary be established to consist of One supreme Tribunal; the Judges of which to be appointed by the second Branch of the National Legislature; to hold their offices during good behaviour; to receive punctually, at stated times, a fixed compensation for their services, in which no encrease or diminution shall be made, so as to affect the persons actually in office at the time of such encrease or diminution.

12. Resolved, That the national Legislature be empowered to appoint inferior Tribunals.

13. Resolved, That the jurisdiction of the national Judiciary shall extend to cases which respect the collection of the national revenue; impeachments of any National officers; and questions which involve the national peace and harmony.

14. Resolved, That provision ought to be made for the admission of States, lawfully arising within the limits of the United States, whether from a voluntary junction of government and territory, or

otherwise, with the consent of a number of voices in the National legislature less than the whole.

15. Resolved, That provision ought to be made for the continuance of Congress and their authorities until a given day after the reform of the articles of Union shall be adopted; and for the completion of all their engagements.

16. Resolved, That a republican Constitution, and its existing laws, ought to be guaranteed to each State by the United States.

17. Resolved, That provision ought to be made for the amendment of the articles of Union, whensoever it shall seem necessary.

18. Resolved, That the Legislative, Executive, and Judiciary powers within the several States ought to be bound by oath to support the articles of Union.

19. Resolved, That the amendments which shall be offered to the confederation by the Convention, ought at a proper time or times, after the approbation of Congress, to be submitted to an assembly or assemblies of representatives, recommended by the several Legislatures, to be submitted to an assembly or assemblies of representatives, recommended by the several Legislatures, to be expressly chosen by the People to consider and decide thereon.

5

THE NEW JERSEY PLAN AS OFFERED BY PATERSON

June 15, 1787

1. RESOLVED, That the articles of Confederation ought to be so revised, corrected and enlarged, as to render the federal Constitution adequate to the exigencies of Government, and the preservation of the Union.

2. Resolved, That in addition to the powers vested in the United States in Congress, by the present existing articles of Confederation, they be authorized to pass acts for raising a revenue, by levying a duty or duties on all goods and merchandizes of foreign growth or manufacture, imported into any part of the United States, by Stamps on paper, vellum, or parchment, and by a postage on all letters and packages passing through the general post-office, to be applied to such federal purposes as they shall deem proper and expedient; to make rules and regulations for the collection thereof; and the same from time to time, to alter and amend in such manner as they shall think proper; to pass Acts for the regulation of trade and commerce, as well with foreign nations as with each other: provided that all punishments, fines, forfeitures, and penalties to be incurred for contravening such rules and regulations shall be adjudged by the Common law Judiciarys of the State in which any offence contrary to the true intent and meaning of such Acts, rules and regulations shall have been committed or perpetrated, with liberty of commencing in the first instance all suits or prosecutions for that purpose, in the superior Common law Judiciary of such State; subject nevertheless, for the correction of all errors, both in law and fact in rendering judgment, to an appeal to the Judiciary of the United States.

3. Resolved, That whenever requisitions shall be necessary, instead of the rule for making requisitions mentioned in the articles of Confederation the United States in Congress be authorized to make such requisitions in proportion to the whole number of white and other free citizens and inhabitants of every age, sex, and condition, including those bound to servitude for a term of years, and three fifths of all other persons not comprehended in the foregoing description, except Indians not paying taxes; that if such requisitions be not complied with, in the time specified therein, to direct the collection

thereof in the non-complying States, and for that purpose to devise and pass acts directing and authorizing the same; provided that none of the powers hereby vested in the United States in Congress shall be exercised without the consent of at least   States; and in that proportion, if the number of confederated States should hereafter be increased or diminished.

4. Resolved, That the United States in Congress be authorized to elect a federal Executive to consist of   persons, to continue in office for the term of   years; to receive punctually at stated times a fixed compensation for their services in which no increase or diminution shall be made so as to affect the persons composing the Executive at the time of such increase or diminution, to be paid out of the federal treasury; to be incapable of holding any other office or appointment during their term of service, and for   years thereafter; to be ineligible a second time, and removable by Congress on application by a majority of the Executives of the several States. That the executive, besides their general authority to execute the federal acts ought to appoint all federal officers not otherwise provided for, and to direct all military operations; provided, that none of the persons composing the federal executive shall on any occasion take command of any troops, so as personally to conduct any military enterprise as General, or in any other capacity.

5. Resolved, That a federal Judiciary be established, to consist of a supreme Tribunal the Judges of which to be appointed by the Executive, and to hold their offices during good behaviour; to receive punctually at stated times a fixed compensation for their services, in which no increase or diminution shall be made, so as to affect the persons actually in office at the time of such increase or diminution. That the Judiciary so established shall have authority to hear and determine in the first instance on all impeachments of federal officers, and by way of appeal in the dernier resort in all cases touching the rights and privileges of Ambassadors; in all cases of captures from an enemy; in all cases of piracies and felonies on the high seas; in all cases in which foreigners may be interested, in the construction of any treaty or treaties, or which may arise on any of the acts for regulation of trade, or the collection of the federal Revenue. That none of the Judiciary shall during the time they remain in Office be capable of receiving or holding any other office or appointment during their term of service, or for   thereafter.

6. Resolved, That all acts of the United States in Congress, made by virtue and in pursuance of the powers hereby and by the articles of confederation vested in them, and all treaties made and ratified under the authority of the United States, shall be the supreme law

of the respective States as far forth as those Acts or Treaties shall relate to the said States or their Citizens; and that the judiciary of the several States shall be bound thereby in their decisions, any thing in the respective laws of the Individual States to the contrary notwithstanding; and if any State, or any body of men in any State, shall oppose or prevent the carrying into execution such acts or treaties, the federal Executive shall be authorized to call forth the powers of the Confederated States, or so much thereof as may be necessary, to enforce and compel an obedience to such Acts, or an Observance of such Treaties.

7. Resolved, That provision be made for the admission of new States into the Union.

8. Resolved, That the rule for naturalization ought to be the same in every State.

9. Resolved, That a citizen of one State committing an offence in another State of the Union shall be deemed guilty of the same offence as if it had been committed by a citizen of the State in which the offence was committed.

6

RESOLUTIONS OF THE CONVENTION
THROUGH JULY 26
Referred to the Committee of Detail

[The text follows that of Farrand's *Records*, II, 129-34]

RESOLVED:
That the Government of the United States ought to consist of a Supreme Legislative, Judiciary and Executive.

That the Legislature of the United States ought to consist of two Branches.

That the Members of the first Branch of the Legislature of the United States ought to be elected by the People of the several States —for the Term of two Years—to be of the Age of twenty five Years at least—to be ineligible to and incapable of holding any Office under the Authority of the United States (except those peculiarly belonging to the Functions of the first Branch) during the Time of Service of the first Branch.

That the Members of the second Branch of the Legislature of the United States ought to be chosen by the Individual Legislatures—to be of the Age of thirty Years at least—to hold their Offices for the Term of six Years; one third to go out biennially—to receive a Compensation for the Devotion of their Time to the public Service—to be ineligible to and incapable of holding any Office under the Authority of the United States (except those peculiarly belong to the Functions of the second Branch) during the Term for which they are elected, and for one Year thereafter.

That each Branch ought to possess the Right of originating Acts.

That the Right of Suffrage in the first Branch of the Legislature of the United States ought not to be according to the Rules established in the Articles of Confederation but according to some equitable Ratio of Representation.

That in the original Formation of the Legislature of the United States the first Branch thereof shall consist of sixty five Members of which Number New Hampshire shall send *three*—Massachusetts *eight* —Rhode Island *one*—Connecticut *five*—New York *six*—New Jersey *four* —Pennsylvania *eight*—Delaware *one*—Maryland *six*—Virginia *ten*— North Carolina *five*—South Carolina *five*—Georgia *three*.

But as the present Situation of the States may probably alter in the Number of their Inhabitants, the Legislature of the United States shall be authorized from Time to Time to apportion the Number of Representatives; and in Case any of the states shall hereafter be divided, or enlarged by Addition of Territory, or any two or more States united, or any new States created within the Limits of the United States, the Legislature of the United States shall possess Authority to regulate the Number of Representatives in any of the foregoing Cases, upon the Principle of the Number of their Inhabitants, according to the Provisions herein after mentioned namely —Provided always that Representation ought to be proportioned according to direct Taxation: And in order to ascertain the Alteration in the direct Taxation, which may be required from Time to Time, by the Changes in the relative Circumstances of the States—

Resolved that a Census be taken, within six years from the first Meeting of the Legislature of the United States, and once within the Term of every ten Years afterwards, of all the Inhabitants of the United States in the Manner and according to the Ratio recommended by Congress in their Resolution of April 18th, 1783—And that the Legislature of the United States shall proportion the direct Taxation accordingly.

Resolved that all Bills for raising or Appropriating Money, and for fixing the Salaries of the Officers of the Government of the United States shall originate in the first Branch of the Legislature of the United States, and shall not be altered or amended by the second Branch; and that no money shall be drawn from the public Treasury but in Pursuance of Appropriations to be originated by the first Branch.

That from the first Meeting of the Legislature of the United States until a Census shall be taken, all Monies for supplying the public Treasury by direct Taxation shall be raised from the several States according to the Number of their Representatives respectively in the first Branch.

That in the second Branch of the Legislature of the United States each State shall have an equal vote.

That the Legislature of the United States ought to possess the legislative Rights vested in Congress by the Confederation; and moreover to legislate in all Cases for the general Interests of the Union, and also in those Cases to which the States are separately incompetent, or in which the Harmony of the United States may be interrupted by the Exercise of Individual Legislation.

That the legislative Acts of the United States made by Virtue and in Pursuance of the Articles of Union, and all Treaties made and ratified under the Authority of the United States shall be the supreme Law of the respective States so far as those Acts or Treaties shall relate to the said States, or their Citizens and Inhabitants; and that the Judicatures of the several States shall be bound thereby in their Decisions, any thing in the respective Laws of the individual States to the contrary notwithstanding.

That a national Executive be instituted to consist of a single Person —to be chosen for the Term of six Years—with Power to carry into Execution the national laws—to appoint to Offices in Cases not otherwise provided for—to be removable on Impeachment and Conviction of mal Practice or Neglect of Duty—to receive a fixed Compensation for the Devotion of his Time to public Service—to be paid out of the public Treasury.

That the national Executive shall have a Right to negative any legislative Act, which shall not be afterwards passed, unless by two third Parts of each Branch of the national Legislature.

That a national Judiciary be established to consist of one Supreme Tribunal—the Judges of which shall be appointed by the second Branch of the national Legislature—to hold their Offices during good Behaviour—to receive punctually at stated Times a fixed Compensation for their Services, in which no Diminution shall be made so as to affect the Persons actually in Office at the Time of such Diminution.

That the Jurisdiction of the national Judiciary shall extend to Cases arising under the Laws passed by the general Legislature, and to such other Questions as involve the national Peace and Harmony.

That the national Legislature be empowered to appoint inferior Tribunals.

That Provision ought to be made for the Admission of States lawfully arising within the Limits of the United States, whether from a voluntary Junction of Government and Territory, or otherwise, with the Consent of a number of Voices in the national Legislature less than the whole.

That a Republican Form of Government shall be guarantied to each State; and that each State shall be protected against foreign and domestic Violence.

That Provision ought to be made for the Amendment of the Articles of Union, whensoever it shall seem necessary.

That the legislative, executive, and judiciary Powers, within the several States, and of the national Government, ought to be bound by Oath to support the Articles of Union.

That the Amendments which shall be offered to the Confederation by the Convention ought at a proper Time or Times, after the Approbation of Congress, to be submitted to an Assembly or Assemblies of Representatives, recommended by the several Legislatures, to be expressly chosen by the People to consider and decide thereon.

That the Representation in the second Branch of the Legislature of the United States consist of two Members of each State, who shall vote *per capita*.

That a National Executive be instituted—to consist of a Single Person—to be chosen by the National Legislature—for a Term of Seven Years—to be ineligible a second time; with power to carry into execution the national Laws; to appoint to Offices in cases not otherwise provided for; to be removable on impeachment and conviction of malpractice or neglect of duty; to receive a fixed compensation for the devotion of his time to public service; to be paid out of the public Treasury.

That it be an instruction of the Committee to whom are referred the proceedings of the Convention for the establishment of a national government, to receive a clause or clauses, requiring certain qualifications of property and citizenship in the United States for the Executive, the Judiciary, and the Members of both branches of the Legislature of the United States.

7

THE CONSTITUTION AS REPORTED
BY THE COMMITTEE OF DETAIL
August 6, 1787

W E THE people of the States of New Hampshire, Massachusetts, Rhode-Island and Providence Plantations, Connecticut, New-York, New-Jersey, Pennsylvania, Delaware, Maryland, Virginia, North-Carolina, South-Carolina, and Georgia, do ordain, declare, and establish the following Constitution for the Government of Ourselves and our Posterity.

ARTICLE I.

The stile of this government shall be, "The United States of America."

ARTICLE II.

The Government shall consist of supreme legislative, executive, and judicial powers.

ARTICLE III.

The legislative power shall be vested in a Congress, to consist of two separate and distinct bodies of men, a House of Representatives and a Senate; each of which shall, in all cases, have a negative on the other. The legislature shall meet on the first Monday in December in every year.

ARTICLE IV.

Sect. 1. The members of the House of Representatives shall be chosen every second year, by the people of the several States comprehended within this Union. The qualifications of the electors shall be the same, from time to time, as those of the electors in the several States, of the most numerous branch of their own legislatures.

Sect. 2. Every member of the House of Representatives shall be of the age of twenty five years at least; shall have been a citizen in the United States for at least three years before his election; and shall be, at the time of his election, a resident of the State in which he shall be chosen.

Sect. 3. The House of Representatives shall, at its first formation, and until the number of citizens and inhabitants shall be taken in the manner herein after described, consist of sixty five Members, of whom three shall be chosen in New Hampshire, eight in Massachusetts, one in Rhode-Island and Providence Plantations, five in Connecticut, six in New-York, four in New Jersey, eight in Pennsylvania, one in Delaware, six in Maryland, ten in Virginia, five in North-Carolina, five in South-Carolina, and three in Georgia.

Sect. 4. As the proportions of numbers in the different States will alter from time to time; as some of the States may hereafter be divided; as others may be enlarged by addition of territory; as two or more States may be united; as new States will be erected within the limits of the United States, the legislature shall, in each of these cases, regulate the number of representatives by the number of inhabitants, according to the provisions hereinafter made, at the rate of one for every forty thousand.

Sect. 5. All bills for raising or appropriating money, and for fixing the salaries of the officers of the government, shall originate in the House of Representatives, and shall not be altered or amended by the Senate. No money shall be drawn from the public Treasury, but in pursuance of appropriations that shall originate in the House of Representatives.

Sect. 6. The House of Representatives shall have the sole power of impeachment. It shall choose its Speaker and other officers.

Sect. 7. Vacancies in the House of Representatives shall be supplied by writs of election from the executive authority of the State, in the representation from which they shall happen.

ARTICLE V.

Sect. 1. The Senate of the United States shall be chosen by the Legislatures of the several States. Each Legislature shall choose two members. Vacancies may be supplied by the Executive until the next meeting of the Legislature. Each member shall have one vote.

Sect. 2. The Senators shall be chosen for six years; but immediately after the first election they shall be divided, by lot, into three classes, as nearly as may be, numbered one, two, and three. The seats of the members of the first class shall be vacated at the expiration of the second year, of the second class, at the expiration of the fourth year, of the third class at the expiration of the sixth year, so that a third part of the members may be chosen every second year.

Sect. 3. Every member of the Senate shall be of the age of thirty years at least; shall have been a citizen in the United States for at least four years before his election; and shall be, at the time of his election, a resident of the State from which he shall be chosen.

Sect. 4. The Senate shall chuse its own President and other officers.

Sect. 1. The times and places, and the manner of holding the elections of the members of each House shall be prescribed by the Legislature of each State; but their provisions concerning them may, at any time, be altered by the Legislature of the United States.

Sect. 2. The Legislature of the United States shall have authority to establish such uniform qualifications of the members of each House, with regard to property, as to the said legislature shall seem expedient.

Sect. 3. In each House a majority of the members shall constitute a quorum to do business; but a smaller number may adjourn from day to day.

Sect. 4. Each House shall be the judge of the elections, returns and qualifications of its own members.

Sect. 5. Freedom of speech and debate in the Legislature shall not be impeached or questioned in any Court or place out of the Legislature; and the members of each House shall, in all cases, except treason, felony, and breach of the peace, be privileged from arrest during their attendance at Congress, and in going to and returning from it.

Sect. 6. Each House may determine the rules of its proceedings; may punish its members for disorderly behaviour; and may expel a member.

Sect. 7. The House of Representatives, and the Senate, when it shall be acting in a legislative capacity, shall keep a journal of their proceedings, and shall, from time to time, publish them: and the yeas and nays of the members of each House, on any question, shall, at the desire of one fifth part of the members present, be entered on the journal.

Sect. 8. Neither House, without the consent of the other, shall adjourn for more than three days, nor to any other place than that at which the two Houses are sitting. But this regulation shall not extend to the Senate, when it shall exercise the powers mentioned in the article.

Sect. 9. The members of each House shall be ineligible to, and incapable of holding any office under the authority of the United States, during the time for which they shall respectively be elected: and the members of the Senate shall be ineligible to, and incapable of holding any such office for one year afterwards.

Sect. 10. The members of each House shall receive a compensation for their services, to be ascertained and paid by the State, in which they shall be chosen.

Sect. 11. The enacting stile of the laws of the United States shall be, "Be it enacted by the Senate and Representatives in Congress assembled."

Sect. 12. Each House shall possess the right of originating bills, except in the cases beforementioned.

Sect. 13. Every bill, which shall have passed the House of Representatives and the Senate, shall, before it becomes a law, be presented to the President of the United States, for his revision: if, upon such revision, he approve of it, he shall signify his approbation by signing it: But if, upon such revision, it shall appear to him improper for being passed into a law, he shall return it, together with his objections against it, to that House in which it shall have originated, who shall enter the objections at large on their journal, and proceed to reconsider the bill. But if after such reconsideration, two thirds of that House shall, notwithstanding the objections of the President, agree to pass it, it shall together with his objections, be sent to the other house, by which it shall likewise be reconsidered, and if approved by two thirds of the other House also, it shall become a law. But in all such cases, the votes of both Houses shall be determined by yeas and nays; and the names of the persons voting for or against the bill shall be entered in the journal of each House respectively. If any bill shall not be returned by the President within seven days after it shall have been presented to him, it shall be a law, unless the legislature by their adjournment, prevent its return; in which case, it shall not be a law.

ARTICLE VII.

Sect. 1. The Legislature of the United States shall have the power to lay and collect taxes, duties, imposts, and excises;

To regulate commerce with foreign nations, and among the several States;

To establish a uniform rule of naturalization throughout the United States;

To coin money;

To regulate the value of foreign coin;

To fix the standard of weights and measures;

To establish Post-offices;

To borrow money, and emit bills on the credit of the United States;

To appoint a Treasurer by ballot;

To constitute tribunals inferior to the Supreme Court;

To make rules concerning captures on land and water;

To declare the law and punishment of piracies and felonies committed on the high seas, and the punishment of counterfeiting the coin of the United States, and of offences against the law of nations;

To subdue a rebellion in any State, on the application of its legislature;

To make war;

To raise armies;

To build and equip fleets;

To call forth the aid of the militia, in order to execute the laws of the Union; enforce treaties, suppress insurrections, and repel invasions;

And to make all laws that shall be necessary and proper for carrying into execution the foregoing powers, and all other powers vested, by this constitution, in the government of the United States, or in any department or officer thereof.

Sect. 2. Treason against the United States shall consist only in levying war against the United States, or any of them; and in adhering to the enemies of the United States, or any of them. The Legislature of the United States shall have power to declare the punishment of treason. No person shall be convicted of treason, unless on the testimony of two witnesses. No attainder of treason shall work corruption of blood, nor forfeiture, except during the life of the person attainted.

Sect. 3. The proportions of direct taxation shall be regulated by the whole number of white and other free citizens and inhabitants of every age, sex, and condition, including those bound to servitude for a term of years, and three fifths of all other persons not comprehended in the foregoing description, (except Indians not paying taxes); which number shall, within six years after the first meeting of the Legislature, and within the term of every ten years afterwards, be taken in such manner as the said Legislature shall direct.

Sect. 4. No tax or duty shall be laid by the Legislature on articles exported from any State; nor on the migration or importation of such persons as the several States shall think proper to admit; nor shall such migration or importation be prohibited.

Sect. 5. No capitation tax shall be laid, unless in proportion to the census hereinbefore directed to be taken.

Sect. 6. No navigation act shall be passed without the assent of two thirds of the members present in each House.

Sect. 7. The United States shall not grant any title of nobility.

ARTICLE VIII.

The acts of the Legislature of the United States made in pursuance of this Constitution, and all treaties made under the authority of the United States shall be the supreme law of the several States, and of their citizens and inhabitants; and the judges in the several States shall be bound thereby in their decisions; any thing in the Constitution or laws of the several States to the contrary notwithstanding.

Sect. 1. The Senate of the United States shall have power to make treaties, and to appoint Ambassadors, and Judges of the Supreme Court.

Sect. 2. In all disputes and controversies now subsisting, or that may hereafter subsist between two or more States, respecting jurisdiction or territory, the Senate shall possess the following powers. Whenever the Legislature, or the Executive authority, or the lawful Agent of any State, in controversy with another, shall by memorial to the Senate, state the matter in question, and apply for a hearing; notice of such memorial and application shall be given by order of the Senate, to the Legislature or the Executive authority of the other State in controversy. The Senate shall also assign a day for the appearance of the parties, by their agents, before that House. The Agents shall be directed to appoint, by joint consent, commissioners or judges to constitute a Court for hearing and determining the matter in question. But, if the Agents cannot agree, the Senate shall name three persons out of each of the several States; and from the list of such persons each party shall alternately strike out one, until the number shall be reduced to thirteen; and from that number not less than seven, nor more than nine names, as the Senate shall direct, shall in their presence, be drawn out by lot; and the persons whose names shall be so drawn, or any five of them shall be commissioners or Judges to hear and finally determine the controversy; provided a majority of the Judges, who shall hear the cause, agree in the determination. If either party shall neglect to attend at any day assigned, without showing sufficient reasons for not attending, or being present shall refuse to strike, the Senate shall proceed to nominate three persons out of each State, and the clerk of the Senate shall strike in behalf of the party absent or refusing. If any of the parties shall refuse to submit to the authority of such Court, or shall not appear to prosecute or defend their claim or cause, the Court shall nevertheless proceed to pronounce judgment. The judgment shall be final and conclusive. The proceedings shall be transmitted to the President of the Senate, and shall be lodged among the public records for the security of the parties concerned. Every Commissioner shall, before he sit in judgment, take an oath, to be administered by one of the judges of the Supreme or Superior Court of the State where the cause shall be tried, "well and truly to hear and determine the matter in question according to the best of his judgment, without favor, affection, or hope of reward."

Sect. 3. All controversies concerning lands claimed under different grants of two or more States, whose jurisdictions as they respect such lands shall have been decided or adjusted subsequent to such grants, or any of them, shall, on application to the Senate, be finally determined, as near as may be, in the same manner as is before prescribed for deciding controversies between different States.

ARTICLE X.

Sect. 1. The Executive Power of the United States shall be vested in a single person. His stile shall be, "The President of the United States of America"; and his title shall be, "His Excellency." He shall be elected by ballot by the Legislature. He shall hold his office during the term of seven years; but shall not be elected a second time.

Sect. 2. He shall, from time to time, give information to the Legislature, of the state of the Union: he may recommend to their consideration such measures as he shall judge necessary and expedient: he may convene them on extraordinary occasions. In case of disagreement between the two Houses, with regard to the time of adjournment, he may adjourn them to such time as he thinks proper: he shall take care that the laws of the United States be duly and faithfully executed: he shall commission all the officers of the United States; and shall appoint officers in all cases not otherwise provided for by this Constitution. He shall receive Ambassadors, and may correspond with the supreme Executives of the several States. He shall have power to grant reprieves and pardons; but his pardon shall not be pleadable in bar of an impeachment. He shall be commander in chief of the Army and navy of the United States, and of the Militia of the several States. He shall, at stated times, receive for his services a compensation, which shall neither be increased nor diminished during his continuance in office. Before he shall enter on the duties of his department, he shall take the following oath or affirmation: "I —————— solemnly swear (or affirm), that I will faithfully execute the office of President of the United States of America." He shall be removed from his office on impeachment by the House of Representatives, and conviction in the Supreme Court, of treason, bribery, or corruption. In case of his removal as aforesaid, death, resignation, or disability to discharge the powers and duties of his office, the President of the Senate shall exercise those powers and duties until another President of the United States be chosen, or until the disability of the President be removed.

ARTICLE XI.

Sect. 1. The Judicial Power of the United States shall be vested in one Supreme Court, and in such inferior Courts as shall, when necessary, from time to time, be constituted by the Legislature of the United States.

Sect. 2. The Judges of the Supreme Court, and of the Inferior Courts, shall hold their offices during good behaviour. They shall, at stated times, receive for their services a compensation, which shall not be diminished during their continuance in office.

Sect. 3. The Jurisdiction of the Supreme Court shall extend to all cases arising under laws passed by the Legislature of the United States; to all cases affecting Ambassadors, other Public Ministers, and Consuls; to the trial of impeachments of Officers of the United States; to all cases of Admiralty and maritime jurisdiction; to controversies between two or more States (except such as shall regard Territory or Jurisdiction), between a State and citizens of another State, between Citizens of different States, and between a State or the citizens thereof and foreign states, citizens, or subjects. In cases of impeachment, cases affecting Ambassadors, other Public Ministers, and Consuls, and those in which a State shall be a party, this jurisdiction shall be original. In all the other cases before mentioned, it shall be appellate, with such exceptions and under such regulations as the Legislature shall make. The Legislature may assign any part of the jurisdiction above mentioned (except the trial of the President of the United States) in the manner and under the limitations which it shall think proper, to such Inferior Courts as it shall constitute from time to time.

Sect. 4. The trial of all criminal offences (except in cases of impeachments) shall be in the State where they shall be committed; and shall be by jury.

Sect. 5. Judgment, in cases of Impeachment, shall not extend farther than to removal from Office, and disqualification to hold and enjoy any office of honor, trust, or profit under the United States. But the party convicted shall, nevertheless, be liable and subject to indictment, trial, judgment, and punishment according to law.

ARTICLE XII.

No State shall coin money; nor grant letters of marque and reprisal; nor enter into any treaty, alliance, or confederation; nor grant any title of Nobility.

ARTICLE XIII.

No State, without the consent of the Legislature of the United States, shall emit bills of credit, or make any thing but specie a tender in payment of debts; nor lay imposts or duties on imports; nor keep troops or ships of war in time of peace; nor enter into any agreement or compact with another State, or with any foreign power; nor engage in any war, unless it shall be actually invaded by enemies, or the danger of invasion be so imminent, as not to admit of a delay, until the Legislature of the United States can be consulted.

ARTICLE XIV.

The Citizens of each State shall be entitled to all privileges and immunities of citizens in the several States.

ARTICLE XV.

Any person charged with treason, felony, or high misdemeanor, in any State, who shall flee from justice, and shall be found in any other State, shall, on demand of the Executive power of the State from which he fled, be delivered up and removed to the State having jurisdiction of the offence.

ARTICLE XVI.

Full faith shall be given in each State to the acts of the Legislatures, and to the records and judicial proceedings of the Courts and Magistrates of every other State.

ARTICLE XVII.

New States lawfully constituted or established within the limits of the United States may be admitted, by the Legislature, into this government; but to such admission the consent of two thirds of the members present in each House shall be necessary. If a new State shall arise within the limits of any of the present States, the consent of the Legislatures of such States shall be also necessary to its admission. If the admission be consented to, the new States shall be admitted on the same terms with the original States. But the legislature may make conditions with the new States concerning the public debt which shall be then subsisting.

ARTICLE XVIII.

The United States shall guaranty to each State a Republican form of Government; and shall protect each State against foreign invasions; and, on the application of its Legislature, against domestic violence.

ARTICLE XIX.

On the application of the Legislatures of two thirds of the States in the Union for an amendment of this Constitution, the Legislature of the United States shall call a Convention for that purpose.

ARTICLE XX.

The members of the Legislatures, and the Executive and Judicial officers of the United States, and of the several States, shall be bound by oath to support this Constitution.

ARTICLE XXI.

The ratification of the Conventions of   States shall be sufficient for organizing this Constitution.

ARTICLE XXII.

This Constitution shall be laid before the United States in Congress assembled, for their approbation; and it is the opinion of this Convention, that it should be afterwards submitted to a Convention chosen in each State, under the recommendation of its legislature, in order to receive the ratification of such Convention.

ARTICLE XXIII.

To introduce this government, it is the opinion of this convention, that each assenting Convention should notify its assent and ratification to the United States in Congress assembled; that Congress, after receiving the assent and ratifications of the Conventions of   States, should appoint and publish a day, as early as may be, and appoint a place for commencing proceedings under this Constitution; that after such publication, the Legislatures of the several States should elect members of the Senate, and direct the election of members of the House of Representatives; and that the members of the Legislature should meet at the time and place assigned by Congress, and should, as soon as may be, after their meeting, choose the President of the United States, and proceed to execute this Constitution.

8

PROCEEDINGS OF THE CONVENTION
THROUGH SEPTEMBER 10

Referred to the Committee of Style

[Articles and Sections identical, except in some cases for immaterial variations in phraseology, with those in the Constitution as reported by the Committee of Detail are here omitted. The text follows that in Farrand's *Records*, II, 565-80]

ARTICLE III

THE LEGISLATIVE power shall be vested in a Congress, to consist of two separate and distinct bodies of men, a House of Representatives, and a Senate. The Legislature shall meet at least once in every year, and such a meeting shall be on the first Monday in December unless a different day shall be appointed by law.

IV

Sect. 2. Every Member of the House of Representatives shall be of the age of twenty-five years at least; shall have been a citizen of the United States for at least seven years before his election; and shall be, at the time of his election, an inhabitant of the State in which he shall be chosen.

Sect. 4. As the proportions of numbers in the different states will alter from time to time; as some of the States may hereafter be divided; as others may be enlarged by addition of territory; as two or more States may be united; as new States will be erected within the limits of the United States, the Legislature shall, in each of these cases, regulate the number of representatives by the number of inhabitants, according to the rule hereinafter made for direct taxation not exceeding the rate of one for every forty thousand. Provided that every State shall have at least one representative.

V

Sect. 1. The Senate of the United States shall be chosen by the Legislatures of the several States. Each Legislature shall chuse two members. Vacancies happening by refusals to accept, resignations or otherwise may be supplied by the Legislature of the State in the representation of which such vacancies shall happen, or by the executive thereof until the next meeting of the Legislature. Each member shall have one vote.

Sect. 3. Every member of the Senate shall be of the age of thirty years at least; shall have been a citizen of the United States for at least nine years before his election; and shall be, at the time of his election, an inhabitant of the State for which he shall be chosen.

VI

Sect. 1. The times and places and the manner of holding the elections of the members of each House shall be prescribed by the Legislature of each State respectively; but regulations in each of the foregoing cases may, at any time, be made or altered by the Legislature of the United States.

Sect. 2. [Struck out by the Convention]

Sect. 3. In each House a majority of the members shall constitute a quorum to do business; but a smaller number may adjourn from day to day, and may be authorised to compel the attendance of absent members in such manner and under such penalties as each House may provide.

Sect. 6. Each House may determine the rules of its proceedings; may punish its members for disorderly behaviour; and may, with the concurrence of two thirds, expel a member.

Sect. 8. During the session of the Legislature neither House, without the consent of the other, shall adjourn for more than three days, nor to any place than that at which the two Houses are sitting.

Sect. 9. The Members of each House shall be ineligible to any civil office under the authority of the United States created, or the emoluments whereof shall have been encreased during the time for which they shall respectively be elected—and no person holding any office under the United States shall be a Member of either House during his continuance in Office.

Sect. 10. The members of each House shall receive a compensation for their services, to be paid out of the Treasury of the United States, to be ascertained by law.

Sect. 12. All Bills for raising revenue shall originate in the House of representatives: but the Senate may propose or concur with amendments as on other bills. No money shall be drawn from the Treasury but in consequence of appropriations made by law.

Sect. 13. [The President shall have "ten days (Sundays excepted)" instead of "seven days" in which to veto a bill sent to him by Congress]

Sect. 14. Every order, resolution or vote, to which the concurrence of the Senate and House of Representatives may be necessary (except on a question of adjournment, and in the cases hereinafter mentioned) shall be presented to the President for his revision; and before the same shall have force, shall be approved by him, or, being disapproved by him, shall be repassed by the Senate and House of representatives, according to the rules and limitations prescribed in the case of a bill.

VII

Sect. 1. The Legislature shall have power to lay and collect taxes, duties, imposts and excises, to pay the debts and provide for the common defence and general welfare of the United States.

To regulate commerce with foreign nations, and among the several States; and with the Indian tribes.

To establish an uniform rule of naturalization throughout the United States;

To coin money;

To regulate the value of foreign coin;

To fix the standard of weights and measures;

To establish post-offices and post-roads;

To borrow money on the credit of the United States;

To appoint a Treasurer by joint ballot;

To constitute tribunals inferior to the supreme court;

To make rules concerning captures on land and water;

To define and punish piracies and felonies committed on the high seas, to punish the counterfeiting of the securities, and current coin of the United States, and offences against the law of nations;

To declare war; and grant letters of marque and reprisal.

To raise and support armies; but no appropriation of money to that use shall be for a longer term than two years.

To provide & maintain a navy;

To make rules for the government and regulation of the land and naval forces.

To provide for calling forth the militia to execute the laws of the Union, suppress insurrections, and repel invasions;

To make laws for organizing, arming, and disciplining the militia, and for governing such part of them as may be employed in the service of the United States reserving to the States, respectively, the appointment of the Officers, and the authority of training the militia according to the discipline prescribed by the United States.

To establish uniform laws on the subject of bankruptcies.

To exercise exclusive legislation in all cases whatsoever over such district (not exceeding ten miles square) as may by cession of particular States and the acceptance of the Legislature become the seat of the Government of the United States, and to exercise like authority over all Places purchased, by the consent of the Legislature of the State, for the erection of Forts, Magazines, Arsenals, Dock Yards and other needful buildings.

To promote the progress of science and useful arts by securing for limited times to Authors and Inventors the exclusive right to their respective writings and discoveries.

And to make all laws that shall be necessary and proper for carrying into execution the foregoing powers, and all other powers vested, by this Constitution, in the government of the United States, or in any department or officer thereof.

All debts contracted and engagements entered into, by or under the authority of Congress shall be as valid against the United States under this constitution as under the confederation.

Sect. 2. Treason against the United States shall consist only in levying war against them, or in adhering to their enemies, giving them aid and comfort. The Legislature shall have power to declare the punishment of treason. No person shall be convicted of treason, unless on the testimony of two witnesses to the same overt act, or on confession in open court. No attainder of treason shall work corruption of blood, nor forfeiture, except during the life of the person attainted. The Legislature shall pass no bill of attainder nor any ex post facto laws.

Sect. 3. [The first census to be taken within three years, not six as formerly, after "the first meeting of the Legislature"]

Sect. 4. No tax or duty shall be laid by the Legislature on articles exported from an ' State. The migration or importation of such persons as the several States now existing shall think proper to admit shall not be prohibited by the Legislature prior to the year 1808—but a tax or duty may be imposed on such importation not exceeding ten dollars for each person. Nor shall any regulation of commerce or revenue give preference to the ports of one State over those of another, or oblige Vessels bound to or from any State to enter, clear, or pay duties in another.

And all duties, imposts, and excises, laid by the Legislature, shall be uniform throughout the United States.

Sect. 6. [Struck out by the Convention]

Sect. 7. The United States shall not grant any title of nobility. No person holding any office of profit or trust under the United States, shall without the consent of the Legislature accept of any present, emolument, office, or title of any kind whatever, from any king, prince or foreign State.

VIII

The Constitution and the Laws of the United States which shall be made in pursuance thereof, and all treaties made or which shall be made under the authority of the United States, shall be the supreme law of the several States, and of their citizens and inhabitants; and the judges in the several States shall be bound thereby in their decisions; any thing in the constitutions or laws of the several States to the contrary notwithstanding.

IX

Sect. 1. The Senate of the United States shall have power to try all impeachments: but no person shall be convicted without the concurrence of two thirds of the Members present: and every Member shall be on oath.

X

Sect. 1. The Executive power of the United States shall be vested in a single person. His stile shall be, "The President of the United States of America;" and his title shall be, "His Excellency." He shall hold his office during the term of four years, and together with the Vice President, chosen for the same term, be elected in the following manner.

Each State shall appoint, in such manner as it's legislature may direct, a number of Electors equal to the whole number of Senators and Members of the House of representatives to which the State may be entitled in the Legislature. But no Person shall be appointed an Elector who is a member of the Legislature of the United States, or who holds any office of profit or trust under the United States.

The Electors shall meet in their respective States and vote by ballot for two Persons of whom one at least shall not be an inhabitant of the same State with themselves.—and they shall make a list of all the Persons voted for, and of the number of votes for each, which list they shall sign and certify, and transmit sealed to the seat of the general Government, directed to the President of the Senate.

The President of the Senate shall in the presence of the Senate and House of representatives open all the certificates and the votes shall then be counted.

The Person having the greatest number of votes shall be the President (if such number be a majority of the whole number of the Electors appointed) and if there be more than one who have such a majority, and have an equal number of votes, then the House of representatives shall immediately choose by ballot one of them for President, the representation from each State having one vote— But if no Person have a majority, then from the five highest on the list, the House of representatives shall, in like manner, choose by ballot the President— In the choice of a President by the House of representatives a quorum shall consist of a Member or Members from two thirds of the States, and the concurrence of a majority of all the States shall be necessary to such choice.—and, in every case after the choice of the President, the Person having the greatest number of votes of the Electors shall be the vice-President: But, if there should remain two or more who have equal votes, the Senate shall choose from them the Vice President.

The Legislature may determine the time of chusing the Electors and of their giving their votes— But the election shall be on the same day throughout the United States.

The Legislature may declare by law what officer of the United States shall act as President in case of the death, resignation, or disability of the President and Vice President; and such Officer shall act accordingly, until such disability be removed, or a President shall be elected.

Sect. 2. No Person except a natural born Citizen or a Citizen of the U. S. at the time of the adoption of this Constitution shall be eligible to the office of President: nor shall any Person be elected to that office, who shall be under the age of 35 years, and who has not been in the whole, at least 14 years a resident within the U. S.

Sect. 3. The Vice President shall be ex officio, President of the Senate, except when they sit to try the impeachment of the President, in which case the Chief Justice shall preside, and excepting also when he shall exercise the powers and duties of President, in which case, and in case of his absence, the Senate shall chuse a President pro tempore— The Vice President when acting as President of the Senate shall not have a vote unless the House be equally divided.

Sect. 4. The President by and with the advice and consent of the Senate, shall have power to make treaties: and he shall nominate and by and with the advice and consent of the Senate shall appoint Ambassadors, other public Ministers and Consuls, Judges of the supreme Court, and all other officers of the U. S. whose appointments are not otherwise herein provided for. But no Treaty shall be made without the consent of two thirds of the Members present.

The President shall have power to fill up all vacancies that may happen during the recess of the Senate by granting commissions which shall expire at the end of the next session of the Senate.

Sect. 2.[1] He shall, from time to time, give to the Legislature in-

---

[1] Original numbering, the sections above numbered 2-4 were insertions.

formation of the State of the Union: and recommend to their consideration such measures as he shall judge necessary, and expedient: he
may convene both or either of the Houses on extraordinary occasions,
and in case of disagreement between the two Houses, with regard to
the time of adjournment, he may adjourn them to such time as he
shall think proper: he shall take care that the laws of the United
States be duly and faithfully executed: he shall commission all the
officers of the United States; and shall appoint to all offices established by this constitution except in cases herein otherwise provided
for, and to all offices which may hereafter be created by law. He
shall receive Ambassadors, other public Ministers and Consuls. He
shall have power to grant reprieves and pardons except in cases of
impeachment. He shall be Commander in Chief of the Army and
Navy of the United States, and of the Militia of the several States
when called into the actual service of the United States; and may
require the opinion in writing of the principal officer in each of the
executive departments upon any subject relating to the duties of their
respective offices. He shall, at stated times, receive for his services, a
compensation, which shall neither be encreased nor diminished during his continuance in office. Before he shall enter on the duties of his
department, he shall take the following Oath or Affirmation, "I _____
solemnly swear (or affirm) that I will faithfully execute the Office of
President of the United States of America, and will to the best of
my judgment and power, preserve, protect and defend the Constitution
of the United States." He shall be removed from his office on impeachment by the House of representatives, and conviction by the
Senate, for treason or bribery or other high crimes and misdemeanors
against the United States; the Vice President and other civil Officers
of the United States shall be removed from Office on impeachment
and conviction as aforesaid; and in case of his removal as aforesaid,
death, absence, resignation or inability to discharge the powers or
duties of his office the Vice President shall exercise those powers and
duties until another President be chosen, or until the inability of the
President be removed.

XI

Sect. 3. The Judicial Power shall extend to all cases both in law
and equity arising under this Constitution and the laws of the United
States, and treaties made or which shall be made under their authority; to all cases affecting Ambassadors, other Public Ministers and
Consuls; to all cases of Admiralty and Maritime Jurisdiction; to Controversies to which the United States shall be a party, to controversies

between two or more States (except such as shall regard Territory and Jurisdiction) between a State and citizens of another State, between citizens of different States, between citizens of the same State claiming lands under grants of different States, and between a State or the citizens thereof and foreign States, citizens or subjects. In cases affecting Ambassadors, other Public Ministers and Consuls, and those in which a State shall be party, the Supreme Court shall have original jurisdiction. In all other cases beforementioned the Supreme Court shall have appellate jurisdiction both as to law and fact with such exceptions and under such regulations as the Legislature shall make.

Sect. 4. The trial of all crimes (except in cases of impeachments) shall be by jury and such trial shall be held in the State where the said crimes shall have been committed; but when not committed within any State then the trial shall be at such place or places as the Legislature may direct.

The privilege of the writ of Habeas Corpus shall not be suspended; unless where in cases of rebellion or invasion the public safety may require it.

XII

No State shall coin money; nor emit bills of credit, nor make anything but gold or silver coin a tender in payment of debts; nor pass any bill of attainder or ex post facto laws; nor grant letters of marque and reprisal, nor enter into any treaty, alliance, or confederation; nor grant any title of nobility.

XIII

No State, without the consent of the Legislature of the United States shall lay imposts or duties on imports or exports, nor with such consent but for the use of the treasury of the United States; nor keep troops or ships of war in time of peace; nor enter into any agreement or compact with another State, or with any foreign power; nor engage in any war, unless it shall be actually invaded by enemies, or the danger of invasion be so imminent, as not to admit of a delay, until the Legislature of the United States can be consulted.

XV

Any person charged with treason, felony, or other crime in any State, who shall flee from justice, and shall be found in any other State, shall, on demand of the Executive Power of the State from which he fled, be delivered up and removed to the State having jurisdiction of the offence.

If any Person bound to service or labor in any of the United States shall escape into another State, He or She shall not be discharged from such service or labor in consequence of any regulations subsisting in the State to which they escape; but shall be delivered up to the person justly claiming their service or labor.

XVI

Full faith and credit shall be given in each State to the public Acts, records, and judicial proceedings of every other State, and the Legislature may by general laws prescribe the manner in which such acts, records, and proceedings shall be proved and the effect thereof.

XVII

New States may be admitted by the Legislature into this Union: but no new State shall be hereafter formed or erected within the jurisdiction of any of the present States, without the consent of the Legislature of such State as well as of the general Legislature. Nor shall any State be formed by the junction of two or more States or parts thereof without the consent of the Legislatures of such States as well as of the Legislature of the United States.

The Legislature shall have power to dispose of and make all needful rules and regulations respecting the territory or other property belonging to the United States: and nothing in this Constitution contained shall be so construed as to prejudice any claims either of the United States or of any particular State.

XVIII

The United States shall guaranty to each State a Republican form of government; and shall protect each State against invasions, and, on the application of its Legislature or Executive, against domestic violence.

XIX

The Legislature of the United States, whenever two thirds of both Houses shall deem necessary, or on the application of two thirds of the Legislatures of the several States, shall propose amendments to this Constitution which shall be valid to all intents and purposes as parts thereof, when the same shall have been ratified by three fourths at least of the Legislatures of the several States, or by Conventions in three fourths thereof, as one or the other mode of ratification may be proposed by the Legislature of the United-States: Provided that no amendments which may be made prior to the year 1808. shall in any manner affect the 4th and 5th Sections or article the 7th.

XX

The Members of the Legislatures, and the executive and judicial officers of the United States, and of the several States, shall be bound by oath or affirmation to support this Constitution.

But no religious test shall ever be required as a qualification to any office or public trust under the authority of the United States.

XXI

The ratification of the Conventions of nine States shall be sufficient for organising this Constitution between the said States.

XXII

This Constitution shall be laid before the United States in Congress assembled, and it is the opinion of this Convention that it should be afterwards submitted to a Convention chosen in each State, under the recommendation of its Legislature, in order to receive the ratification of such Convention.

XXIII

[The same as before except that the first Congress assembled under the Constitution would not "choose the President of the United States"]

That it be an instruction to the Committee to prepare an address to the People to accompany the present constitution, and to be laid with the same before the United States in Congress.[1]

Mr. Randolph moved to refer to the Committee also a motion relating to pardons in cases of Treason—which was agreed to nem: con:[1]

[1] Action taken by the Convention at the close of the proceedings on September 10.

9

THE CONSTITUTION
OF THE UNITED STATES

(The official text as compared with the original manuscript and
published by the Government Printing Office)

WE THE PEOPLE of the United States, in Order to form a more
perfect Union, establish Justice, insure domestic Tranquility,
provide for the common defence, promote the general Welfare, and
secure the Blessings of Liberty to ourselves and our Posterity, do
ordain and establish this CONSTITUTION for the United States of
America.

ARTICLE I.

SECTION 1. All legislative Powers herein granted shall be vested
in a Congress of the United States, which shall consist of a Senate
and House of Representatives.

SECTION 2. The House of Representatives shall be composed of
Members chosen every second Year by the People of the several States,
and the Electors in each State shall have the Qualifications requisite
for Electors of the most numerous Branch of the State Legislature.

No Person shall be a Representative who shall not have attained to
the Age of twenty five Years, and been seven Years a Citizen of the
United States, and who shall not, when elected, be an Inhabitant of
that State in which he shall be chosen.

Representatives and direct Taxes shall be apportioned among the
several States which may be included within this Union, according
to their respective Numbers, which shall be determined by adding to
the whole Number of free Persons, including those bound to Service
for a Term of Years, and excluding Indians not taxed, three fifths of
all other Persons. The actual Enumeration shall be made within three
Years after the first Meeting of the Congress of the United States, and
within every subsequent Term of ten Years, in such Manner as they
shall by Law direct. The Number of Representatives shall not exceed
one for every thirty Thousand, but each State shall have at Least one
Representative; and until such enumeration shall be made, the State
of New Hampshire shall be entitled to chuse three, Massachusetts
eight, Rhode-Island and Providence Plantations one, Connecticut five,

New-York six, New Jersey four, Pennsylvania eight, Delaware one, Maryland six, Virginia ten, North Carolina five, South Carolina five, and Georgia three.

When vacancies happen in the Representation from any State, the Executive Authority thereof shall issue Writs of Election to fill such Vacancies.

The House of Representatives shall chuse their Speaker and other Officers; and shall have the sole Power of Impeachment.

SECTION 3. The Senate of the United States shall be composed of two Senators from each State, chosen by the Legislature thereof, for six Years; and each Senator shall have one Vote.

Immediately after they shall be assembled in Consequence of the first Election, they shall be divided as equally as may be into three Classes. The Seats of the Senators of the first Class shall be vacated at the Expiration of the second Year, of the second Class at the Expiration of the fourth Year, and of the third Class at the Expiration of the sixth Year, so that one third may be chosen every second Year; and if Vacancies happen by Resignation, or otherwise, during the Recess of the Legislature of any State, the Executive thereof may make temporary Appointments until the next Meeting of the Legislature, which shall then fill such Vacancies.

No Person shall be a Senator who shall not have attained to the Age of thirty Years, and been nine Years a Citizen of the United States, and who shall not, when elected, be an Inhabitant of that State for which he shall be chosen.

The Vice President of the United States shall be President of the Senate, but shall have no Vote, unless they be equally divided.

The Senate shall chuse their other Officers, and also a President pro tempore, in the Absence of the Vice President, or when he shall exercise the Office of President of the United States.

The Senate shall have the sole Power to try all Impeachments. When sitting for that Purpose, they shall be on Oath or Affirmation. When the President of the United States is tried, the Chief Justice shall preside: And no Person shall be convicted without the Concurrence of two thirds of the Members present.

Judgment in Cases of Impeachment shall not extend further than to removal from Office, and disqualification to hold and enjoy any Office of honor, Trust or Profit under the United States: but the Party convicted shall nevertheless be liable and subject to Indictment, Trial, Judgment and Punishment, according to Law.

SECTION 4. The Times, Places and Manner of holding Elections for Senators and Representatives, shall be prescribed in each State by the Legislature thereof; but the Congress may at any time by Law make or alter such Regulations, except as to the Places of chusing Senators.

The Congress shall assemble at least once in every Year, and such Meeting shall be on the first Monday in December, unless they shall by Law appoint a different Day.

SECTION 5. Each House shall be the Judge of the Elections, Returns and Qualifications of its own Members, and a Majority of each shall constitute a Quorum to do Business; but a smaller Number may adjourn from day to day, and may be authorized to compel the Attendance of absent Members, in such Manner, and under such Penalties as each House may provide.

Each House may determine the Rules of its Proceedings, punish its Members for disorderly Behaviour, and, with the Concurrence of two thirds, expel a Member.

Each House shall keep a Journal of its Proceedings, and from time to time publish the same, excepting such Parts as may in their Judgment require Secrecy; and the Yeas and Nays of the Members of either House on any question shall, at the desire of one fifth of those Present, be entered on the Journal.

Neither House, during the Session of Congress, shall, without the Consent of the other, adjourn for more than three days, nor to any other Place than that in which the two Houses shall be sitting.

SECTION 6. The Senators and Representatives shall receive a Compensation for their Services, to be ascertained by Law, and paid out of the Treasury of the United States. They shall in all Cases, except Treason, Felony and Breach of the Peace, be privileged from Arrest during their Attendance at the Session of their respective Houses, and in going to and returning from the same; and for any Speech or Debate in either House, they shall not be questioned in any other Place.

No Senator or Representative shall, during the Time for which he was elected, be appointed to any civil Office under the Authority of the United States, which shall have been created, or the Emoluments whereof shall have been encreased during such time; and no Person holding any Office under the United States, shall be a Member of either House during his Continuance in Office.

SECTION 7. All Bills for raising Revenue shall originate in the House of Representatives; but the Senate may propose or concur with Amendments as on other Bills.

Every Bill which shall have passed the House of Representatives and the Senate, shall, before it become a Law, be presented to the President of the United States; If he approve he shall sign it, but if not he shall return it, with his Objections to that House in which it shall have originated, who shall enter the Objections at large on their Journal, and proceed to reconsider it. If after such Reconsideration two thirds of that House shall agree to pass the Bill, it shall be sent, together with the Objections, to the other House, by which it shall likewise be reconsidered, and if approved by two thirds of that House, it shall become a Law. But in all such Cases the Votes of both Houses shall be determined by yeas and Nays, and the Names of the Persons voting for and against the Bill shall be entered on the Journal of each House respectively. If any Bill shall not be returned by the President within ten Days (Sundays excepted) after it shall have been presented to him, the Same shall be a Law, in like Manner as if he had signed it, unless the Congress by their Adjournment prevent its Return, in which Case it shall not be a Law.

Every Order, Resolution, or Vote to which the Concurrence of the Senate and House of Representatives may be necessary (except on a question of Adjournment) shall be presented to the President of the United States; and before the Same shall take Effect, shall be approved by him, or being disapproved by him, shall be repassed by two thirds of the Senate and House of Representatives, according to the Rules and Limitations prescribed in the Case of a Bill.

SECTION 8. The Congress shall have Power To lay and collect Taxes, Duties, Imposts and Excises, to pay the Debts and provide for the common Defence and general Welfare of the United States; but all Duties, Imposts and Excises shall be uniform throughout the United States;

To borrow Money on the credit of the United States;

To regulate Commerce with foreign Nations, and among the several States, and with the Indian Tribes;

To establish an uniform Rule of Naturalization, and uniform Laws on the subject of Bankruptcies throughout the United States;

To coin Money, regulate the Value thereof, and of foreign Coin, and fix the Standard of Weights and Measures;

To provide for the Punishment of counterfeiting the Securities and current Coin of the United States;

To establish Post Offices and post Roads;

To promote the Progress of Science and useful Arts, by securing for limited Times to Authors and Inventors the exclusive Right to their respective Writings and Discoveries;

To constitute Tribunals inferior to the supreme Court;

To define and punish Piracies and Felonies committed on the high Seas, and Offences against the Law of Nations;

To declare War, grant Letters of Marque and Reprisal, and make Rules concerning Captures on Land and Water;

To raise and support Armies, but no Appropriation of Money to that Use shall be for a longer Term than two Years;

To provide and maintain a Navy;

To make Rules for the Government and Regulation of the land and naval Forces;

To provide for calling forth the Militia to execute the Laws of the Union, suppress Insurrections and repel Invasions;

To provide for organizing, arming, and disciplining, the Militia, and for governing such Part of them as may be employed in the Service of the United States, reserving to the States respectively, the Appointment of the Officers, and the Authority of training the Militia according to the discipline prescribed by Congress;

To exercise exclusive Legislation in all Cases whatsoever, over such District (not exceeding ten Miles square) as may, by Cession of particular States, and the Acceptance of Congress, become the Seat of the Government of the United States, and to exercise like Authority over all Places purchased by the Consent of the Legislature of the State in which the Same shall be, for the Erection of Forts, Magazines, Arsenals, dock-Yards, and other needful Buildings;—And

To make all Laws which shall be necessary and proper for carrying into Execution the foregoing Powers, and all other Powers vested by this Constitution in the Government of the United States, or in any Department or Officer thereof.

SECTION 9. The Migration or Importation of such Persons as any of the States now existing shall think proper to admit, shall not be prohibited by the Congress prior to the Year one thousand eight hundred and eight, but a Tax or duty may be imposed on such Importation, not exceeding ten dollars for each Person.

The Privilege of the Writ of Habeas Corpus shall not be suspended, unless when in Cases of Rebellion or Invasion the public Safety may require it.

No Bill of Attainder or ex post facto Law shall be passed.

No Capitation, or other direct, Tax shall be laid, unless in Proportion to the Census or Enumeration herein before directed to be taken.

No Tax or Duty shall be laid on Articles exported from any State.

No Preference shall be given by any Regulation of Commerce or Revenue to the Ports of one State over those of another: nor shall Vessels bound to, or from, one State, be obliged to enter, clear, or pay Duties in another.

No Money shall be drawn from the Treasury, but in Consequence of Appropriations made by Law; and a regular Statement and Account of the Receipts and Expenditures of all public Money shall be published from time to time.

No Title of Nobility shall be granted by the United States: And no Person holding any Office of Profit or Trust under them, shall, without the Consent of the Congress, accept of any present, Emolument, Office, or Title, of any kind whatever, from any King, Prince, or foreign State.

SECTION 10. No State shall enter into any Treaty, Alliance, or Confederation; grant Letters of Marque and Reprisal; coin Money; emit Bills of Credit; make any Thing but gold and silver Coin a Tender in Payment of Debts; pass any Bill of Attainder, ex post facto Law, or Law impairing the Obligation of Contracts, or grant any Title of Nobility.

No State shall, without the Consent of the Congress, lay any Imposts or Duties on Imports or Exports, except what may be absolutely necessary for executing its inspection Laws: and the net Produce of all Duties and Imposts, laid by any State on Imports or Exports, shall be for the Use of the Treasury of the United States; and all such Laws shall be subject to the Revision and Controul of the Congress.

No State shall, without the Consent of Congress, lay any Duty of Tonnage, keep Troops, or Ships of War in time of Peace, enter into any Agreement or Compact with another State, or with a foreign Power, or engage in War, unless actually invaded, or in such imminent Danger as will not admit of delay.

ARTICLE II.

SECTION 1. The executive Power shall be vested in a President of the United States of America. He shall hold his Office during the Term of four Years, and, together with the Vice President, chosen for the same Term, be elected, as follows

Each State shall appoint, in such Manner as the Legislature thereof may direct, a Number of Electors, equal to the whole Number of Senators and Representatives to which the State may be entitled in the Congress: but no Senator or Representative, or Person holding an Office of Trust or Profit under the United States, shall be appointed an Elector.

The Electors shall meet in their respective States, and vote by Ballot for two Persons, of whom one at least shall not be an Inhabitant of the same State with themselves. And they shall make a List of all the Persons voted for, and of the Number of Votes for each; which List they shall sign and certify, and transmit sealed to the Seat of the Government of the United States, directed to the President of the Senate. The President of the Senate shall, in the Presence of the Senate and House of Representatives, open all the Certificates, and the Votes shall then be counted. The Person having the greatest Number of

Votes shall be the President, if such Number be a Majority of the whole Number of Electors appointed; and if there be more than one who have such Majority, and have an equal Number of Votes, then the House of Representatives shall immediately chuse by Ballot one of them for President; and if no Person have a Majority, then from the five highest on the List the said House shall in like Manner chuse the President. But in chusing the President, the Votes shall be taken by States, the Representation from each State having one Vote; A quorum for this Purpose shall consist of a Member or Members from two thirds of the States, and a Majority of all the States shall be necessary to a Choice. In every Case, after the Choice of the President, the Person having the greatest Number of Votes of the Electors shall be the Vice President. But if there should remain two or more who have equal Votes, the Senate shall chuse from them by Ballot the Vice President.

The Congress may determine the Time of chusing the Electors, and the Day on which they shall give their Votes; which Day shall be the same throughout the United States.

No Person except a natural born Citizen, or a Citizen of the United States, at the time of the Adoption of this Constitution, shall be eligible to the Office of President; neither shall any Person be eligible to that Office who shall not have attained to the Age of thirty five Years, and been fourteen Years a Resident within the United States.

In Case of the Removal of the President from Office, or of his Death, Resignation, or Inability to discharge the Powers and Duties of the said Office, the Same shall devolve on the Vice President, and the Congress may by Law provide for the Case of Removal, Death, Resignation or Inability, both of the President and Vice President, declaring what Officer shall then act as President, and such Officer shall act accordingly, until the Disability be removed, or a President shall be elected.

The President shall, at stated Times, receive for his Services, a Compensation, which shall neither be encreased nor diminished during the Period for which he shall have been elected, and he shall not receive within that Period any other Emolument from the United States, or any of them.

Before he enter on the Execution of his Office, he shall take the following Oath or Affirmation:— "I do solemnly swear (or affirm) that I will faithfully execute the Office of President of the United States, and will to the best of my Ability, preserve, protect and defend the Constitution of the United States."

SECTION 2. The President shall be Commander in Chief of the Army and Navy of the United States, and of the Militia of the several States, when called into the actual Service of the United States; he may require the Opinion, in writing, of the principal Officer in each of the executive Departments, upon any Subject relating to the Duties of their respective Offices, and he shall have Power to grant Reprieves and Pardons for Offences against the United States, except in Cases of Impeachment.

He shall have Power, by and with the Advice and Consent of the Senate, to make Treaties, provided two thirds of the Senators present concur; and he shall nominate, and by and with the Advice and Consent of the Senate, shall appoint Ambassadors, other public Ministers and Consuls, Judges of the supreme Court, and all other Officers of the United States, whose Appointments are not herein otherwise provided for, and which shall be established by Law: but the Congress may by Law vest the Appointment of such inferior Officers, as they think proper, in the President alone, in the Courts of Law, or in the Heads of Departments.

The President shall have Power to fill up all Vacancies that may happen during the Recess of the Senate, by granting Commissions which shall expire at the End of their next Session.

SECTION 3. He shall from time to time give to the Congress Information of the State of the Union, and recommend to their Consideration such Measures as he shall judge necessary and expedient; he may, on extraordinary Occasions, convene both Houses, or either of them, and in Case of Disagreement between them, with Respect to the Time of Adjournment, he may adjourn them to such Time as he shall think proper; he shall receive Ambassadors and other public Ministers; he shall take Care that the Laws be faithfully executed, and shall Commission all the Officers of the United States.

SECTION 4. The President, Vice President and all civil Officers of the United States, shall be removed from Office on Impeachment for, and Conviction of, Treason, Bribery, or other high Crimes and Misdemeanors.

ARTICLE III

SECTION 1. The judicial Power of the United States, shall be vested in one supreme Court, and in such inferior Courts as the Congress may from time to time ordain and establish. The Judges, both of the supreme and inferior Courts, shall hold their Offices during good Behaviour, and shall, at stated Times, receive for their Services, a Compensation, which shall not be diminished during their continuance in Office.

SECTION 2. The judicial Power shall extend to all Cases, in Law and Equity, arising under this Constitution, the Laws of the United States, and Treaties made, or which shall be made, under their Authority;—

to all Cases affecting Ambassadors, other public Ministers and Consuls;—to all Cases of admiralty and maritime Jurisdiction;—to Controversies to which the United States shall be a Party;—to Controversies between two or more States;—between a State and Citizens of another State;—between Citizens of different States,—between Citizens of the same State claiming Lands under Grants of different States, and between a State, or the Citizens thereof, and foreign States, Citizens or Subjects.

In all Cases affecting Ambassadors, other public Ministers and Consuls, and those in which a State shall be Party, the supreme Court shall have original Jurisdiction. In all the other Cases before mentioned, the supreme Court shall have appellate Jurisdiction, both as to Law and Fact, with such Exceptions, and under such regulations as the Congress shall make.

The Trial of all Crimes, except in Cases of Impeachment, shall be by Jury; and such Trial shall be held in the State where the said Crimes shall have been committed; but when not committed within any State, the Trial shall be at such Place or Places as the Congress may by Law have directed.

SECTION 3. Treason against the United States, shall consist only in levying War against them, or in adhering to their Enemies, giving them Aid and Comfort. No person shall be convicted of Treason unless on the Testimony of two Witnesses to the same overt Act, or on Confession in open Court.

The Congress shall have Power to declare the Punishment of Treason, but no Attainder of Treason shall work Corruption of Blood, or Forfeiture except during the Life of the Person attainted.

ARTICLE IV.

SECTION 1. Full Faith and Credit shall be given in each State to the public Acts, Records, and judicial Proceedings of every other State. And the Congress may by general Laws prescribe the Manner in which such Acts, Records and Proceedings shall be proved, and the Effect thereof.

SECTION 2. The Citizens of each State shall be entitled to all Privileges and Immunities of Citizens in the several States.

A Person charged in any State with Treason, Felony, or other Crime, who shall flee from Justice, and be found in another State, shall on demand of the executive Authority of the State from which he fled, be delivered up, to be removed to the State having Jurisdiction of the Crime.

No Person held to Service or Labour in one State, under the Laws thereof, escaping into another, shall, in Consequence of any Law or Regulation therein, be discharged from such Service or Labour, but shall be delivered up on Claim of the Party to whom such Service or Labour may be due.

SECTION 3. New States may be admitted by the Congress into this Union; but no new State shall be formed or erected within the Jurisdiction of any other State; nor any State be formed by the Junction of two or more States, or Parts of States, without the Consent of the Legislatures of the States concerned as well as of the Congress.

The Congress shall have Power to dispose of and make all needful Rules and Regulations respecting the Territory or other Property belonging to the United States; and nothing in this Constitution shall be so construed as to Prejudice any Claims of the United States, or of any particular State.

SECTION 4. The United States shall guarantee to every State in this Union a Republican Form of Government, and shall protect each of them against Invasion; and on Application of the Legislature, or of the Executive (when the Legislature cannot be convened) against domestic Violence.

ARTICLE V.

The Congress, whenever two thirds of both Houses shall deem it necessary, shall propose Amendments to this Constitution, or, on the Application of the Legislatures of two thirds of the several States, shall call a Convention for proposing Amendments, which, in either Case, shall be valid to all Intents and Purposes, as Part of this Constitution, when ratified by the Legislatures of three fourths of the several States, or by Conventions in three fourths thereof, as the one or the other Mode of Ratification may be proposed by the Congress; Provided that no Amendment which may be made prior to the Year One thousand eight hundred and eight shall in any Manner affect the first and fourth Clauses in the Ninth Section of the first Article; and that no State, without its Consent, shall be deprived of it's equal Suffrage in the Senate.

ARTICLE VI.

All Debts contracted and Engagements entered into, before the Adoption of this Constitution, shall be valid against the United States under this Constitution, as under the Confederation.

This Constitution, and the Laws of the United States which shall be made in Pursuance thereof; and all Treaties made, or which shall be made, under the Authority of the United States, shall be the supreme

Law of the Land; and the Judges in every State shall be bound thereby, any Thing in the Constitution or Laws of any State to the Contrary notwithstanding.

The Senators and Representatives before mentioned, and the Members of the several State Legislatures, and all executive and judicial Officers, both of the United States and of the several States, shall be bound by Oath or Affirmation, to support this Constitution; but no religious Test shall ever be required as a Qualification to any Office or public Trust under the United States.

ARTICLE VII.

The Ratification of the Conventions of nine States, shall be sufficient for the Establishment of this Constitution between the States so ratifying the Same.

The Word, "the", being interlined between the seventh and eighth Lines of the first Page, The Word "Thirty" being partly written on an Erazure in the fifteenth Line of the first Page, The Words "is tried" being interlined between the thirty second and thirty third Lines of the first Page and the Word "the" being interlined between the forty third and forty fourth Lines of the second Page.

[*Note.* The interlined and rewritten words mentioned in the above explanation, are in this edition printed in their proper places in the text.]

DONE in Convention by the Unanimous Consent of the States present the Seventeenth Day of September in the Year of our Lord one thousand seven hundred and Eighty seven and of the Independence of the United States of America the Twelfth *In Witness* whereof We have hereunto subscribed our Names,

G⁰: WASHINGTON — *Presidt.*
and deputy from Virginia

Attest WILLIAM JACKSON *Secretary*

New Hampshire { JOHN LANGDON
NICHOLAS GILMAN }

Massachusetts { NATHANIEL GORHAM
RUFUS KING }

Connecticut { WM: SAML. JOHNSON
ROGER SHERMAN }

New York . . . ALEXANDER HAMILTON

New Jersey
WIL: LIVINGSTON
DAVID BREARLEY
WM. PATERSON
JONA: DAYTON

Pennsylvania
B FRANKLIN
THOMAS MIFFLIN
ROBT. MORRIS
GEO. CLYMER
THOS. FITZ SIMONS
JARED INGERSOLL
JAMES WILSON
GOUV MORRIS

Delaware
GEO: READ
GUNNING BEDFORD jun
JOHN DICKINSON
RICHARD BASSETT
JACO: BROOM

Maryland
JAMES MCHENRY
DAN OF ST THOS. JENIFER
DANL CARROLL

Virginia
JOHN BLAIR
JAMES MADISON JR.

North Carolina
WM: BLOUNT
RICHD. DOBBS SPAIGHT
HU WILLIAMSON

South Carolina
J. RUTLEDGE
CHARLES COTESWORTH PINCKNEY
CHARLES PINCKNEY
PIERCE BUTLER

Georgia
WILLIAM FEW
ABR BALDWIN

10

RESOLUTION OF THE CONVENTION
September 17, 1787

In Convention Monday September 17th, 1787

PRESENT, *The States of New-Hampshire, Massachusetts, Connecticut, Mr. Hamilton from New-York, New Jersey, Pennsylvania, Delaware, Maryland, Virginia, North Carolina, South Carolina, and Georgia.*

Resolved, That the preceding Constitution be laid before the United States in Congress assembled, and that it is the opinion of this convention, that it should afterwards be submitted to a convention of delegates, chosen in each State by the people thereof, under the recommendation of its legislature, for their assent and ratification; and that each convention assenting to, and ratifying the same should give notice thereof to the United States in Congress assembled.

Resolved, That it is the opinion of this convention, that as soon as the conventions of nine States shall have ratified this Constitution, the United States in Congress assembled should fix a day on which electors should be appointed by the States which shall have ratified the same, and a day on which the electors should assemble to vote for the President, and the time and place for commencing proceedings under this Constitution; that after such publication the electors should be appointed, and the senators and representatives elected; that the electors should meet on the day fixed for the election of the President, and should transmit their votes certified, signed, sealed, and directed, as the Constitution requires, to the secretary of the United States in Congress assembled; that the senators and representatives should convene at the time and place assigned; that the senators should appoint a president of the Senate, for the sole purpose of receiving, opening and counting the votes for President; and that after he shall be chosen, the Congress, together with the President, should without delay proceed to execute this Constitution.

By the unanimous order of the convention.

GEORGE WASHINGTON, *President.*

WILLIAM JACKSON, *Secretary.*

LETTER OF THE CONVENTION
TO CONGRESS

In Convention, September 17, 1787

S**IR,**
   WE HAVE now the honor to submit to the consideration of the
United States in Congress assembled, that Constitution which has
appeared to us the most advisable.

The friends of our country have long seen and desired, that the
power of making war, peace, and treaties, of levying money and regulating commerce, and the correspondent executive and judicial authorities should be fully and effectually vested in the general government
of the Union: but the impropriety of delegating such extensive trust
to one body of men is evident— Hence results the necessity of a different organization.

It is obviously impracticable in the federal government of these
States, to secure all rights of independent sovereignty to each, and yet
provide for the interest and safety of all— Individuals entering into
society, must give up a share of liberty to preserve the rest. The
magnitude of the sacrifice must depend as well on situation and circumstances as on the object to be obtained. It is at all times difficult
to draw with precision the line between those rights which must be
surrendered, and those which may be reserved; and on the present
occasion this difficulty was increased by a difference among the several
States as to their situation, extent, habits, and particular interests.

In all our deliberations on this subject we kept steadily in our view,
that which appears to us the greatest interest of every true American,
the consolidation of our Union, in which is involved our prosperity,
felicity, safety, perhaps our national existence. This important consideration, seriously and deeply impressed on our minds, led each State
in the Convention to be less rigid on points of inferior magnitude, than
might have been otherwise expected; and thus the Constitution, which
we now present, is the result of a spirit of amity, and of that mutual
deference and concession which the peculiarity of our political situation rendered indispensable.

That it will meet the full and entire approbation of every State is
not perhaps to be expected; but each will doubtless consider, that
had her interest alone been consulted, the consequences might have
been particularly disagreeable or injurious to others; that it is liable

311

to as few exceptions as could reasonably have been expected, we hope and believe; that it may promote the lasting welfare of that country so dear to us all, and secure her freedom and happiness, is our most ardent wish.

With great respect,

We have the honor to be

SIR,

Your Excellency's most

Obedient and Humble Servants,

GEORGE WASHINGTON, President

By Unanimous Order of the Convention

HIS EXCELLENCY

THE PRESIDENT OF CONGRESS

THE BILL OF RIGHTS:
FIRST TEN AMENDMENTS

[Since most of the opponents of the Constitution had objected to the omission from it of a Bill of Rights, and several of the state conventions had proposed that such a Bill be included, the First Congress at its first session agreed on twelve "Articles in addition to, and amendment of, the Constitution of the United States of America," to be "proposed by Congress, and ratified by the legislatures of the several states, pursuant to the Fifth Article of the Constitution." The first two Articles were rejected by various states, with the result that the third in the original series became the first amendment. Although no formal announcement was ever made, the ten amendments adopted appear to have been in force from December 15, 1791. The rejected Articles were: (I) "After the first enumeration required by the first article of the Constitution, there shall be one representative for every thirty thousand, until the number shall amount to one hundred, after which the proportion shall be so regulated by Congress, that there shall not be less than one hundred representatives, nor more than one representative for every forty thousand persons, until the number of representatives shall amount to two hundred, after which the proportion shall be so regulated by Congress, that there shall not be less than two hundred representatives, nor more than one representative for every fifty thousand; (II) "No law varying the compensation for services of the senators and representatives shall take effect, until an election of representatives shall have intervened." The ten amendments accepted and ratified by the states, eventually numbered I to X, were not officially named a Bill of Rights but have commonly been called that.]

ARTICLE I

Congress shall make no law respecting an establishment of religion, or prohibiting the free exercise thereof; or abridging the freedom of speech, or of the press; or the right of the people peaceably to assemble, and to petition the Government for a redress of grievances.

ARTICLE II

A well regulated Militia, being necessary to the security of a free

State, the right of the people to keep and bear Arms, shall not be infringed.

ARTICLE III

No Soldier shall, in time of peace be quartered in any house, without the consent of the Owner, nor in time of war, but in a manner to be prescribed by law.

ARTICLE IV

The right of the people to be secure in their persons, houses, papers, and effects, against unreasonable searches and seizures, shall not be violated, and no Warrants shall issue, but upon probably cause, supported by Oath or affirmation, and particularly describing the place to be searched, and the persons or things to be seized.

ARTICLE V

No person shall be held to answer for a capital, or otherwise infamous crime, unless on a presentment or indictment of a Grand Jury, except in cases arising in the land or naval forces, or in the Militia, when in actual service in time of War or public danger; nor shall any person be subject for the same offence to be twice put in jeopardy of life or limb; nor shall be compelled in any Criminal Case to be a witness against himself, nor be deprived of life, liberty, or property, without due process of law; nor shall private property be taken for public use, without just compensation.

ARTICLE VI

In all criminal prosecutions, the accused shall enjoy the right to a speedy and public trial, by an impartial jury of the State and district wherein the crime shall have been committed, which district shall have been previously ascertained by law, and to be informed of the nature and cause of the accusation; to be confronted with the witnesses against him; to have compulsory process for obtaining witnesses in his favor, and to have the Assistance of Counsel for his defence.

ARTICLE VII

In Suits at common law, where the value in controversy shall exceed twenty dollars, the right of trial by jury shall be preserved, and no fact tried by a jury, shall be otherwise re-examined in any Court of the United States, than according to the rules of the common law.

ARTICLE VIII

Excessive bail shall not be required, nor excessive fines imposed, nor cruel and unusual punishments inflicted.

ARTICLE IX

The enumeration in the Constitution, of certain rights, shall not be construed to deny or disparage others retained by the people.

ARTICLE X

The powers not delegated to the United States by the Constitution, nor prohibited by it to the States, are reserved to the States respectively, or to the people.

LATER AMENDMENTS

ARTICLE XI
[January 8, 1798]

The Judicial power of the United States shall not be construed to extend to any suit in law or equity, commenced or prosecuted against one of the United States by Citizens of another State, or by Citizens or Subjects of any Foreign State.

ARTICLE XII
[September 25, 1804]

The Electors shall meet in their respective states, and vote by ballot for President and Vice President, one of whom, at least, shall not be an inhabitant of the same state with themselves; they shall name in their ballots the person voted for as President, and in distinct ballots the person voted for as Vice-President, and they shall make distinct lists of all persons voted for as President, and of all persons voted for as Vice-President, and of the number of votes for each, which lists they shall sign and certify, and transmit sealed to the seat of the government of the United States, directed to the President of the Senate;— The President of the Senate shall, in presence of the Senate and House of Representatives, open all the certificates and the votes shall then be counted;— The person having the greatest number of votes for President, shall be the President, if such number be a majority of the whole number of Electors appointed; and if no person have such majority, then from the persons having the highest numbers not exceeding three on the list of those voted for as President, the House of Representatives shall choose immediately, by ballot, the President. But in choosing the President, the votes shall be taken by states, the representation from each state having one vote; a quorum for this purpose shall consist of a member or members from two-thirds of the states, and a majority of all the states shall be necessary to a choice. And if the House of Representatives shall not choose a President whenever the right of choice shall devolve upon them, before the fourth day of March next following, then the Vice-President shall act as President, as in the case of the death or other constitutional disability of the President. The person having the greatest number of votes as Vice-President, shall be the Vice-President, if such number be a majority of the whole number of Electors appointed, and if no person have a majority, then from the two highest numbers on the list, the Senate shall choose the Vice-President; a quorum for the purpose shall consist of two-thirds of the whole number of Senators, and a majority of the whole number shall be necessary to a choice. But no person constitutionally ineligible to the office of President shall be eligible to that of Vice-President of the United States.

ARTICLE XIII
[December 18, 1865]

Section 1. Neither slavery nor involuntary servitude, except as a punishment for crime whereof the party shall have been duly convicted, shall exist within the United States, or any place subject to their jurisdiction.

Section 2. Congress shall have power to enforce this article by appropriate legislation.

ARTICLE XIV
[July 21, 1868]

Section 1. All persons born or naturalized in the United States, and subject to the jurisdiction thereof, are citizens of the United States and of the State wherein they reside. No State shall make or enforce any law which shall abridge the privileges or immunities of citizens of the United States; nor shall any State deprive any person of life, liberty, or property, without due process of law; nor deny to any person within its jurisdiction the equal protection of the laws.

Section 2. Representatives shall be apportioned among the several States according to their respective numbers, counting the whole number of persons in each State, excluding Indians not taxed. But when the right to vote at any election for the choice of electors for President and Vice President of the United States, Representatives in Congress, the Executive and Judicial officers of a State, or the members of the Legislature thereof, is denied to any of the male inhabitants of such State, being twenty-one years of age, and citizens of the United States, or in any way abridged, except for participation in rebellion, or other crime, the basis of representation therein shall be reduced in the proportion which the number of such male citizens shall bear to the whole number of male citizens twenty-one years of age in such State.

Section 3. No person shall be a Senator or Representative in Congress, or elector of President and Vice President, or hold any office, civil or military, under the United States, or under any State, who, having previously taken an oath, as a member of Congress, or as an officer of the United States, or as a member of any State legislature, or as an executive or judicial officer of any State, to support the Constitution of the United States, shall have engaged in insurrection or rebellion against the same, or given aid or comfort to the enemies thereof. But Congress may by a vote of two-thirds of each House, remove such disability.

Section 4. The validity of the public debt of the United States, authorized by law, including debts incurred for payment of pensions and bounties for services in suppressing insurrection or rebellion, shall not be questioned. But neither the United States nor any State shall assume or pay any debt or obligation incurred in aid of insurrection or rebellion against the United States, or any claim for the loss or emancipation of any slave; but all such debts, obligations and claims shall be held illegal and void.

Section 5. The Congress shall have power to enforce, by appropriate legislation, the provisions of this article.

ARTICLE XV
[March 30, 1870]

Section 1. The right of citizens of the United States to vote shall not be denied or abridged by the United States or by any State on account of race, color, or previous condition of servitude.

Section 2. The Congress shall have power to enforce this article by appropriate legislation.

ARTICLE XVI
[February 25, 1913]

The Congress shall have the power to lay and collect taxes on incomes, from whatever source derived, without apportionment among the several States, and without regard to any census or enumeration.

ARTICLE XVII
[May 31, 1913]

Section 1. The Senate of the United States shall be composed of two Senators from each State, elected by the people thereof, for six years; and each Senator shall have one vote. The electors in each State shall have the qualifications requisite for electors of the most numerous branch of the State Legislatures.

Section 2. When vacancies happen in the representation of any State in the Senate, the executive authority of such State shall issue writs of election to fill such vacancies; Provided, That the Legislature of any State may empower the executive thereof to make temporary appointment until the people fill the vacancies by election as the Legislature may direct.

Section 3. This amendment shall not be so construed as to affect the election or term of any Senator chosen before it becomes valid as part of the Constitution.

ARTICLE XVIII
[January 29, 1919]

Section 1. After one year from the ratification of this article, the manufacture, sale, or transportation of intoxicating liquors within, the importation thereof into, or the exportation thereof from the United States and all territory subject to the jurisdiction thereof, for beverage purposes, is hereby prohibited.

Section 2. The Congress and the several States shall have concurrent power to enforce this article by appropriate legislation.

Section 3. This article shall be inoperative unless it shall have been ratified as an amendment to the Constitution by the legislatures of the several States, as provided in the Constitution, within seven years from the date of the submission hereof to the States by the Congress.

ARTICLE XIX
[August 26, 1920]

Section 1. The rights of citizens of the United States to vote, shall not be denied or abridged by the United States or by any State on account of sex.

Section 2. Congress shall have power to enforce this article by appropriate legislation.

ARTICLE XX
[February 6, 1933]

Section 1. The terms of the President and Vice President shall end at noon on the twentieth day of January, and the terms of Senators and Representatives at noon on the third day of January, of the years in which such terms would have ended if this article had not been ratified; and the terms of their successors shall then begin.

Section 2. The Congress shall assemble at least once in every year, and such meeting shall begin at noon on the third day of January, unless they shall by law appoint a different day.

Section 3. If, at the time fixed for the beginning of the term of the President, the President elect shall have died, the Vice President elect shall become President. If a President shall not have been chosen before the time fixed for the beginning of his term, or if the President elect shall have failed to qualify, then the Vice President elect shall act as President until a President shall have qualified; and the Congress may by law provide for the case wherein neither a President elect nor a Vice President elect shall have qualified, declaring who shall then act as President, or the manner in which one who is to act shall be selected, and such person shall act accordingly until a President or Vice President shall have qualified.

Section 4. The Congress may by law provide for the case of the death of any of the persons from whom the House of Representatives may choose a President whenever the right of choice shall have devolved upon them, and for the case of the death of any of the persons from whom the Senate may choose a Vice President whenever the right of choice shall have devolved upon them.

Section 5. Sections 1 and 2 shall take effect on the fifteenth day of October following the ratification of this article.

Section 6. This article shall be inoperative unless it shall have been ratified as an amendment to the Constitution by the legislatures of three-fourths of the several States within seven years from the date of its submission.

ARTICLE XXI
[December 5, 1933]

Section 1. The eighteenth article of amendment to the Constitution of the United States is hereby repealed.

Section 2. The transportation or importation into any State, Territory, or possession of the United States for delivery or use therein of intoxicating liquors, in violation of the laws thereof, is hereby prohibited.

Section 3. This article shall be inoperative unless it shall have been ratified as an amendment to the Constitution by conventions in the several States, as provided in the Constitution, within seven years from the date of the submission hereof to the States by the Congress.

SOURCES AND ACKNOWLEDGMENTS

Y EARS of intimate, inquisitive familiarity with hundreds of histories, biographies, monographs, official minutes, letters, and newspapers of or concerning the times of the American Revolution and Constitution have gone into the making of this book. To list the uncounted titles which have furnished many or few details would give a wrong impression of its character. It is based essentially on the original records of the Federal Convention of 1787 and of the state conventions which ratified or rejected the Constitution. Max Farrand's *The Records of the Federal Convention* (revised edition, 4 vols., 1937) supersedes all previous works dealing with its subject. Jonathan Elliot's *The Debates in the Several State Conventions on the Adoption of the Federal Constitution* (revised edition, 5 vols., 1836-45, and later reprints) deserves to be thoroughly re-edited, but as it stands is indispensable. Paul Leicester Ford's *Pamphlets on the Constitution* (1888) and *Essays on the Constitution* (1892) include valuable published writings of the years 1787-88. The most satisfactory history of the Federal Convention is Charles Warren's *The Making of the Constitution* (1928), a day-by-day account. Charles A. Beard's *An Economic Interpretation of the Constitution of the United States* (1913) lays important stress on an aspect of the Convention which had been neglected before that and has since been overemphasized. Of the general histories of the period the most useful, for the purposes of the present narrative, is Allan Nevins's *The American States during and after the Revolution 1775-1789* (1924).

The best study of a state convention is Hugh Blair Grigsby's *The History of the Virginia Federal Convention of 1788* (2 vols., 1890-91): supplemented by the graphic account by Albert J. Beveridge in Volume I of *The Life of John Marshall* (4 vols., 1916-19). Other studies of state conventions are: O. G. Libby, *The Geographical Distribution of the Vote of the Thirteen States on the Federal Constitution* (1894); J. B. Walker, *A History of the New Hampshire Convention for the Investigation, Discussion, and Decision of the Federal Constitution* (1888); S. B. Harding, *The Contest over the Ratification of the Federal Constitution in the State of Massachusetts* (1896); B. C. Steiner, "Connecticut's Ratification of the Federal Constitution," *Proceedings of the American Antiquarian Society*, New Series, XXV (1915), 70-127; C. E. Miner, *The Ratification of the Federal Consti-*

tution by the State of New York (1921); J. B. McMaster and F. D. Stone, *Pennsylvania and the Federal Constitution 1787-1788* (1888), which reprints numerous fugitive publications; B. C. Steiner, "Maryland's Adoption of the Federal Constitution," *American Historical Review*, V (1899-1900), 22-44, 207-224; P. A. Crowl, "Antifederalism in Maryland, 1787-1788," *William and Mary Quarterly*, 3rd Series, IV (October 1947), 409-69; L. I. Trenholme, *The Ratification of the Federal Constitution in North Carolina* (1932).

Acknowledgments are due, and are gratefully made, to the Yale University Press for permission to quote extensively from the text of Farrand's *Records of the Federal Convention;* to the Library Company of Philadelphia for permission to reprint letters from the Dillwyn and Rush Papers; and to the Historical Society of Pennsylvania for permission to print a letter from the Gratz Autograph Collection: individual sources are indicated in footnotes.

It is a special pleasure to thank these friends for generous encouragement and advice: Julian P. Boyd, L. H. Butterfield, Thomas K. Finletter, Alan Green, Selma Hirsh, George Holt, J. H. Powell, and Mark Van Doren; Mary Barnard for tireless and expert assistance in research; and the members of all the departments of The Viking Press for such skill, taste, and kindness as makes a writer's work with them a delight.

INDEX